access to history

The British Experience of Warfare 1790–1918

ALAN FARMER

SECOND EDITION

ccess to history

The British Experience of Warfare 1790–1918

ALAN FARMER

SECOND EDITION

HODDER
EDUCATION
AN HACHETTE UK COMPANY

The Publishers would like to thank Robin Bunce for his contribution to the Study Guide.

Although every effort has been made to ensure that website addresses are correct at time of going to press, Hodder Education cannot be held responsible for the content of any website mentioned in this book. It is sometimes possible to find a relocated web page by typing in the address of the home page for a website in the URL window of your browser.

Hachette UK's policy is to use papers that are natural, renewable and recyclable products and made from wood grown in sustainable forests. The logging and manufacturing processes are expected to conform to the environmental regulations of the country of origin.

Orders: please contact Bookpoint Ltd, 130 Milton Park, Abingdon, Oxon OX14 4SB. Telephone: +44 (0)1235 827720. Fax: +44 (0)1235 400454. Lines are open 9.00a.m.–5.00p.m., Monday to Saturday, with a 24-hour message answering service. Visit our website at www.hoddereducation.co.uk

© Alan Farmer
Second edition © Alan Farmer 2015

First published in 2011 by
Hodder Education
An Hachette UK Company
Carmelite House, 50 Victoria Embankment
London EC4Y 0DZ

Impression number   10 9 8 7 6 5 4 3 2 1
Year   2019 2018 2017 2016 2015

Cover photo: For King and Country (1917), by E.F. Skinner, © Imperial War Museum (IWM_ART_006513)
Produced, illustrated and typeset in Palatino LT Std by Gray Publishing, Tunbridge Wells
Printed and bound by CPI Group (UK) Ltd, Croydon CR0 4YY

A catalogue record for this title is available from the British Library

ISBN 978 1471838880

Contents

Dedication

Keith Randell (1943–2002)

The *Access to History* series was conceived and developed by Keith, who created a series to 'cater for students as they are, not as we might wish them to be'. He leaves a living legacy of a series that for over 20 years has provided a trusted, stimulating and well-loved accompaniment to post-16 study. Our aim with these new editions is to continue to offer students the best possible support for their studies.

CHAPTER 1

The British Navy and the French Wars 1793–1815

The French Revolutionary Wars (1793–1802) and the Napoleonic Wars (1803–15) lasted for over twenty years, with a short break following the Peace of Amiens (March 1802 to May 1803). The wars were world wars in all but name, fought not just in Europe but in the Caribbean, Africa and India. On several occasions Britain faced the threat of invasion. In the event, Britain survived and won. This chapter will examine the contribution made by the Royal Navy and the nation as a whole to British victory. It will do so by examining the following themes:

★ The Royal Navy

★ The naval war 1793–7

★ The Nelson touch 1798–1805

★ The Royal Navy 1806–15

★ The British war effort 1793–1815

Key dates

1793		France declared war on Britain	**1797**	**Oct.**	Battle of Camperdown
1794		Battle of the Glorious First of June	**1798**		Battle of the Nile
			1801		Battle of Copenhagen
1797	**Feb.**	Battle of Cape St Vincent	**1802–3**		Peace of Amiens
	April–May	Naval mutinies at Spithead and the Nore	**1805**		Battle of Trafalgar
			1812–14		The War of 1812

 ## The Royal Navy

▶ *How well prepared for war was the navy in 1793?*

For almost half the eighteenth century, Britain was engaged in military conflict with France. Britain was generally successful. However, the War of American Independence (1775–83) had ended in British defeat. While Britain lost its American colonies, the Royal Navy ensured that Britain escaped invasion and clung on to the rest of its empire. After 1783, Britain, unlike all other European countries, kept a considerable number of ships at sea. In 1792, there were 125 ships in commission, ensuring that 20,000 officers and seamen maintained their skills.

Naval warfare in the late eighteenth century

The navy's ships were built of wood and were dependent on sails for movement. The main battleships were called ships of the line. Usually carrying more than 70 guns, they had crews of many hundreds of men. The navy also relied on frigates. These were smaller but faster ships, usually carrying 28–36 guns. Frigates were in continual action, patrolling, scouting or conveying **merchantmen**. There were also smaller ships – sloops and gunboats – which were used on convoy and blockade duty.

In battle, warships raked the enemy with **broadsides**. If ships came together, they might be boarded by crews and **marines** from the other side. Captured ships were repaired, given a new name and then put back into use.

Blockade

The navy tried to prevent enemy ships from leaving port. Two methods were used:

- A close blockade, where the main fleet sailed near to the enemy port.
- An open blockade, where the main fleet was in a home port or miles away at sea and frigates patrolled the coast off the enemy port. If enemy ships put to sea, some of the frigates informed the fleet.

Gunnery

Since 1745 every Royal Navy ship was obliged to perform daily gunnery practice (see Source A). Most British ships carried 32-pounder guns which could fire a cannon ball weighing approximately 32 pounds (14.5 kg). Each gun was manned by a team of seven sailors. A gun captain was responsible for aiming and firing. Guns weighed three tons and recoiled on firing. They then had to be hauled back to the gun-port. This laborious work was conducted by men in a crouching position: the maximum height below decks was five feet six inches (168 cm). The speed at which guns fired usually determined the outcome of naval battles. British seamen could unleash a broadside every minute and a half – much faster than their enemies.

SOURCE A

Francis Spilsbury, a ship's surgeon, describing gun drill in 1805, quoted in Ben Wilson, _Empire of the Deep_, Weidenfeld & Nicolson, 2013, p. 390.

On the beat of a drum, the men immediately fly to their quarters; and their being so constant in that point of duty, increases their agility, gives them confidence in their own powers, and prevents much of that confusion, which with those less disciplined must necessarily ensue – even the little powder-boy would be ashamed of being reproached by his ship mates, for not knowing his duty. On these occasions, a general silence prevails, all attentively listening for the word of command.

? According to Source A, why were British naval gunnery crews so good?

Naval officers

Most British naval officers came from the professional middle classes. Many were sons or relations of naval officers. Usually embarking on their naval careers at an early age, they learned the ropes (literally) as lowly midshipmen. As well as getting practical experience in all aspects of naval life, midshipmen were taught crucial skills: mathematics, astronomy and navigation. Family influence could ensure that some officers (like Horatio Nelson, for example) were fast-tracked.

British officers born in the 1750s and 1760s had gained valuable experience of naval warfare in the American War of Independence. So too had French naval officers. But many of the latter had fled the country or been guillotined during the **French Revolution**. Thus, French officers after 1793 usually lacked the experience of their British counterparts.

Naval crews

After 1793 the navy's strength was usually around 120,000 men, climbing to over 140,000 sailing in 1000 vessels by 1812.

Recruitment

Britain did not impose conscription. Given that voluntary recruitment did not provide enough men to service the fleet in wartime, the navy relied on impressment. Although most Britons opposed conscription, impressment was accepted as it was seen as vital for the navy and thus for the nation's survival. The Impressment Service had the power to force seafarers aged between 15 and 55 to join the Royal Navy. Press gangs were sent out to round up suitable men in and around ports. Captains were also allowed to press into service seamen from merchant ships at sea, provided they replaced the men they took with men from their own ships – invariably malcontents or **landsmen**. By 1805 half the Royal Navy's crews were made of pressed men. In addition to impressment, Britain used the Quota System, whereby each county was required to supply a certain number of volunteers, based on its population and the number of its seaports. In order to meet their quotas, counties frequently offered criminals the option of volunteering for the navy rather than completing their sentences.

Many sailors were not British. HMS *Caledonia*, for example, had Swedes, Frenchmen, Portuguese, North Americans, West Indians, Brazilians, Germans, Italians, Africans and Russians on board.

Conditions

Able-bodied naval seamen in 1793 were paid 22*s.* 6*d.* (£1.12½) a month. (Merchant seamen were usually paid twice as much.) There had been no wage increase since 1652 and pay was often months in arrears. Life on board a warship was not pleasant:

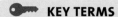 **KEY TERMS**

French Revolution
The term used to describe the political turbulence in France 1789–94. These years saw the overthrow (and execution) of King Louis XVI and an attempted destruction of the aristocracy.

Landsmen Men with no seafaring or riverboat experience.

- Sailors, who slept in hammocks, were permitted a width of just 14 inches (35 cm) per man.
- Food, while plentiful by the standards of the day, tended to be monotonous. But at least there was a realisation that sailors needed to have fresh fruit and vegetables to prevent **scurvy**.
- Work was hard physically.
- Discipline was harsh. Those who broke the rules could expect to be flogged with the **cat-o'-nine-tails**.
- Sailors could be at sea for years at a time.

Sailors' main hope was capturing an enemy ship and winning **prize money**.

Discipline and teamwork

The foundation of Britain's naval strength was the discipline and teamwork shown by thousands of seamen. While some operated guns, others worked aloft, furling and unfurling sails. The Royal Navy's strength was based on ships that hummed like well-oiled machines, each part contributing to the smooth running of the whole. It was no easy matter teaching raw recruits and discontented pressed men to accept the need for the unquestioning obedience that made a ship safe at sea and fit for battle. This could be achieved by driving seamen to work with the continual threat of punishment. Other officers preferred to win the love and respect of their crews.

The navy 1783–93

The British Navy ruled the waves for most of the eighteenth century, principally because of the superiority of British seamanship and gunnery. While the navy had retained its dominance for most of the American War of Independence, that conflict had exposed some shortcomings, and efforts were made to address these in the decade before 1793.

In the 1780s the Conservative (Tory) Prime Minister **William Pitt** the Younger developed a good working relationship with the **Comptroller of the Navy**, Rear Admiral Charles Middleton, a determined reformer:

- Dockyards were more closely supervised to eliminate waste and corruption.
- Middleton was the brains behind **coppering** the fleet, which meant that warships needed fewer repairs.
- Massive stocks of timber and rope were built up.
- New docks were constructed at Portsmouth and Plymouth.

Great strides were also made in naval gunnery. The carronade, developed by the Carron ironworks in Falkirk, was a triumph of industrial innovation. Light, able to swivel and with a short, fat muzzle, the carronade was fitted to the **forecastles** and sterns of warships. Nicknamed the 'smasher', it could be fired rapidly. When loaded with **grapeshot**, it made mincemeat of sailors and marines on an opposing ship's upper decks. The French failed to produce a close-range weapon as good as the carronade.

KEY TERMS

Scurvy A disease caused by deficiency of vitamin C. The symptoms are weakness and aching joints and muscles, progressing to bleeding of the gums and other organs.

Cat-o'-nine-tails A whip with nine knotted tails.

Prize money Captured enemy ships were sold. The money made was then allotted to the men. Officers took the lion's share but ordinary crewmen did receive something.

Comptroller of the Navy The man who headed the Navy Board, which was responsible for building and maintaining ships.

Coppering Covering a ship's hull with copper sheeting to protect it from wear and tear.

Forecastle The raised deck at the front of a ship.

Grapeshot Iron shot, contained in a canvas bag, that scattered widely when fired.

KEY FIGURE

William Pitt (the Younger) (1759–1806)

Entered Parliament in 1781. He became chancellor of the exchequer in 1782 and was twice prime minister, in 1783–1801 and 1804–6.

Long-range guns were also developed:

- The **Ordnance Board** insisted that every new gun was fired 30 times before it was accepted.
- **Gunlocks** replaced **slowmatches**. Slowmatches had to be held against a gun's priming powder. Thus, gun captains had to position themselves beside the gun and hope the gunpowder ignited and fired. Gunlocks were more efficient because the gun captain stood back from the gun, aimed, and when the time was ripe yanked on a **lanyard** that set off a firing mechanism. Broadsides became faster and more accurate as a result.

Thanks to Middleton's administrative zeal and Pitt's willingness to spend money on naval defence, the Royal Navy was better prepared for war in 1793 than the navies of France and Spain.

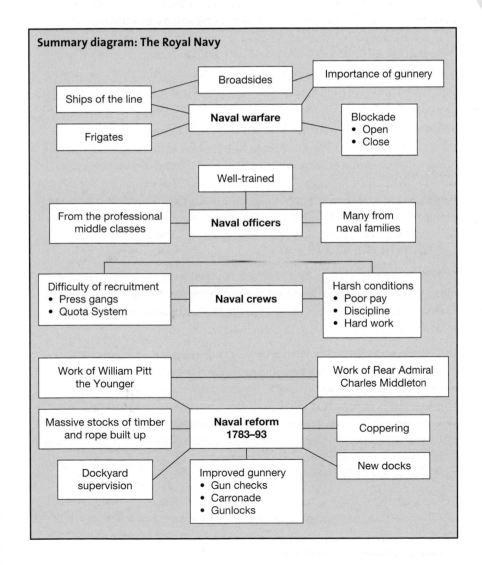

Summary diagram: The Royal Navy

- Ships of the line
- Broadsides
- Importance of gunnery
- Frigates
- **Naval warfare**
- Blockade
  - Open
  - Close

- From the professional middle classes
- **Naval officers**
- Well-trained
- Many from naval families

- Difficulty of recruitment
  - Press gangs
  - Quota System
- **Naval crews**
- Harsh conditions
  - Poor pay
  - Discipline
  - Hard work

- Work of William Pitt the Younger
- Work of Rear Admiral Charles Middleton
- Massive stocks of timber and rope built up
- **Naval reform 1783–93**
- Coppering
- Dockyard supervision
- Improved gunnery
  - Gun checks
  - Carronade
  - Gunlocks
- New docks

KEY TERMS

Ordnance Board The government agency responsible for arms, armaments and munitions.

Gunlock The mechanism in some guns by which the charge is exploded.

Slowmatch A slow-burning rope used for firing a gun.

Lanyard A short piece of rope.

② The naval war 1793–7

▶ *How dominant was the Royal Navy between 1793 and 1797?*

In February 1793 Revolutionary France declared war on Britain. At first the Royal Navy's task looked easy, given that the French Navy had been allowed to run down and many of its officers were inexperienced (see page 3). However, retaining supremacy proved a major challenge for the Royal Navy.

Toulon

In August 1793 Admiral Hood, who commanded the British Mediterranean fleet, seized Toulon, the main French naval base in the Mediterranean. The arrival of a French army forced him to abandon the port in December. Before departing, he captured or destroyed a large number of French ships.

The Battle of the Glorious First of June

The Royal Navy blockaded French ports on the Atlantic coast, particularly Brest. In 1794, Lord Howe, who commanded the blockading fleet, heard that a grain convoy was returning to France from the USA, escorted by a large fleet. Howe sailed west to give battle. The two fleets met 400 miles (640 km) out in the Atlantic on 1 June 1794. The French had 26 ships of the line, the British 25. Howe's fleet captured or sank seven enemy ships. Some 7000 French sailors were killed or taken prisoner. The British sustained 1200 casualties. But the battle was not a total success for Howe: the grain ships succeeded in reaching France, their cargoes helping to avert famine.

Developments in 1795–6

In 1795 Sir John Jervis took over command in the Mediterranean, replacing Hood. Jervis, who loathed inefficiency, set about whipping the fleet into shape. He forged an excellent relationship with those officers (like Nelson) whom he trusted and respected.

In 1796 the situation deteriorated when the Netherlands and Spain changed sides, joining France against Britain. The Royal Navy, now facing far more enemy ships, was seriously strained. The main British fleet was stationed at Spithead (off Portsmouth), leaving just fifteen battleships to blockade Brest, where double that number of French ships was preparing to break out. In December 1796, 44 French ships (seventeen of them ships of the line) carrying 14,000 troops sailed from Brest, aiming to land in Ireland. Fortunately for Britain, after a week of gales, the French fleet abandoned its mission and returned to Brest.

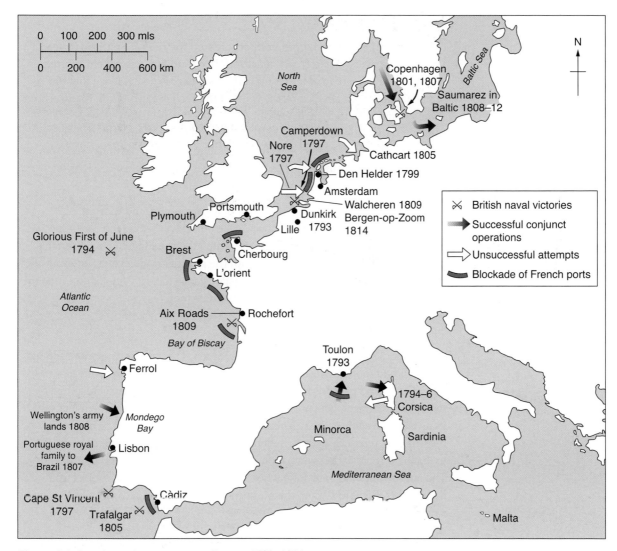

Figure 1.1 British naval actions against Europe 1793–1814.

The Battle of Cape St Vincent

Jervis stationed the bulk of his force off Càdiz, facing the main Spanish fleet. On 14 February 1797 Jervis's fleet encountered a Spanish force almost twice the size of his own at the Battle of Cape St Vincent. Confident in the skills of his men, Jervis attacked, his ships cutting through the enemy line. Nelson played a major role. Acting with speed and courage, he boarded and captured the much larger *San Josef*. He immediately became the darling of the Royal Navy, stealing the limelight from other heroes of the battle – Thomas Troubridge, Cuthbert Collingwood and James Saumarez. Jervis, who had captured four ships and driven the enemy back into Càdiz, was ennobled as the Earl of St Vincent.

The Spithead Mutiny

On 16 April 1797 Admiral Lord Bridport ordered the fleet at Spithead to sea. The crews of every ship refused the admiral's command. Discontent centred on pay, the quality of food and brutal officers. There is no evidence that the seamen were much affected by the spirit of the French Revolution. Many officers sympathised with their men, and the 'mutiny' – it was more a strike – was conducted in a civilised way. A petition was sent to the Admiralty describing 'the many hardships and oppressions we have laboured under for many years'. In response, the government agreed to raise wages and made concessions on some of the other issues.

Things then soured as legislation to improve matters ground through Parliament. On 7 May a fresh mutiny broke out. It was led by the backbone of the navy, the **petty officers**, who presented their demands in a reasonable manner. Lord Howe dealt in person with the mutineers' delegates, entertaining them at a banquet on 15 May. He also visited each ship, re-establishing trust by guaranteeing that the men's demands would be met.

The Nore Mutiny

On 12 May 1797 the ships at the **Nore** mutinied. This mutiny was more serious. The men had more far-reaching demands: the power of veto over officers, longer leave and pardons for all deserters. The Nore mutineers were joined by the North Sea Fleet, which was responsible for blockading the Dutch Navy. In an effort to achieve their demands, the mutineers attempted to blockade the Thames, refusing entry to merchant ships. Pitt's government, determined to make no more concessions, took steps to isolate and starve the mutineers. The mutiny ended in mid-June when moderate sailors wrested control from the radicals. Richard Parker, the mutiny's leader, was hanged, as were 28 other ringleaders.

The mutinies were serious. It seemed that the Royal Navy's most valuable asset – its discipline – was on the verge of collapse.

The Battle of Camperdown

The Royal Navy's reputation was restored by a victory at the Battle of Camperdown on 11 October 1797. Admiral Lord Duncan's North Sea Fleet, consisting of sixteen ships of the line, encountered a similar number of Dutch ships off the Dutch coast. Duncan's ships, in two unevenly sized divisions, smashed the enemy line, capturing eleven battleships and three frigates.

While Camperdown provided an immense boost to national morale, Britain's outlook remained bleak:

KEY TERMS

Petty officers Seamen who were not commissioned officers but who had some authority.

Nore The area at the mouth of the River Thames.

- The country continued to be threatened by French invasion.
- Austria made peace with France in 1797, which meant that Britain had no major ally in Europe.
- A large French army and fleet at Toulon was preparing to sail – no one was quite sure where.

The British government faced a hard choice. If ships were sent back to the Mediterranean to blockade the fleet at Toulon it would deprive the Channel Fleet of the strength it might need to fend off invasion. In the event, Nelson, with three ships of the line and three frigates, was sent to the Mediterranean to discover the intentions of the Toulon Fleet.

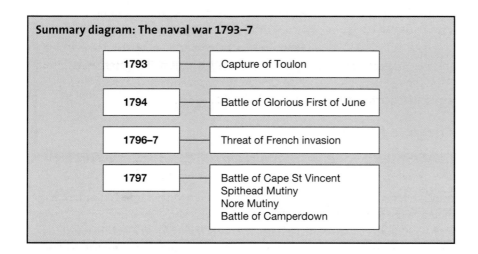

Summary diagram: The naval war 1793–7

1793	—	Capture of Toulon
1794	—	Battle of Glorious First of June
1796–7	—	Threat of French invasion
1797	—	Battle of Cape St Vincent Spithead Mutiny Nore Mutiny Battle of Camperdown

3 The Nelson touch 1798–1805

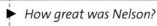

▶ *How great was Nelson?*

The Battle of Cape St Vincent made Nelson's reputation. In the eight years that followed he was to greatly enhance his standing.

The Battle of the Nile

In May 1798 **Napoleon** left Toulon with thirteen battleships and 280 transports carrying nearly 50,000 men. His destination was Egypt. Nelson was unaware of this; nor, initially, was there much he could have done about it. However, in June his fleet was reinforced by eleven ships of the line. Hearing rumours that the French had taken Malta, Nelson gambled on the fact that Napoleon was making for Egypt. He sailed eastwards, arriving at Alexandria on 29 June. There was no sign of the French. Weighing anchor, he set off to search elsewhere. As bad luck would have it, Napoleon reached Alexandria on 1 July – the day after Nelson sailed away.

 **KEY FIGURE**

Napoleon Bonaparte (1769–1821)

A French soldier who made his reputation in Italy in 1796–7. In 1799 he became first consul in France. By 1804 he was emperor and by 1807 he controlled most of Europe. His power declined after 1812 and, after his defeat at Waterloo in 1815, he was exiled to the island of St Helena in the South Atlantic.

Horatio Nelson

1758	Born at Burnham Thorpe in Norfolk
1779	Became captain of the frigate *Hinchinbrook*
1793	Took command of the 64-gun *Agamemnon*
1794	Lost the sight of his right eye at the siege of Calvi on the island of Corsica
1795	The *Agamemnon* captured a much larger French ship, *Ca Ira*
1797	Served with distinction at the Battle of Cape St Vincent in February. Lost his right arm during a failed attack on Santa Cruz de Tenerife in July
1798	Battle of the Nile
1801	Battle of Copenhagen
1803	Appointed to command the Mediterranean Fleet
1805	Died at the Battle of Trafalgar

Nelson was a naturally gifted commander who inspired men and fellow officers, winning their trust, respect and affection. One seaman said: 'he was easy of access and his manner was particularly agreeable and kind. No man was ever afraid of displeasing him, but everybody was afraid of not pleasing him.' In command of large numbers of ships after 1797, he spent time meeting all his captains, talking through his ideas and his expectations. All the officers who served under him knew that he aimed for complete annihilation of the enemy and expected them to show aggression, initiative and courage. His hallmark as a fleet commander was simplicity of tactics: get in close to the enemy and let the British naval guns do the talking. Nelson's **pell-mell** tactics were not new. Duncan's tactics at Camperdown were very similar to those used later by Nelson.

KEY TERM

Pell-mell An aggressive, confused head-to-head brawl.

A month later, on 1 August, Nelson found the French fleet in Aboukir Bay at the mouth of the River Nile. The thirteen enemy battleships were anchored in a line with both flanks close to shoals. The two fleets had the same number of ships but the French had one exceptionally large 120-gun ship – the *Orient* – and two 80-gun ships. Nelson's ships, with the exception of the 50-gun *Leander*, were all 74s.

Although it was nearing nightfall, Nelson gave battle – against the conventional rules of naval warfare. He simply ordered his captains to get close to the enemy and fight. Soon after 6.00p.m. the *Goliath*, commanded by Thomas Foley, sailed round the leading French ship so as to attack from the shore side. Foley believed the French would not have prepared their port-side guns because they would not expect the British to risk sailing so close to the shoals. Other ships followed the *Goliath* and the rest opened fire from the starboard side. Some French ships were thus attacked from two sides.

Superior British gunnery devastated the French. At 9.37p.m. the French flagship, the *Orient*, ablaze for 30 minutes, exploded. The fight continued through the night. By morning it was clear that Nelson's 'band of brothers' (as he referred to his captains) had done him proud. Of the thirteen French ships only two escaped.

It was a stunning victory:

- In one night the Royal Navy regained control of the Mediterranean.
- Napoleon and his army were trapped in Egypt. (Napoleon managed to escape in 1799.)
- Austria, Russia, Naples and Turkey joined Britain in a new coalition.

Dazed by a slight wound, Nelson did not do much in the actual battle. His influence on events had been before the fighting:

- He had brought about the battle.
- He had inspired his officers and men.
- He had not over-complicated matters with detailed orders and endless signals. (He raised only nine signals before and during the battle.)

Nelson now became a national hero.

The Mediterranean 1798–1801

French and Spanish ships continued to pose a major threat in 1798–9. British naval forces remained severely overstretched. Angry that Admiral Keith was appointed commander-in-chief of the Mediterranean Fleet rather than himself, Nelson embarked on a long sulk, sometimes refusing to take orders. Naval officers and ministers at home were scandalised by his affair with Emma Hamilton, the wife of his friend Sir William Hamilton. By 1800, it seemed that Nelson was more attracted by Lady Hamilton's charms than by life at sea. He eventually asked Keith for permission to return home. Keith agreed. Under the methodical Keith, the Royal Navy made significant gains, taking Malta in 1800.

The Atlantic 1798–1801

The Earl of St Vincent, the new head of the Channel Fleet, blockaded Brest as closely as possible. This was no easy matter:

- It was hard providing British ships with supplies of food, water and alcohol.
- Several ships were wrecked on dangerous rocks around Brest.
- There was no rest for anyone, only constant watchfulness and manoeuvring.

But the blockade prevented the French venturing out. St Vincent was made first lord of the admiralty in 1801.

The Baltic threat

The British blockade of French and Spanish ports deprived Baltic nations of markets. In 1800 Tsar Paul of Russia put pressure on Denmark, Sweden and Prussia to join a League of Armed Neutrality that would challenge British arrogance on the high seas. This posed a serious threat to Britain:

- The Baltic powers had nearly 100 warships between them.
- It was possible that the League would keep Britain out of the Baltic, where it obtained most of its naval stores: timber, pitch, tar and hemp.

Admiral Sir Hyde Parker, old and vacillating, was given command of a British Baltic Fleet. His orders were to sail to Copenhagen and either force the Danes into concessions or destroy their fleet. He was then to attack the Russian Navy. Nelson was appointed as second-in-command.

KEY TERM

Bomb vessels Small ships that carried mortars – short guns that fired heavy shells.

Parker gave Nelson the task of leading the attack on Copenhagen. Nelson's force, comprising eleven ships of the line, five frigates, four sloops and seven **bomb vessels**, had to enter the King's Channel, a narrow strip of shallow water, which was lined with Danish warships, gun batteries on rafts and shore forts on the city side. On 31 March 1801, Nelson outlined his plan to his captains. The first ship would enter the Channel, anchor opposite a Danish ship or floating battery and open fire. The next ship would pass outside the first and fire at the next target, and so on. Once the shore defences were overcome, the bomb vessels would shell the city and its dockyards.

On 2 April the attack began. While several leading ships ran aground, most of the rest made it through and by noon all were engaged. The Danes suffered a pounding but continued to fight back, the floating gun platforms being particularly effective, At 1.15p.m. Parker, five miles (8 km) away, fretting at Danish resistance, raised a signal: 'Discontinue the action'. Nelson saw it. 'I have only one eye', he said, 'and I have a right to be blind sometimes'. Placing his telescope to his blind eye, he declared: 'I really do not see the signal.'

If Nelson had obeyed Parker's order, the Battle of Copenhagen would have been a major disaster. As it was, most of the Danish ships had surrendered by 2.00p.m. Nevertheless, the batteries continued to inflict serious damage on Nelson's ships. Nelson now sent a letter to the Crown Prince of Denmark, implying that the Danes had been beaten and that if they continued to resist, he would have no option but to set fire to the floating batteries without rescuing the Danish prisoners. The Crown Prince agreed to a truce. This enabled Nelson to get his damaged ships out of range of the enemy guns and float his grounded ships. He was also able to secure the prizes he had captured. Two Danish ships had been sunk, one had exploded and twelve were taken. The Battle of Copenhagen further enhanced Nelson's reputation. He now replaced Parker as commander of the Baltic fleet.

Nelson and Britain were fortunate. Alexander I, who became Russian tsar following Paul's assassination, had no wish to fight a naval war with Britain. Thus, matters in the Baltic were peacefully settled – in Britain's favour.

The situation 1802–5

In March 1802 Britain and France signed the Peace of Amiens, ending hostilities. St Vincent set about trying to reform the royal dockyards, which he regarded as nests of corruption. Seeking to save money, he cancelled shipbuilding contracts and dismissed hundreds of workers.

In May 1803 war recommenced. Napoleon began gathering an army of 100,000 men at Boulogne to invade Britain. As a result of St Vincent's war on contractors, vital work in the yards had ground to a halt. Thus, in 1803 admirals found that their fleets were short of men, ships and supplies. Keith took command of the North Sea Fleet while Lord Cornwallis commanded the blockade of Brest.

Nelson was given command of the Mediterranean Fleet. HMS *Victory* – a 100-gun ship – became his flagship. He did not leave her for two years. His main task was to keep watch on the French Fleet in Toulon. Employing an open blockade, Nelson hoped to entice the French out to sea where he could pounce. But the French remained in port.

In December 1804 the situation deteriorated when Spain allied with France. The two countries had 102 battleships between them. The Royal Navy had just 83 in serviceable condition. If Napoleon could concentrate his ships in the English Channel, a French invasion was a serious possibility.

The chase

Napoleon's plan was for Vice Admiral Pierre Charles Villeneuve, who commanded the Toulon Fleet, to evade Nelson, lure him across the Atlantic to the Caribbean, lose him and sail back to Spain, uniting with French and Spanish ships at Vigo and Càdiz. The combined fleets would then join with the French fleets at Rochefort and Brest, overwhelm the British Channel Fleet and enable Napoleon's army at Boulogne to invade Britain.

In April 1805 Villeneuve's fleet left Toulon. Escaping Nelson's trap, it joined up with a Spanish fleet and headed towards the Caribbean. Nelson gave chase. He had eleven ships of the line; Villeneuve had eighteen. Nelson reached Barbados on 4 June. He would have caught up with Villeneuve but false intelligence sent him south instead of north. Villeneuve now set sail for Europe, hoping to put Napoleon's plan into operation. Learning of Villeneuve's move, Nelson recrossed the Atlantic, sending a fast frigate ahead to warn of the danger.

On 22 July a British fleet under Sir Robert Calder intercepted Villeneuve off Cape Finisterre. Calder captured two Spanish ships but Villeneuve made it into Ferrol. Calder, savaged by the British press, was ordered home to explain himself. But Napoleon's plan of bringing Villeneuve to Boulogne had failed. Rather than heading north, Villeneuve sailed south to Càdiz. Nelson and Calder's fleets joined Cornwallis off Brest. On 18 August Nelson returned to Britain. On 23 August Napoleon left Boulogne. The threat of invasion had lifted.

The Battle of Trafalgar

Having spent less than a month in Britain, Nelson was given command of the fleet off Càdiz. Hoping to lure Villeneuve out of port, he kept his ships 50 miles (80 km) offshore. A line of frigates reported any enemy movement. Nelson set about inspiring confidence in his captains. He stressed the importance of getting into battle quickly and not firing until they were only yards away from the enemy: 'in case signals can neither be seen nor perfectly understood, no captain can do very wrong if he places his ship alongside that of the enemy', he wrote.

On 19 October 1805 Villeneuve, obeying Napoleon's orders to sail for Italy, left Càdiz. Nelson immediately gave chase. He had 27 battleships, 17,000 men and 2148 guns. Villeneuve had 33 battleships, 30,000 men and 2568 guns. Early on 21 October both fleets sighted each other. With insufficient wind to sail back to Càdiz, Villeneuve ordered his ships into a makeshift line. Nelson formed his fleet into two divisions, one led by himself in the *Victory*, the other by Collingwood in the *Royal Sovereign*.

At 11.40a.m. Nelson signalled the fleet: 'England expects that every man will do his duty.' Soon afterwards, he raised his favourite signal: 'Engage the enemy more closely.' Given the light wind, his leading ships inched forwards, receiving heavy fire from the enemy which they were unable to return. Thankfully for the British ships, the enemy aim was poor.

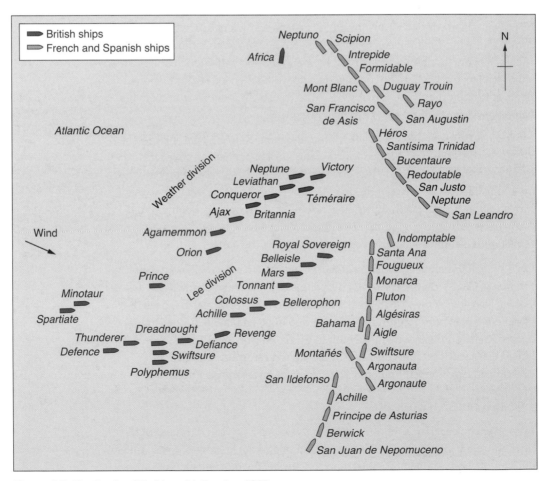

Figure 1.2 The Battle of Trafalgar, 21 October 1805.

The 60 ships preparing to fight carried a huge weight of armament. If all the cannons of all the armies at the battle of Waterloo (see pages 58–9) were lumped together with the guns from the two fleets at Trafalgar, just seven per cent of the total would be contributed by the land forces. HMS *Victory* alone carried armaments equivalent to 67 per cent of the British Army's artillery at Waterloo.

The *Royal Sovereign* reached the enemy line first. Collingwood was on the **quarterdeck**, the most dangerous place on the ship, the target for every sharpshooter. But it was a point of honour for officers to lead their men from that exposed position. At 12.10, with the *Royal Sovereign* only yards from the enemy, Collingwood, nonchalantly eating an apple, gave the order to open fire.

Before the *Victory* opened fire she was under fire from five ships for 40 minutes, losing over 50 men. Her rigging and sails were cut to pieces and her steering mechanism blasted to bits as she approached the centre of the enemy's line. At 12.35 she found a gap astern of Villeneuve's flagship, the *Bucentaure*. The *Victory's* forecastle carronade caused devastation on *Bucentaure's* quarterdeck, while her main guns raked the enemy's stern with a broadside which put some 400 Frenchmen and twenty guns out of action. The *Victory* then encountered two other French ships – the *Redoutable* and the *Neptune*. Nelson's flagship became so entangled with the *Redoutable* that French sailors looked set to board her but carronade fire from the *Victory* and from the *Temeraire*, the second ship in Nelson's column, held the boarders at bay.

For several minutes the *Royal Sovereign*, the *Belleisle* (the second ship in Collingwood's column), the *Victory* and the *Temeraire* suffered huge damage. But as more British ships arrived, Villeneuve's fleet took a pounding as British gunnery overwhelmed the enemy at exceptionally close quarters (see Source B).

SOURCE B

French Lieutenant Gicquel des Touches, aboard the *Intrepide* at Trafalgar, quoted in P. Warwick, *Tales from the Front Line: Trafalgar*, David & Charles, 2011, pp. 169–70.

*The audacity with which Admiral Nelson had attacked us, and which had so completely succeeded, arose from the complete scorn which, not without reason, he professed for the effects of our gunfire. At that time our principle was to aim at the masts and, in order to produce any real damage, we wasted masses of projectiles which, if they had been aimed at the hulls, would have felled a proportion of the crews. Thus our losses were always incomparably higher than those of the English, who fired horizontally and hit our wooden sides, letting fly splinters which were more murderous than the cannon ball itself. We were still using the **linstock** match to fire our guns, which dispatched the ball with an excruciating delay, so that if the ship was rolling, as it was on October 21, complete broadsides flew over the enemy's mastheads without causing the slightest damage. The English had **flintlocks**, rather than our crude linstocks.*

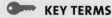

KEY TERMS

Quarterdeck Part of the deck behind the main mast, used by officers.

Linstock A staff holding a lighted match for firing a cannon.

Flintlock A gunlock or gun with a flint from which a spark is struck to ignite gunpowder.

Why, according to Source B, was the French fire so poor at Trafalgar?

Conditions below deck were appalling. Gun decks turned into noisy, smoky furnaces. Men slipped on the blood of their crewmates as they loaded, hauled and fired – over and over again.

At 1.15p.m. Nelson was shot through the shoulder by a sharpshooter stationed in the *Redoutable*'s rigging. The ball punctured his lung and passed through his spine. In great agony, he was carried below. Soon after 1.45p.m. the *Bucentaure*, with 99 fit men out of a crew of 643, surrendered. Other French–Spanish ships did the same. At 2.35p.m. Captain Hardy visited Nelson. Nelson asked how the battle was going. 'Very well', Hardy replied, 'We have got twelve or fourteen of the enemy's ships in our possession'.

Nelson died at 4.30p.m. His fleet eventually took eighteen of Villeneuve's battleships. Of these, four were lost in the storm that followed the battle, three were scuttled, one exploded, two were burned and the *Redoutable* sank; the rest were prizes. Four of the enemy ships that escaped were captured off Cape Ortegal on 4 November. Of the eleven that made it back to Càdiz, only five were considered seaworthy. Not one British ship had been lost. Four hundred and fifty-nine Britons died, including Nelson, and 1208 were wounded. There were 2218 French deaths and 1155 wounded. The Spanish had 1025 killed and 1383 wounded. Some 8000 French and Spaniards were taken prisoner.

Trafalgar was a decisive victory. It did not prevent a French invasion, which had already been postponed. Nor did it have much impact on the remainder of the **War of the Third Coalition**. Two months later Napoleon triumphed at Austerlitz, knocking Austria out of the war. Prussia and Russia were both defeated by 1807. However, after Trafalgar the Royal Navy achieved an aura of invincibility and was not seriously challenged by the French for the remainder of the French Wars.

Nelson's importance

John Sugden in his *Nelson: The Sword of Albion* (2012) considered Nelson's importance:

> *Perhaps his greatest contribution to the navy was to lift its standing to unprecedented heights. Nelson knew that he had a fine weapon, but it had to be tested to reach its true potential. That, in effect, meant stretching the navy sometimes beyond what we would now call its 'comfort zone'. He was by no means the only admiral to attack the boundaries. The close blockades of St Vincent and Cornwallis wore down ships and men, but they took seamanship to new levels. More spectacularly, Nelson took the navy where few admirals would have dared go. As a young officer he led naval forces into engagements ashore that even some members of the military did not think were winnable. The other two flag officers of the Baltic fleet would not have attacked the Danish position at Copenhagen, and there is no evidence that Collingwood had a clear tactical plan to cope with Villeneuve. On all of these occasions Nelson placed men and ships where they had to fight for their survival, but in the doing they won victories that raised the morale and reputation of the service and reached new horizons.*

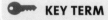 **KEY TERM**

War of the Third Coalition In 1805 Britain was allied with Austria and Russia against France. Prussia joined the coalition in 1806.

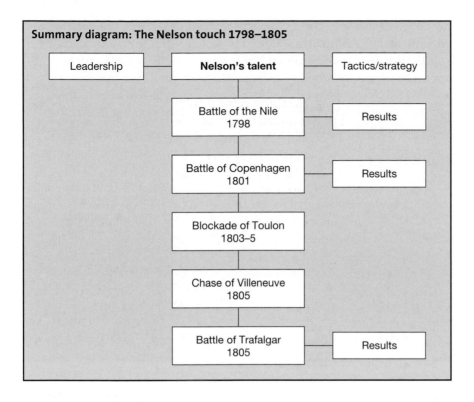

Summary diagram: The Nelson touch 1798–1805

4 The Royal Navy 1806–15

▶ *How did Britain make use of its naval supremacy after Trafalgar?*

After Trafalgar, while Britain ruled the waves, Napoleon ruled most of Europe between 1806 and 1812. The possible revival of the French Navy could not therefore be ignored, particularly as Napoleon ordered a large-scale shipbuilding programme. He controlled a host of European dockyards and had a vast reservoir of trained manpower from Europe's idle merchant fleets at his command. It was conceivable that he could build a fleet that could swamp the Royal Navy by sheer force of numbers. Antwerp became the centre of the French shipbuilding effort after 1807, necessitating a British blockade of the River Scheldt.

The Continental System

In 1806, hoping to destroy Britain commercially, Napoleon introduced the Berlin Decrees forbidding Europe to trade with Britain. This attempt at economic blockade came to be known as the Continental System. In June 1807 Napoleon and Tsar Alexander I signed the Treaties of Tilsit. Alexander agreed to outlaw Russian trade with Britain. Thus, virtually the whole of Europe was closed to British merchants. Napoleon believed that this would force Britain to make peace.

But Britain did not surrender. Nor was it brought to its knees economically (see pages 24–5). In 1807 Britain hit back, banning trade with any ports complying with the Berlin Decrees. The Royal Navy was allowed to stop and search any neutral ship it suspected of trading with the enemy. Given that the navy now had to blockade far more European ports, large numbers of small ships were built. Europe, starved of imports from around the world, suffered more economic hardship than Britain.

Naval actions

- At Tilsit, Napoleon and Alexander I agreed that Denmark should come under French control. Fearing that the Danish Fleet would fall into French hands, in July 1807 Britain sent seventeen ships of the line, 21 frigates and 18,000 troops to attack Copenhagen (see Source C). British soldiers besieged the Danish capital while British ships bombarded the city. In September the Danes capitulated, surrendering their entire fleet – 70 ships, including seventeen ships of the line.
- Admiral Sir James Saumarez ensured free passage of British ships into the Baltic, enabling Britain to acquire vital materials (see page 11).
- From 1808 to 1814, the Royal Navy helped to transport troops and supplies to (and from) Spain and Portugal (see pages 47–57).
- In 1809 the navy co-operated with the army in the Walcheren debacle (see page 45). Its hopes of seizing Antwerp and destroying battleships being built in the River Scheldt were thwarted.
- British frigates terrorised European coastlines, damaging local trade and tying down large numbers of enemy troops. A number of aggressive frigate captains, like Lord Cochrane, made their reputations (and their fortunes) raiding enemy ports and taking scores of prizes.
- After 1805 Britain seized Cape Colony, **Ceylon**, Sierra Leone, Tobago, Trinidad, Java and Mauritius from the Netherlands and France.

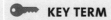 **KEY TERM**

Ceylon Present-day Sri Lanka.

? Why, according to Source C, was Perceval able to justify an attack on Denmark?

SOURCE C

Scribbled memorandum by Spencer Perceval, chancellor of the exchequer, 22 July 1807, quoted in R. Knight, *Britain Against Napoleon: The Organization of Victory 1793–1815*, Penguin, 2014, p. 285.

But for the justification of a hostile armament against Denmark we must look for other reasons. I trust, however, that the world will feel that we have them … Intelligence from so many and such varied sources of B[onaparte]'s intention to force or seduce D[enmark] into an active confederacy against this country, leaves no doubt of his design. Nay, the fact that he has openly avowed such intention in an interview with the E[mperor] of R[ussia] is brought to this country in such a way as it cannot be doubted. Under such circumstances it would be madness, it would be idiotic … to wait for an overt act.

- After 1811 the French Navy posed no threat as money for French shipbuilding dried up. Between 1812 and 1815 only four French ships of the line were launched.

The War of 1812

Britain's blockade of Europe angered American merchants who had profited from the Napoleonic Wars. So did the fact that British sailors boarded American merchant ships, searching for British seamen who had deserted. There were a number of incidents before the USA declared war in June 1812. From Britain's point of view the war with America (known as the War of 1812) was a sideshow. The USA had only fourteen small warships in 1812. American frigate captains initially out-fought their British counterparts in a number of actions, largely because US frigates were larger and carried more guns than their British equivalents. Nevertheless, by 1813–14 the Royal Navy had successfully blockaded most American ports.

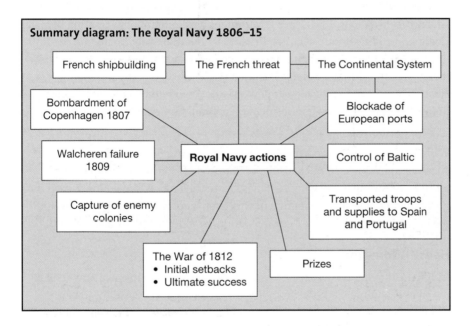

Summary diagram: The Royal Navy 1806–15

5 The British war effort 1793–1815

▶ *How did Britain's entire population contribute to the war effort?*

While the officers and seamen of the Royal Navy win most of the plaudits for Britain's survival and ultimate success in the 22-year conflict with France, British victory was the result of many other factors. Historian Roger Knight has recently emphasised the degree to which the efforts of virtually the whole British population – politicians, industrialists, farmers, shipbuilders, gunsmiths and gunpowder manufacturers, bankers and traders of the City of London – ensured British success.

British governments

At the centre of the British war effort was Parliament. The British parliamentary system, far from democratic at this time, was also far from perfect. British politicians often supported overambitious war plans and appointed men who were not up to the job. But for all its faults, the parliamentary system proved itself better at waging war than Napoleon's dictatorship.

William Pitt the Younger

William Pitt the Younger had been a successful peacetime prime minister, restoring Britain's finances after the American War of Independence. He was an able but not inspiring war leader. Pitt, Henry Dundas (secretary of state for war) and Lord Grenville (foreign secretary) largely controlled Britain's war strategy from 1793 to 1801. Pitt's government was influential in creating the First Coalition in 1793: Britain, Austria, Prussia, the Netherlands, Spain and Sardinia united against Revolutionary France. Large British **subsidies** held the coalition together until 1797. The Second Coalition (1799–1801), comprising Britain, Austria, Russia and several lesser powers, was negotiated by Pitt and Grenville. Both coalitions collapsed as a result of French military success.

The Whig Party was generally critical of Pitt (a Conservative, or Tory). Several Whig leaders favoured appeasing France and making peace. But in 1794, some 60 moderate Whigs led by the Duke of Portland, disliking the sympathetic attitude of leading Whig Charles James Fox to the French Revolution, joined the government's side. This realignment effectively kept the Whigs from power for the next 40 years, except for one brief administration in 1806–7 (see below).

Henry Addington

In 1801, Pitt resigned over King George III's opposition to his measure to relax the rules excluding Catholics from the armed forces. Henry Addington formed a new government, even though many of Pitt's friends would have nothing to do with him. Addington made peace with the French at Amiens in March 1802. This was hardly a great triumph. Britain had to return all French overseas possessions captured in the war. When war recommenced in May 1803, Pitt came out in opposition, attacking Addington for the Earl of St Vincent's naval administration (see page 12). Addington fell from power in May 1804.

Pitt's return

Pitt returned as prime minister. He formed the Third Coalition with Austria and Russia in 1805. Henry Dundas, ennobled in 1802 as Lord Melville, became first lord of the admiralty. He immediately reversed St Vincent's policies. Stores' contracts were quickly renewed and private contractors employed to repair and

KEY TERM

Subsidies Sums of money given to Britain's allies.

build ships (see page 26). Unfortunately, Melville's reputation was ruined by a monetary scandal in 1805 and he was forced to resign. In January 1806, Pitt, worn out by his exertions, died aged 46.

The Ministry of All the Talents

Grenville, allying with Whig leader Charles James Fox, formed a new government in February 1806. Grenville had long wanted a ministry that would 'comprehend all the talents and character' in public life. Although the term 'Ministry of All the Talents' was used ironically by his opponents, it is the term by which Grenville's government is generally known. Efforts to make peace with Napoleon came to nothing. In 1807 Grenville revived Pitt's 1801 initiative to appease Catholics by enabling them to join the military services. Again, the king would not have it and Grenville resigned.

The Duke of Portland

The Tories formed a new government, led by the 70-year-old Duke of Portland. Sick and ineffectual, Portland had little control over his cabinet. But with **Castlereagh** as secretary of state for war, Canning as foreign secretary and Lord Mulgrave at the Admiralty, the government was a stronger team than the Talents. Unfortunately, Portland's 'team' was not united. A plot by Canning (who had prime ministerial ambitions) to demote Castlereagh culminated in a duel between the two men in September 1809. Canning was hit in the thigh by Castlereagh's second shot. As a result, both men resigned from their posts.

SOURCE D

From *The Morning Chronicle*, 22 September 1809, quoted in R. Knight, *Britain Against Napoleon: The Organization of Victory 1793–1815*, Penguin, 2014, p. 213.

The distractions of the Cabinet have at last burst into open and public violence. It will scarcely be credited by posterity that two of His Majesty's principal Secretaries of State should so far forget the duty that they owed to their Sovereign and the example they ought to give to the country in obedience to its laws, to fight a duel. Yet the fact is actually so … [It is] most serious that His Majesty should have committed the affairs of State to persons whose intemperate passions were so little under the control of reason.

Spencer Perceval

Portland died in October 1809. He was replaced by Spencer Perceval. Perceval proved himself a capable leader. He kept his nerve during difficult times and ensured that his fragile government provided the funds for war, notably in Spain and Portugal (see pages 47–57). The political situation was rendered unstable by the fact that King George III's mind gave way in 1810. The role of his son George, the Prince Regent, was formalised by Parliament in February 1811, with the proviso that he should do nothing irreversible for a year. After many years

KEY FIGURE

Robert Stewart, Viscount Castlereagh (1769–1822)
Secretary of state for war 1805–6 and again 1807–9. As foreign secretary (1812–22), he played an important role in the peace-making process at the end of the Napoleonic Wars.

Why was Source D critical of the actions of Canning and Castlereagh?

of friendship with the Whigs, it was expected that, when the year was over, he would ask the Whigs to form a government. But the Whigs were divided and the Prince Regent gradually changed his loyalties. In February 1812 he backed the Tories, in what Roger Knight describes as 'an uncharacteristic attack of common sense'.

Lord Liverpool

In May 1812 Perceval was assassinated in the lobby of the House of Commons by a deranged merchant. Lord Liverpool, secretary of state for war 1809–12, now formed a government. Prudent, able, discreet and trusted, he remained prime minister until his death in 1827.

Government bureaucracy

Corruption and inefficiency in government was a major problem. The growing scale and complexity of the war put an enormous strain on the bureaucratic machinery (today's civil service). The number of officials and clerks in every department swelled. But office systems, particularly with regard to auditing and accounting, were weak. **Patronage** often resulted in men with inadequate skills being appointed or promoted.

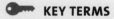

KEY TERMS

Patronage The process of bestowing jobs and offices.

Sinecures Well-paid jobs without much work.

Financial and administrative reform really gathered pace only after 1806. Two lengthy parliamentary commissions, the Commission of Naval Revision and the Commission of Military Enquiry, exposed corruption and administrative incompetence in both the navy and army. The commissions' recommendations were quickly adopted. Ancient customs were abandoned, money was saved, and **sinecures** diminished as younger, more able men rose to the top. Stricter systems and accounting methods led to a reduction in corruption.

As the talents of senior officials improved, so did the skills of government clerks. The productivity of the state industrial establishments (see below) increased sharply. Relations between government officials and private contractors were governed by an increasingly sophisticated contract system. This enabled government technicians and the officials who ran the treasury, army, ordnance, navy, transport and victualling boards, together with the officers of the various state yards, to maintain and control quality. According to Knight, between 1806 and 1815, 'A silent revolution had taken place across government … the quiet triumph of the "men of business"'.

Between 1793 and 1815 there were six British prime ministers, ten foreign secretaries, seven secretaries of state for war and ten first lords of the admiralty. Not all these men were successful or particularly talented, but Britain did produce some able wartime leaders, including Pitt, Dundas, Canning, Castlereagh, Perceval and Liverpool. Knight also highlights the work of a host of politicians and civil servants, serving as secretaries and officials in the major departments: men of 'youth, intelligence and formidable industry' like Viscount Palmerston (see page 89), who helped to reform the army.

Financing the war

How to pay for the war was the central issue in British politics between 1793 and 1815.

Loans

In 1793 Pitt, assuming that the war would be short, believed that the government could pay for it by raising loans from the City of London. While vast sums were raised, thanks to the help of the Bank of England and the Banking House of Benjamin and Abraham Goldsmid, it was soon apparent that borrowing alone would be insufficient to meet the costs of the war.

New taxes

At least 21 goods and services were newly taxed during the war, including salt, beer, spirits, thread and lace, auctions, ships' hulls, windows, carriages, stage coaches, farm horses, silk, hops, servants, newspapers, dogs and hair powder. Over the 22 years of war, taxes on spirits yielded £51 million. Even the tax on farm horses raised £9 million.

In 1799 Pitt took the art of raising revenue to a new level by persuading Parliament to impose a graduated income tax for the first time in Britain's history. It was to be paid by all those who earned more than £60 a year. The immensely unpopular tax raised a great deal of money – £155 million by 1815.

Before 1793 around £18 million a year was raised in taxes. An additional £12 million on average was extracted every year between 1793 and 1815. The increase in taxation hit mainly the rich.

The City of London

As the war progressed, the mutual dependence of politicians and merchants and bankers in the City of London was magnified. While the government needed to borrow money from the City, as well as to purchase many of the commodities in which the merchants specialised, the merchants required warships to escort the convoys carrying their goods to protect them from enemy **privateers**. The fact that over 100 MPs were themselves bankers, insurers, merchants and industrialists helped to strengthen the ties.

The close relationship between the government and powerful capital markets gave Britain a considerable advantage over France. No other city in the world had the power and reach of London, the centre of many worldwide markets. With large numbers of continental merchants and bankers coming to London to escape the Napoleonic blockade (see page 17), the City's international aspect became even more pronounced. By 1815, nearly two-thirds of all merchants in the City were of continental origins. Several of these immigrants played crucial roles in raising money for the government, most notably Nathan Meyer Rothschild, a banker of German origin, who organised the finance for Wellington's advance through Spain and France in 1813–14 (see pages 56–7).

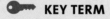

KEY TERM

Privateers Private vessels commissioned to seize and plunder an enemy's ships in wartime.

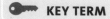
Government expenditure and income in 1811

Not until 1811 did **Hansard** print an easily understood table of annual public expenditure. Total government expenditure in 1811 came to just over £85 million. £43 million was spent on the army, navy and ordnance combined. Interest on the national debt totalled £35 million. The remainder consisted of civil costs and subsidies to continental allies.

Government income in 1811 was as follows:

- Land-assessed taxes, property and income taxes: £26.8 million.
- Customs and excise duties: £39.4 million.
- Profits from the Post Office: £1.7 million.

With other small sources of income, the government raised £69.2 million. This meant there was a spending deficit of nearly £16 million. The government had to rely on loans to meet the shortfall.

Financial success 1808–15

When Grenville left office in 1807 he was convinced that Britain could not afford to finance a significant army on the continent. The Tory (Conservative) administrations of Portland, Perceval and Liverpool proved him wrong. These governments met the expenses of Wellington's army in the Peninsula. They also subsidised their allies, ensuring that coalition armies remained operational against Napoleon. Between 1793 and 1815 nearly £66 million was paid in subsidies. Over half this total was paid in the last five years of the war. In 1814 alone Britain spent £10 million on subsidies.

The British economy

Britain's growing economy enabled the government to finance the war. Between 1783 and 1802 Britain's economy grew at an annual rate of nearly six per cent, a greater pace than at any time during the previous century.

Industrial growth

Britain's industries made spectacular advances during the war:

- Cotton production increased threefold between 1793 and 1813.
- Iron and steel manufacturing output increased fourfold during the same period.
- While most of British industry was still powered by watermill and windmills, steam-power was becoming more popular. In 1805, 112 steam engines were operating in London. While they were used mainly for pumping water, steam power was beginning to be applied to manufacturing.

Agricultural growth

Throughout the war, Britain had to import grain, mainly from northern Europe and North America. High wartime prices for foodstuffs created prosperity for farmers and encouraged investment in farming. Common land and wasteland was cultivated and corn output increased by over a fifth between 1790 and 1810. The Board of Agriculture and Internal Improvement, managed by its industrious chairman John Sinclair and able secretary Arthur Young, encouraged improvements in breeding, crop rotation and ploughing techniques.

Canals

Britain had begun to develop its canal network in the late eighteenth century. That development continued during the war years. The Grand Junction Canal, for example, which joined the Midlands to London, was started in 1793. It was operational by 1805. The opening up of more canals greatly reduced the cost of transporting bulk goods.

British trade

Given that a large proportion of government income derived from customs duties, overseas trade was vital to the war effort. British trade expanded during the war. (Between 1793 and 1815 Britain's registered merchant ships increased from 14,500 to 22,000.) Cotton textiles led the export drive. By 1815 their value was six times greater than in 1793. Exports of manufactured goods also increased considerably. Despite the Continental System, between 1808 and early 1810 trade flourished as new markets were found in South America and the Caribbean. But between late 1810 and 1812 imports and exports declined and bankruptcies nearly doubled. Poor harvests and war with the USA (see page 19) added to the economic gloom. However, after Napoleon's defeat in Russia in 1812, the Continental System began to collapse, ensuring that British goods were again shipped to Europe.

The East India Company

The East India Company greatly assisted the British war effort:

- It exported great quantities of British goods to India and China.
- Its ships brought back vital materials, including saltpetre – an essential ingredient in gunpowder manufacture.
- Its ships were chartered to transport troops abroad.
- It swelled the government's coffers through the payment of high duties on Asian imports, especially tea.

The convoy system

British merchant ships relied on the Royal Navy for protection from privateers. **Convoys** became compulsory after 1798, a provision even more stringently applied after 1803. The convoy system proved highly effective in the later stages of the war, ensuring that fewer ships were lost to privateers.

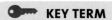 **KEY TERM**

Convoys Groups of merchant ships sailing in formation and protected by warships.

The situation in 1815

If anything, Britain's economy was strengthened by the war. By 1815 manufacturing and mining industries were thriving, shipyards were busy, agricultural prices were high and new markets abroad had opened up.

Military production

The critical task for British politicians and administrators was to translate the buoyant economy and the resulting wealth into an efficient military machine. Throughout the war, the government had its own military establishments producing warships, weapons and gunpowder. However, state ordnance yards and dockyards lacked the capacity to achieve the increased levels of production that were required. The private sector came to the government's aid. Privately owned shipyards, foundries and factories, working on government contracts, ultimately built more ships and manufactured more weapons than the state.

Shipbuilding

Since wooden ships had a limited life, the Royal Navy's warship construction and refitting programme had to be continual to maintain fleet numbers.

Royal dockyards

The government maintained six home dockyards which:

- built the largest warships, which were beyond the capacity of most private yards to build
- repaired and refitted ships
- acted as storage and distribution depots for equipment and raw materials.

The inspector-general of naval works, Samuel Bentham, helped to enlarge and speed up the royal dockyards' building and maintenance capacity.

Private shipyards

By 1815 more than three-quarters of Britain's 10,000 shipwrights were employed in over 500 private shipyards. The shipyards around the Newcastle area, with over 2000 shipwrights, built both warships and merchant ships. So did shipyards in Liverpool, Leith, Hull, Whitby and Bristol. Private yards built their (admittedly) smaller ships faster than the government yards. During the course of the war, private shipyards built 436 warships (228,176 tons) while the royal dockyards built only 82 warships (94,960 tons). A further 52 ships were built in Bermuda, Canada, India and Malaysia.

New developments

The search to reduce costs in war production was continuous:

- In 1804 the navy began to build frigates from fir timber. Although such ships had a shorter sea-life, they were cheaper and easier to construct than hardwood ships.

- The traditional method of repair involved replacing each rotten timber with a new one. Lord Melville (see pages 20–1), against the Navy Board's wishes, ordered 23 warships to be 'doubled and strengthened with riders'. This involved laying a timber bottom over the existing ship's hull and strengthening the internal timbers with diagonal braces fastened with iron pieces. The method worked. 'It might be thought perhaps going too far to say that the Battle of Trafalgar would not have taken place if the new mode of repairing ships had not been adopted,' wrote Sir John Barrow, a leading Admiralty civil servant. 'Instead of 34 sail of the line, the Mediterranean Fleet would not possibly have exceeded 24 sail of the line at the time the action happened … by the ordinary method of repairing ships.'
- The block mills in the royal dockyards at Portsmouth were the first example of mass, standardised production in the world. They were designed by Marc Isambard Brunel, father of the great Victorian engineer Isambard Kingdom Brunel. Blocks (or pullies), small and large, were an essential part of a ship's equipment. A 74-gun ship, for example, was equipped with 920 blocks for running rigging and another 450 for working the guns. After 1807 the steam-driven Portsmouth mills could produce blocks more cheaply and faster than before.
- New docks were built in London: the West India Dock (1802), the London Dock (1805) and the East India Dock (1806). Steam pumps kept the docks dry during building. When completed, steam dredgers, invented by Samuel Bentham, kept them from silting up.

The Board of Ordnance

The Board of Ordnance oversaw the manufacture of munitions of all kinds, including cannon, shot and gunpowder. Like the navy, it managed large industrial concerns, staffed by thousands of employees. Great quantities of gunpowder, for example, were produced in the state mills of Faversham and Waltham Abbey. Elaborate testing of all gunpowder was conducted throughout wartime and improvements continued, ensuring that British gunpowder was superior to that of the French. The Royal Laboratory at Woolwich manufactured cartridges. In 1804 new laboratories were established at Portsmouth and Plymouth.

Nevertheless, private contractors enabled the state to expand war production:

- Cannon were provided by Walker's of Rotherham and the Carron Company of Scotland.
- Birmingham was the chief area for small-arms manufacture. From July 1808 to July 1810 Birmingham gunsmiths supplied 1,045,000 barrels and locks for assembly into firearms.

Britain, as well as arming its troops in the Iberian Peninsula, was able to distribute huge quantities of arms and munitions to its allies. In 1813, for example, 100,000 muskets were sent to both Prussia and Russia.

The Victualling Board

The Victualling Board was responsible for provisioning tens of thousands of men in the Royal Navy and the British Army abroad. This was an enormous logistical task. The domestic market supplied most military provisions. The Victualling Board's main yard and distribution centre was at Deptford, on the south bank of the River Thames. In the yard were bakers, slaughtermen, brewers, coopers and labourers. From this central yard, provisions were distributed to smaller yards at the naval bases of Dover, Chatham, Portsmouth and Plymouth. These yards supplied warships and army transports.

Most of the Victualling Board's food and services were provided by private contractors. The advantages that stemmed from a competitive market-based system, with open and fairly administered contract tendering by the government, gave Britain an advantage over its antagonists in both price and supply. French and Spanish forces, dependent on the monopoly of individuals or the state, had an inferior supply chain. Nelson's fleet, off Càdiz in October 1805 (see page 13), was supported by a succession of victualling convoys. In contrast, French and Spanish crews, in harbour at Càdiz, were poorly supplied and many suffered from scurvy. Accordingly, Nelson's seamen, as they went into battle at Trafalgar, were in better health than their opponents.

The Transport Board

The Transport Board was responsible for chartering the merchant ships needed for expeditions overseas. In the period 1793–1802 alone, 135,000 troops were transported successfully from Britain. That figure rose considerably after 1803. The Board ensured that the government was able to launch all its operations.

Discontent in Britain

By and large, Britain remained united throughout the war. But there were occasions when the government feared that revolution was about to spread across the Channel.

1794–5

There was domestic unrest in 1794–5, mainly caused by high food prices. In October 1795 King George III was jeered as he went to open Parliament. On his return, he had to be rescued from a threatening crowd by troops. As a result, Pitt pushed the **Treasonable Practices Act 1796** and the **Seditious Meetings Act 1796** through Parliament. In the late 1790s he ran a repressive state, complete with Home Office spies and anti-labour legislation contained in the **Combination Acts 1799 and 1800**.

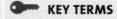 **KEY TERMS**

Treasonable Practices Act 1796 This expanded the definitions of treason to include attempts to coerce Parliament or attacks on the constitution.

Seditious Meetings Act 1796 This banned lectures or meetings of more than 50 people unless permitted by local magistrates.

Combination Acts 1799 and 1800 These acts, designed to prevent strikes, made it illegal for workers to gather together in large numbers.

Ireland

A major rebellion broke out in Ireland in May 1798. Large numbers of troops were sent to deal with the unrest. The defeat of the Irish rebels at Vinegar Hill in County Wexford on 21 June was the turning point of the uprising. Hundreds of rebels were executed.

Luddites

High unemployment in the Midlands and northern England in 1811–12 led to widespread unrest, particularly among skilled weavers who lost their jobs as the result of the introduction of power looms. So-called **Luddites** smashed new machines and threatened mill and factory owners. The government passed legislation declaring that destruction of machines was a capital offence and moved troops to the centres of protest. The execution or transportation of Luddite leaders led to the end of disturbances in 1813.

 **KEY TERM**

Luddites The people who destroyed labour-saving machinery in 1811–12. They took their name from a mythical leader, Ned Ludd.

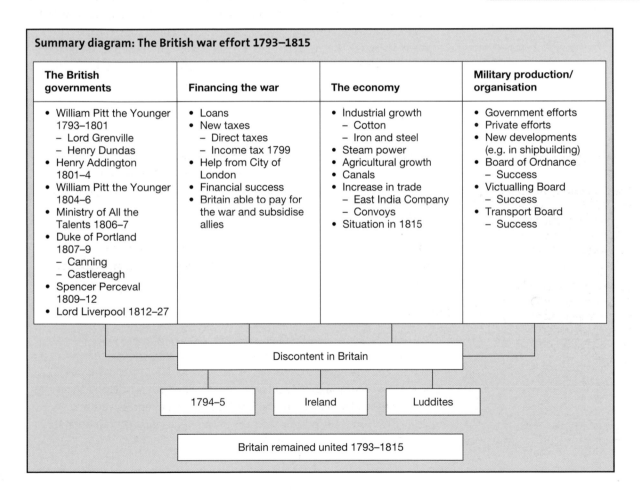

Summary diagram: The British war effort 1793–1815

The British governments	Financing the war	The economy	Military production/ organisation
• William Pitt the Younger 1793–1801 – Lord Grenville – Henry Dundas • Henry Addington 1801–4 • William Pitt the Younger 1804–6 • Ministry of All the Talents 1806–7 • Duke of Portland 1807–9 – Canning – Castlereagh • Spencer Perceval 1809–12 • Lord Liverpool 1812–27	• Loans • New taxes – Direct taxes – Income tax 1799 • Help from City of London • Financial success • Britain able to pay for the war and subsidise allies	• Industrial growth – Cotton – Iron and steel • Steam power • Agricultural growth • Canals • Increase in trade – East India Company – Convoys • Situation in 1815	• Government efforts • Private efforts • New developments (e.g. in shipbuilding) • Board of Ordnance – Success • Victualling Board – Success • Transport Board – Success

Discontent in Britain

1794–5   Ireland   Luddites

Britain remained united 1793–1815

Chapter summary

The fact that Britain survived the war with France was largely due to the Royal Navy. Superior British seamanship and gunnery ensured that the navy maintained its supremacy, successfully blockading both French and Spanish ports for much of the war and defeating enemy fleets when they ventured forth, for example at the Battle of the Glorious First of June (1794) and the Battle of Cape St Vincent (1797). The mutinies at Spithead and the Nore in 1797 were resolved and the Royal Navy went on to win the Battle of Camperdown (1797). Nelson was the navy's greatest hero, winning victories at the Battle of the Nile (1798), the Battle of Copenhagen (1801) and the Battle of Trafalgar (1805). The Royal Navy continued to rule the waves after Nelson's death.

The whole nation, however, and not just the navy, contributed to British victory. Politicians, public servants, naval and army officers all worked for the improvement and growth of Britain's financial, naval and military effectiveness. Thanks to Britain's dynamic and innovative economy, the government found the money to finance the war. Private manufacturers helped to expand war production. Despite some unrest, most Britons supported the war effort.

Refresher questions

Use these questions to remind yourself of the key material covered in this chapter.

1 Why was the Royal Navy well prepared for war in 1793?

2 Why was naval recruitment a problem?

3 How dominant was the navy between 1793 and 1797?

4 How serious were the mutinies at Spithead and the Nore?

5 How great was Nelson?

6 Why did Britain win the Battle of Trafalgar?

7 To what extent did Britain rule the waves after the Battle of Trafalgar?

8 How well was Britain governed from 1793 to 1815?

9 How did Britain finance the war?

10 Why was the British economy so strong?

11 How was Britain able to use its economic strength to military advantage?

12 What were the main internal threats to Britain?

Question practice

ESSAY QUESTIONS

1 How accurate is it to say that the Royal Navy ruled the waves in the years 1793–1815?

2 To what extent was the entire British population involved in the wars against France in the years 1793–1815?

3 How far do you agree with historian John Sugden's view that Nelson's greatest contribution to the navy was 'to lift its standing to unprecedented heights' in the years 1798–1805?

4 How far was Britain economically and financially successful during the Revolutionary and Napoleonic Wars between 1793 and 1815?

SOURCE ANALYSIS QUESTION

1 Assess the value of Source 1 for revealing the nature of Nelson's leadership and the reasons for the Royal Navy's success at the Battle of Trafalgar. Explain your answer, using the source, the information given about its origin and your own knowledge about the historical context.

SOURCE 1

Vice Admiral Cuthbert Collingwood's dispatch, sent from HMS *Euryalus*, off Cape Trafalgar, 22 October 1805, quoted in Peter Warwick, *Tales from the Front Line: Trafalgar*, David & Charles, 2011, pp. 15–16.

The ever-to-be lamented death of vice-Admiral Lord Viscount Nelson, who, in the late conflict with the enemy, fell in the hour of victory, leaves to me the duty of informing My Lords Commissioners of the Admiralty, that on the 19th instant [of this month], it was communicated to the Commander-in-Chief, from the ships watching the motions of the enemy in Cadiz, that the Combined fleets had put to sea; as they sailed with light winds westerly, His Lordship concluded their destination was the Mediterranean, and immediately made all sail for the Straits' entrance, with the British squadron, consisting of twenty seven ships, three of them sixty-fours, where His Lordship was informed by Captain Blackwood … that they had not yet passed the Straits.

On Monday 21st instant, at daylight when Cape Trafalgar bore E. by S. about seven leagues, the enemy was discovered six or seven miles to the eastwards; the wind was west, and very light; the Commander-in-Chief immediately made the signal for the fleet to bear up in two columns, as they are formed in order of sailing; a mode of attack His Lordship had previously directed, to avoid the inconvenience and delay in forming a line of battle in the usual manner. The enemy's line consisted of thirty-three ships (of which eighteen [actually seventeen] were French, and fifteen [actually sixteen] Spanish, commanded-in-chief by Admiral Villeneuve; the Spaniards, under the direction of Gravina, wore, with their heads to northwards, and formed their line of battle with great closeness and correctness … .

As the mode of our attack had been previously determined on, and communicated to flag officers, and captains, few signals were necessary, and none were made, except to direct the close order as the lines bore down.

The Commander-in-Chief, in the VICTORY, led the weather column, and the ROYAL SOVEREIGN, which bore my flag, the lee.

The action began at twelve o'clock, by the leading ships of the columns breaking through the enemy's line.

The British Army and the French Wars 1793–1815

While the Royal Navy ensured Britain's security and while politicians managed Britain's economic and financial resources to good effect, the British Army also played a major part in the eventual defeat of Napoleon. This chapter will explore that role by examining the following themes:

★ The British Army

★ The military situation 1793–1809

★ Wellington's role in the defeat of the French

The key debate on *page 61* of this chapter asks the question: To what extent was Wellington's leadership responsible for Britain's success in the Peninsular War?

Key dates

1808	Start of Peninsular War		**1812**	Battle of Salamanca
1809	Retreat from Corunna		**1813**	Battle of Vitoria
1809	Battle of Talavera		**1815**	Battle of Waterloo

 ## The British Army

▶ *What were the strengths and weaknesses of the British Army after 1793?*

Defeat in the American War of Independence had tarnished the British Army's image and morale. The army did not improve in the decade that passed between the end of the American conflict in 1783 and the outbreak of war with France in 1793. 'Our army was lax in its discipline, entirely without system, and very weak in numbers', recalled one contemporary soldier. Yet by 1815 Britain's army was the envy of the world; the only military force in Europe not to suffer a major defeat at the hands of Napoleonic France. How had this transformation come about?

The problem of recruitment

France, which had a system of conscription, was able to muster armies of hundreds of thousands. Britain could not match such numbers. In 1793 its army amounted to 40,000 men. Conscription was regarded as an unacceptable imposition on the liberties of freeborn Britons and no press gangs operated on the army's behalf. Thus, all Britain's regular soldiers were volunteers. A major problem for the army in (and after) 1793 was how to find the requisite manpower to meet its growing commitments; no easy matter given that army life was not particularly attractive.

Pay

Soldiers were paid less than farm workers. However, the army did offer food, drink, shelter and the prospect of loot. On top of this was a bounty – a signing-on fee – of up to £40, an important motivating factor for recruits. In most cases, however, the bounty was quickly spent on purchasing kit and buying drinks for the recruiting party.

Marriage

Soldiers were allowed but not encouraged to marry. Those who did marry housed their families in communal barrack rooms, with only a blanket hung up as a screen for privacy. Only a few wives were allowed to accompany their husbands on active service overseas, and they usually drew lots for the privilege.

High death rate

In 1794, 18,596 soldiers died on active service. Over the next two years 40,639 men were discharged on account of wounds or infirmity. These trends persisted throughout the wars, with Britain incurring 16,000–24,000 casualties every year between 1793 and 1815.

Drill

Army life was dominated by drill. Troops were taught to perform strictly defined actions; actions driven home by repetitive practice until they became almost a conditioned reflex.

The recruits

Most recruits were from poor families. Soldiers were considered to be on the same level as common criminals; indeed, some were just that. Caught and convicted, they had been offered a choice between prison or the army. The army, the Duke of Wellington (see page 45) famously stated, was 'composed of the scum of the earth … fellows who have enlisted for drink – that is the plain fact'. In reality, he was exaggerating the situation (see below).

Discipline

Army discipline was brutal. Flogging was the usual punishment for most 'crimes'. Sentences varied from 25 to 1200 strokes. The maximum was rarely inflicted but anything up to 700 lashes was common. The brutal spectacle was performed before the entire regiment. The prisoner was tied to an iron frame and flogged with a cat-o'-nine-tails.

Some officers favoured a more humanitarian approach. Sir John Moore (see pages 49–50), for example, argued that soldiers treated with dignity and kindness would be better motivated than those whipped into obedience. Wellington had little sympathy for such views. He stated that he had 'no idea of any great effect being produced on soldiers by anything but the fear of immediate corporal punishment'. Most officers agreed with him.

Recruiting

Given the high wastage from campaign and disease, there was an insatiable demand for recruits. Recruiting parties toured the country. A common trick was to get a man drunk, slip a shilling (the initial payment for signing on) into his pocket, and then swear that he had enlisted.

The militia

The militia, which made up a fifth of Britain's land forces, was restricted solely to home defence operations. Recruits were selected by ballot and had to serve for five years unless they paid for a substitute. Given that militia substitutes could command a £25 bounty, many would-be soldiers preferred to serve in the militia than in the regular army. But after 1805, following the fading of the French invasion scare, many militiamen volunteered for regular service. From 1808 militia recruits were given an extra bounty if they enlisted with the regular army – a further incentive. Between 1807 and 1812, some 74,000 men transferred from the militia to regular units. These men were particularly useful because they had already undergone basic military training.

Given the number of former militiamen in the army, it is something of a myth that the army's ranks were filled by criminals and men lured into the service when drunk. Many soldiers were motivated by patriotism and the prospect of adventure.

Foreign recruitment

Given the shortage of British recruits, there was large-scale recruitment of foreigners. After 1714 British kings were also rulers of **Hanover**, and Hanoverian troops fought alongside the British throughout the eighteenth century. When Napoleon occupied Hanover in 1803, many Hanoverians and men from other German states fled to Britain and joined the King's German Legion (KGL). Recruits to the KGL soon included Europeans of all descriptions,

KEY TERM

Hanover A small German state.

especially deserters from French armies. The KGL, thoroughly professional in military terms, provided Britain with some of its best soldiers. By 1813 there were 52,000 foreigners in the army; one-fifth of the entire force.

Army service

Most men were deployed to defend Britain and Ireland. In the absence of a police force, innumerable detachments of soldiers were drawn into the day-to-day maintenance of law and order. Other troops were needed to defend Britain's overseas possessions. Comparatively few men could thus be spared for offensive action. On only one occasion during the French wars were two armies of significant size simultaneously deployed on the continent. In 1809, 44,000 troops participated in the Walcheren expedition (page 45) while a similar number were in Spain and Portugal (see pages 47–57).

Army officers

A battalion or regiment (900–2000 men) was usually commanded by a lieutenant-colonel, with two majors. Each company (80–100 men) was led by a captain with two lieutenants or ensigns. Two, three or four battalions were combined into a brigade commanded by a colonel or a major general. Two or more brigades formed a division commanded by a general.

The purchase of commissions

Few officers received any formal training. Traditionally, most were from the landed gentry. Rich fathers often bought sons an ensign's commission. The sons then bought successive promotions as vacancies appeared when more senior officers retired or transferred to another regiment. Commissions were thus bought and sold like expensive property. The system was manifestly unfair; wealth mattered more than talent.

The purchase system's impact can be exaggerated:

- When a vacancy occurred in a regiment, it was first offered to the most senior officer in that regiment of the rank below. If he declined, the vacancy was offered to the next senior and so on. Only if no one within the regiment purchased the vacancy was it sold to someone outside the regiment.
- Commissions were not purchased in the Royal Artillery or the Royal Engineers. Candidates for commissions in these arms attended the Royal Military Academy at Woolwich. After a two-year course, they were commissioned. Thereafter, promotion was by seniority.
- The Duke of York (see page 41) initiated a number of reforms ensuring that officers had to serve two years before they could purchase a captaincy and six years before they could become a major.

- During the Peninsular War less than a fifth of officers were promoted by means of purchase.
- By 1808 the purchase system stopped at the rank of lieutenant-colonel. Promotion above this point was strictly by seniority.
- Without the purchase system, Wellington would not have risen to high rank early enough in his career to command an army.

Senior officers

The date on which a man achieved his lieutenant-colonelcy dictated his seniority thereafter. Lieutenant-colonels could expect to become generals if they lived long enough, irrespective of whether they saw action. However, command of an army did not depend on seniority. Generals-in-command were formally appointed by the king but usually selected by the cabinet and recommended by the commander-in-chief.

The officer class

The long war had a considerable impact on the officer class. By 1814 there were 10,000 officers. This meant that the army was compelled to open its doors to a broader swathe of society than the aristocracy and gentry. While officers were expected to be 'gentlemen', this referred to their character and conduct rather than their social standing. By 1815, most officers came from the professional classes. They were the sons of doctors, lawyers and clergymen, or had fathers who had been (or still were) army officers. New commissions could be attained by enlisting 40 militiamen; a fifth of commissions came this way. Men could also rise from the ranks, usually as a result of bravery in action, but only about one officer in twenty had done so. On balance, the system produced an effective officer corps. Most officers led courageously and effectively.

The branches of the army

The organisation of the various branches of the army barely altered between 1793 and 1815.

Artillery

The artillery was divided into horse and foot artillery. Horse artillery crews rode rather than marched alongside the guns, and were consequently more mobile. Each gun, whether horse or foot artillery, was pulled by eight horses. The artillery was administered by the Board of Ordnance. While artillery officers received a thorough training, this limited the rate at which the artillery corps could be expanded. Moreover, there was no artillery militia on which to draw. Thus, although Britain had the industrial resources to produce artillery, the lack of trained gunners limited the number of guns which could be employed in the field.

Types of guns

British batteries had six guns, usually five cannon and one howitzer. Cannon had a flat trajectory, making it impossible to fire over the heads of friendly troops unless the guns were sited at a higher level. The short-barrelled howitzer was used to lob projectiles on top of the enemy. Cannon were classified into types, depending on the weight of the projectile: a nine-pounder fired a round shot weighing nine pounds (4 kg). Most British cannon were four- or six-pounders.

Types of projectiles

Guns could hit a target at 1000 yards (914 m) but their range was dependent on the elevation at which they were fired, the amount of gunpowder used and the type of projectile fired:

- The commonest form of projectile was round shot: a solid iron ball capable of knocking down whole files of men.
- Canister consisted of small cast-iron balls within a metal can which disintegrated on discharge, spreading shot over a large area. Canister's effective range was 300 yards (274 m) or less.
- British gunners used a new shrapnel shell, named after its inventor, Major Henry Shrapnel. Effective at 700 yards (640 m), it consisted of a metal ball filled with musket balls, fused to explode above and in front of its target.

Congreave's rockets

William Congreave developed a new weapon – rockets. By 1806 his 32-pound (14.5 kg) rockets had a range of 3000 yards (2740 m). Unfortunately, accuracy was not their strong point. Never popular with the regular army, Congreave's rockets were rarely used.

Heavy artillery

Throughout the war, the army was short of heavy guns which could batter down the walls of towns and fortresses. This made it hard to undertake sieges.

Engineers

Given the scale of Britain's commitments, the number of Royal Engineers was far too small – just a few hundred men. The building of the lines of Torres Vedras (see page 53) was overseen by a handful of qualified engineers.

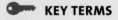

KEY TERMS

Sappers Soldiers skilled in digging trenches.

Pontoon A flat boat that can be used as a bridge.

Why, according to Source A, was the army badly prepared for the Peninsular War (1808–14)?

SOURCE A

From Charles William Vane, Marquess of Londonderry, *Narrative of the Peninsular War from 1808 to 1813* (first published in 1828), quoted in Ian C. Robertson, *Wellington at War in the Peninsula 1808–1814*, Pen & Sword Books, 2000, pp. 29–30.

*Ours was, perhaps the only army in Europe which possessed no corps of **sappers** or miners, nor any body of men peculiarly trained to carry on the more intricate details of a siege … We had no **pontoons** or pontooners; our breaching artillery, chiefly of Portuguese manufacture, was both meagre and* *badly supplied; and our entrenching tools consisted simply of the most common description of spades, bill-hooks and pick-axes. The truth is that the British government having never having contemplated the possibility of its armies being engaged in a serious continental war, and feeling secure against invasion from the decided superiority of its fleets, never bestowed attention on the organisation of means, without which the bravest troops in the world will be liable to disaster.*

The Royal Waggon Train

The Royal Waggon Train, responsible for the movement of supplies, was neglected by the government. In Spain and Portugal, Wellington had to hire local mules and waggons.

Cavalry

By 1808, Britain had some twenty cavalry regiments. At full strength each had just over 900 men. However, no cavalry regiment had more than one battalion so men had to be left at home to make up a depot for recruitment purposes. The result, coupled with sickness among men and horses, was that a regiment in the field rarely had more than 650 men.

Cavalry was divided into heavy and light regiments:

- Heavy cavalry, normally large men mounted on big horses and armed with straight swords, were intended for shock action.
- Light cavalry troopers rode smaller mounts, carried a sabre and were intended primarily for missions like screening, reconnaissance, escort and pursuit.

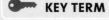

KEY TERM

Carbine A short-barrelled, light gun.

As well as a sword or a sabre, all cavalrymen carried a **carbine**, which had a short range and was not very accurate.

Wellington was generally unimpressed by the quality and intelligence of his cavalry officers. He believed that they tended to regard cavalry action in the same way they regarded fox-hunting, and accused them of 'galloping at everything, and … galloping back as fast'.

Infantry

In 1808 the British infantry was divided into 103 regiments. Most were described by numbers: and most also had a territorial designation. The 5th, for example, was also called the Northumberland Foot Regiment. But, apart from the Irish and Highland regiments (which drew their recruits specifically from those areas), most regiments accepted men from anywhere. No infantry regiment went to war as a body. While one battalion served abroad, the other – the second battalion – would usually be at home at the regimental depot. In theory, the first battalion was supposed to have about 950 officers and men, but disease and casualties meant that battalions often went into battle with about 550 men. The first battalion's numbers were kept up by taking men from the second battalion, which in turn took in new recruits.

Standardisation of procedures was clearly crucial if battalions were to act in concert when brought together. David Dundas's *Principles of Military Movements*, which first appeared in 1788, shaped the manoeuvres of the infantry until beyond the end of the Napoleonic War.

Uniform

Infantrymen wore red coats. Some Scottish regiments wore the military tailor's idea of traditional Highland dress, principally a kilt and a feathered bonnet.

> ## Brown Bess
>
> Most infantrymen were armed with a flintlock musket, known familiarly as Brown Bess. It had been in service in various models since 1716 and remained in service until the 1840s. Just under five feet (152 cm) long, it could be fitted with a 17-inch (43 cm) bayonet. The ammunition for one shot was held in a paper cartridge, which contained the right amount of gunpowder and a lead ball. To load the musket the soldier bit off the end of the cartridge, poured some gunpowder into the pan of his musket lock, which was then closed, poured the remainder down the barrel, spat the ball after it, and inserted the paper tube, all of which was rammed down with an iron ramrod. The soldier then cocked the musket by pulling back the hammer holding the flint. When he pulled the trigger, the hammer fell down and flint struck on steel, showering sparks on to the powder inside the pan. This caused the musket to discharge with a loud bang, clouds of smoke and a vicious recoil. Even experienced soldiers could rarely fire more than three shots a minute.
>
> The musket was only accurate up to 100 yards (91 m). Given the weapon's inaccuracy, the best tactic was for troops to fire simultaneously in a volley, sending a hail of bullets in the direction of the enemy.

Line versus column

In a defensive battle, British infantry stood shoulder to shoulder in a line usually two ranks deep. Drummers and **bandsmen** stood behind the line ready to act as stretcher-bearers.

The French invariably attacked in column. Columns, often 170 wide and 24 ranks deep, were an awesome spectacle and some continental armies fled as they approached. The problem with the column was that only its first two ranks – 340 men out of 3000 for example – could fire effectively. In contrast, every musket in the British line could fire. Not surprisingly, attackers in column rarely broke through a British line. Wellington wrote in 1811, 'I do not desire better sport than to meet one of their columns *en masse* with our line.'

 **KEY TERM**

Bandsmen Most battalions had a small band, useful in attracting recruits at home and maintaining morale on the march and in action.

The square

When attacked by cavalry, infantry battalions formed into squares. Each side would be four to six ranks deep. Those in the outer rank would kneel, holding their musket butts on the ground at an angle, making a bristling hedge of bayonets which deterred horses. It was rare for cavalry to break a square. However, being a dense target, a square was vulnerable to enemy artillery and infantry attack.

Light infantry

The French were among the first to field large numbers of light infantry. Making use of any available cover, these *tirailleurs* aimed to weaken the opposing battle line before French columns approached. British military reformers realised it was necessary to match the enemy's skirmishers with light troops of equal or greater skill. In 1799 the Duke of York ordered the formation of an Experimental Rifle Corps. In 1802 this unit became a regiment of light infantry – the 95th. Its men:

- wore a distinctive dark green uniform – a better colour than red for camouflage purposes
- were armed with the Baker rifle (while the weapon was difficult to load, it was accurate at up to 200 yards)
- were trained in the art of sharpshooting and using cover. They usually scouted or held positions ahead of the army or fought in the rear during a retreat. In battle, riflemen fought in front of the line, skirmishing with *tirailleurs* and targeting enemy officers.

The wounded and sick

Each battalion had a surgeon and two assistants. They plied their trade with crude tools – forceps, saws and knives. Amputation was the standard practice for badly damaged limbs. This was done to avert the threat of **gangrene**. Limbs were lopped off without antiseptics or anaesthetics. Statistics compiled in 1814 showed that more than one in nine operations ended in death.

Disease was a far greater danger than the enemy. During the Peninsular campaigns the British Army lost 8889 men from enemy action and 24,930 from disease. **Dysentery** was a common cause of death.

Civilised warfare

The Peninsular War (see pages 47–57) saw a contrast between dreadful cruelty on the part of Spanish **guerrillas** and Portuguese partisans on French troops and French troops on local populations, and remarkable courtesy between French and British troops. Both Britain and France treated prisoners of war relatively humanely. A system of exchange ensured that officers were freed quite quickly.

KEY TERMS

Gangrene This can result from infected wounds or frostbite. Lack of blood, usually to an arm or a leg, causes body tissue to decay.

Dysentery An infection of the bowel causing painful diarrhoea. This results in dehydration, which can be fatal. Dysentery occurs wherever there is poor sanitation.

Guerrillas Irregular forces that harass an enemy. The word was coined by the Spanish during the Peninsular War.

Reform

The commander-in-chief had responsibility for the upkeep of discipline, the regulation and training of the cavalry and infantry, and the appointment and promotion of officers. Despite his title, he did not have total control over the army. He shared responsibility with a number of officials, including the master-general of the ordnance, the adjutant-general and the secretary at war.

Frederick, Duke of York, second son of King George III, became commander-in-chief in 1795. He had led an expeditionary force, not very successfully, in Flanders in 1793–4 and is best remembered for the nursery rhyme, 'The Grand Old Duke of York'. Nevertheless, he proved himself a capable administrator, helping to transform the service into a formidable fighting machine.

York's reforms included:

- stamping out the worst excesses of the purchase system (see pages 35–6)
- establishing a Military College and a school for cadets (which evolved into the Royal Military Academy Sandhurst)
- standardising tactical drills and manoeuvres
- creating light infantry regiments (see page 40).

Forced to resign in 1809 over a scandal involving his mistress and the sale of commissions, he was soon reinstated and continued his policy of cautious reform until 1815. In the view of military historian Sir John Fortescue (1920), York had done 'more for the Army than any one man has done for it in the whole of its history'.

Fighting Napoleon

Napoleon likened his struggle with Britain to a struggle between a whale and an elephant. Each was incapable of challenging the other outside its natural environment. As long as its navy controlled the sea, Britain could not be defeated. But Britain was unable to match France's military resources on land. French armies were also generally well led, particularly after Napoleon Bonaparte's emergence. Napoleon first rose to prominence in campaigns in Italy in the late 1790s. By a mixture of luck, military genius and political opportunism, he became first consul in 1799. In 1804 he assumed the imperial title, concentrating power in his hands.

British politicians realised that Britain's best hope of defeating Napoleon was to use its financial wealth to subsidise coalitions of European powers – especially Austria, Russia and Prussia – who might have the military potential to defeat France. The British Army's contribution was to fight on the fringes of Europe where, supported by the Royal Navy, it could avoid exposure to France's full strength.

In 1805 Napoleon smashed the Austro-Russian army at the Battle of Austerlitz. In 1806 he defeated Prussia and in 1807 he forced Russia to make peace. By 1807 he controlled most of Europe.

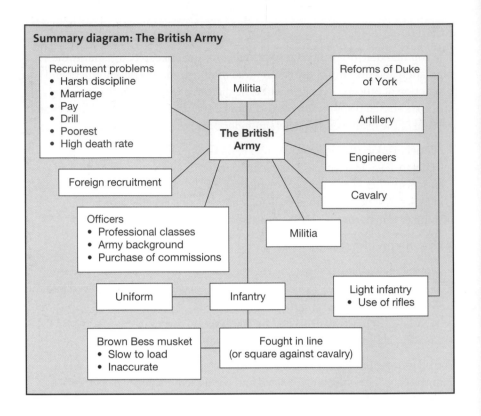

Summary diagram: The British Army

2 The military situation 1793–1809

▶ *How successful was the British Army from 1793 to 1809?*

Between 1793 and 1809 the British Army was engaged in campaigns in Europe and around the world. Britain's main success came in India, where Arthur Wellesley, the future Duke of Wellington, made his reputation.

The French Revolutionary War 1793–1802

The main British effort in the early days of war was against French possessions in the Caribbean. Not only were French islands valuable for their plantations but they were also used by privateers preying on British merchant ships. By 1798 British forces had captured a number of French islands, including St Lucia and Grenada, as well as islands owned by Spain and the Netherlands – France's allies. But 40,000 British soldiers died of yellow fever and other tropical diseases during these campaigns and another 40,000 were dismissed as no longer fit for service.

In 1795 a combined British Army and naval force captured Dutch Cape Colony, a vital strategic point on the voyage to India. Another British force captured the Dutch colony of Trincomalee in Ceylon.

British forces were less successful on the continent. British troops formed part of an allied army in Flanders (with Hanoverians, Dutch, Austrians and Prussians) in 1793, which was eventually pushed back from the French border. British troops were evacuated from Germany in 1795.

In 1801 a British Army defeated French forces, left in Egypt after the Battle of the Nile (see page 9), at the Battle of Alexandria.

British success in India

For much of the 1790s the East India Company (see page 25) was at war in India with the Kingdom of Mysore, which was supported by France. British regiments were the core of the East India Company's army. Forces under the command of Lord Cornwallis eventually captured Mysore's main city, Seringapatam, in 1793, compelling Mysore to make peace on terms favourable to Britain.

In 1797 Arthur Wellesley (see page 45) was sent on military duty to India. He was fortunate that his elder brother Richard arrived in Calcutta as governor-general the following year. Richard, determined to expand British influence, realised – and soon relied on – the military ability of his brother. In 1799 Wellesley assisted in the capture of Seringapatam. In 1800 he engaged in his first campaign as an independent commander, an operation against a powerful brigand, Doondia Wao. Wellesley defeated Doondia's much greater force at Conagul in September 1800.

In 1803 war broke out with the Mahratta Confederacy, a loose association of princes in central India. Wellesley was given command of an army comprising 19,000 men, most of whom were **sepoys**. In September 1803, with 7000 men, Wellesley attacked an Indian army of 40,000 at Assaye and won a major victory. Two months later he triumphed again at Argaum, his 11,000 men defeating 30,000 enemy troops (see Source B). The remnants of the Mahratta Army took refuge in Gawilghar. Wellesley's men stormed the fortress in December 1803. These victories, coupled with General Lake's success in the north, forced the Mahratta Confederacy to make peace.

 **KEY TERM**

Sepoys Indian soldiers who were trained and employed by the East India Company.

SOURCE B

Wellesley (Wellington) writing a few days after the Battle of Argaum, quoted in Michael Glover, *Wellington as Military Commander*, Sphere Books, 1973, pp. 43–4.

What do you think of nearly three entire battalions, who behaved so admirably in the battle of Assaye being broke and running off, when the cannonade commenced at Argaum, which was not to be compared with that at Assaye? Luckily, I happened to be at no great distance from them, and I was able to rally them and to re-establish the battle. If I had not been there, I am convinced we should have lost the day … I formed the army into two lines: the infantry in the first, the cavalry in the second, and supporting the right; and the Mysore and Mogul [irregular] cavalry the left … When formed, the whole advanced in the

According to Source B, how did Wellesley win the Battle of Argaum?

greatest order; the 74th and 79th regiments were attacked by a large body (supposed to be Persians), and all these were destroyed … and their whole line retired in disorder before our troops, leaving in our hands thirty-eight pieces of cannon and all their ammunition. The British cavalry then pursued them for several miles, destroyed great numbers, took many elephants and camels and much baggage.

In 1804 Wellesley was knighted for his exploits. While his career had been assisted by his brother's position, he had also displayed immense ability. There were some who claimed that military reputations were easy to win in India. Those who claimed this had not served in India!

Figure 2.1 India in c.1800.

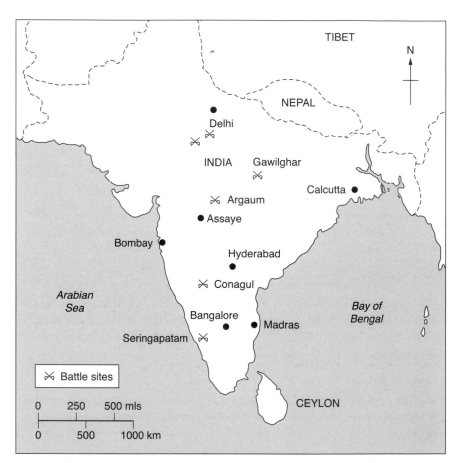

The Napoleonic War 1803–9

When war recommenced in 1803, British forces set about recapturing colonies returned to France and its allies by the Treaty of Amiens (1802). French, Spanish and Dutch islands in the Caribbean were taken, as were Dutch Cape Colony, Dutch possessions in the Far East and French islands in the Indian Ocean.

Arthur Wellesley, the Duke of Wellington

1769	Born in Dublin, fourth son of the Earl of Mornington
1781	Educated at Eton College; achieved little scholastically
1787	Joined the army
1797	Arrived in India
1803	Won the Battles of Assaye and Argaum
1806	Became Tory MP for Rye
1807	Appointed chief secretary for Ireland
1808	Won the Battle of Vimeiro
1809–14	Led allied forces in the Peninsular War
1815	Defeated Napoleon at the Battle of Waterloo
1828–30	Served as prime minister
1851	Died

In 1787 Wellesley decided to make his career in the army. His family had sufficient influence and funds to push him in his profession, enabling him to take command of the 33rd foot in 1793. In 1794 he took part in the ill-fated campaign in Flanders (see page 43). He led his battalion effectively enough. He claimed later that the campaign had taught him 'how not to do it, which is always something'. He made his military reputation in India (see pages 43–4). While he had his admirers, the higher ranks of the army initially mistrusted him because he was a politician. Nor did they have much confidence in his Indian victories. The **Horse Guards**, Wellesley remarked, 'thought very little of anyone who had served in India. An Indian victory was not only no grounds for confidence, but it was actually grounds for suspicion.'

However, Castlereagh (see page 21) recognised Wellesley's ability. His support ensured that Wellesley was given command of British forces in Portugal in 1809. He led those forces brilliantly and went on to defeat Napoleon at Waterloo.

Historian Rory Muir wrote in 2006:

> As both a strategist and a tactician [Wellington] showed a natural boldness, subdued when necessary by the need for caution. He nurtured his army, building its confidence, while looking after its material needs and preserving its discipline … On the day after Waterloo he told a friend, 'By God! I don't think it would have done if I had not been there!' And the remark is at least as true of the war in the Peninsula. Wellington was the final, indispensable, ingredient of victory.

Other expeditions had mixed success. In 1805, 15,000 men were sent to Hanover but soon had to be evacuated. A British army, commanded by General Stuart, won a victory at Maida in Sicily in 1806, an engagement that proved that the British line could be effective against French columns. British efforts to capture Spanish colonies in what is today Argentina and Uruguay ended in failure in 1807. However, in 1807 an expedition was sent to Copenhagen to seize the Danish fleet (see page 18). Troops, led by Wellesley, routed a Danish force at Køge.

In 1809 Austria declared war on Napoleon. To provide a diversion, 44,000 British troops were dispatched to capture the Dutch ports of Flushing (Vlissingen in Dutch) and Antwerp. The British force landed on the island of Walcheren. The place proved to be malaria ridden. Although the army captured Flushing, some 4000 soldiers died of disease and a further 11,000 were put on the sick list before the army was brought back to Britain.

 KEY TERM

Horse Guards
The administrative headquarters of the British Army in Whitehall.

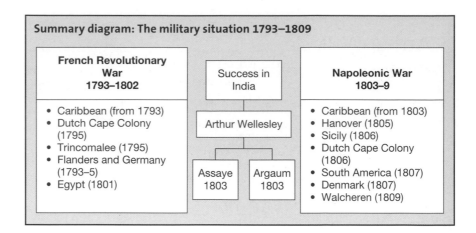

Summary diagram: The military situation 1793–1809

French Revolutionary War 1793–1802	Success in India	Napoleonic War 1803–9
• Caribbean (from 1793) • Dutch Cape Colony (1795) • Trincomalee (1795) • Flanders and Germany (1793–5) • Egypt (1801)	Arthur Wellesley Assaye 1803 Argaum 1803	• Caribbean (from 1803) • Hanover (1805) • Sicily (1806) • Dutch Cape Colony (1806) • South America (1807) • Denmark (1807) • Walcheren (1809)

③ Wellington's role in the defeat of the French

▶ *Why were British forces so successful in the Peninsular War?*

Between 1808 and 1814 British troops were engaged in the Peninsular War, a campaign fought in Portugal, Spain and the south of France. While sometimes seen as a sideshow when compared to the great campaigns in Russia and Germany in 1812–13, the Peninsular War was a constant drain on French resources. It tied down hundreds of thousands of French troops. After 1815 Napoleon said that the roots of his defeat could be traced to the Peninsular War.

The start of the Peninsular War

Napoleon, committed to bringing Britain to its knees, was determined to enforce his Continental System (see page 17). In 1807, a French army under Junot marched through Spain and seized control of Portugal, which was still trading with Britain. Napoleon now determined to bring Spain under his control. Early in 1808 French troops poured into Spain, taking over key cities, on the pretext of supporting Junot in Portugal. In April 1808 Napoleon 'persuaded' the Spanish king, Charles, and his son Ferdinand, to abdicate. Joseph Bonaparte, Napoleon's elder brother, was proclaimed the new Spanish king. Napoleon, who had assumed there would be little opposition to Joseph, had miscalculated. Most Spaniards had no wish to be ruled by France. By June 1808, the whole of Spain was up in arms. Local assemblies – juntas – emerged and began raising forces.

Junot, in Portugal, was now totally cut off from France. French arrogance and shameless plunder had alienated the Portuguese. In mid-June 1808 rebellion broke out at Oporto and quickly spread. Junot's hold on Portugal shrank to the vicinity of Lisbon. The British government realised that the situation in Spain and Portugal offered a wonderful opportunity to strike a blow against Napoleon.

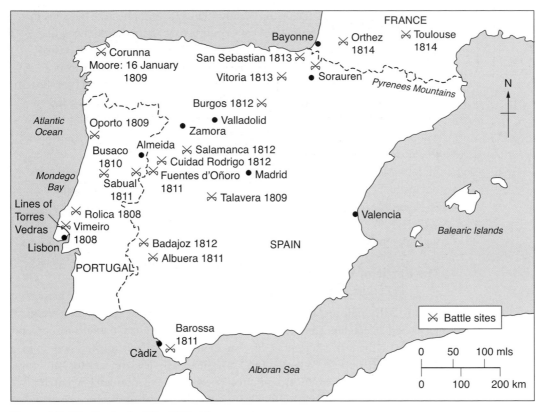

Figure 2.2 The Peninsular War 1808–14.

Portugal 1808

A force of 9000 men was already assembling at Cork to attack Venezuela, a Spanish colony. Castlereagh now ordered this force, commanded by Wellesley, to sail to the Iberian Peninsula.

SOURCE C

Wellesley, speaking to John Wilson Croker in early July 1808, quoted in E. Longford, *The Years of the Sword*, World Books, 1971, p. 162.

I have not seen the French since the campaign in Flanders when they were capital soldiers, and a dozen years of victory under Bonaparte must have made them better still. They have a new system of tactics which has outmanoeuvred and overwhelmed all the armies of Europe … they may overwhelm me, but I don't think they will outmanoeuvre me. First because I am not afraid of them, as everybody else seems to be; secondly, because if what I hear about their system of manoeuvres be true, I think it is a false one against steady troops. I suspect that all the Continental armies were more than half beaten before the battle was begun – I, at least, will not be frightened beforehand.

> Why, according to Source C, was Wellesley confident of success in 1808?

Wellesley's transports left Cork on 12 July 1808. He went ahead of his force in a fast frigate. Informed by the junta at Corunna that Spain did not need his assistance, he decided his army should sail to Portugal. On 1 August British forces began disembarking at Mondego Bay. Wellesley's army was soon reinforced with 5000 men. A further 15,000 also prepared to set sail from Britain. While this was good news for the army, it was bad news for Wellesley. Given the size of the force, the Duke of York (see page 41) had decided that it must be commanded by a general senior in rank to Wellesley. Indeed, Wellesley learned that no fewer than three senior officers were on their way to Portugal. One was Sir John Moore. Moore, a Whig, was held in high esteem by the Duke of York but loathed by many Tory ministers. The government, therefore, appointed 58-year-old Sir Hew Dalrymple as overall commander. He had only once seen active service. Sir Harry Burrard, a loyal Tory who was similarly inexperienced, was appointed second in command.

The Battle of Vimeiro

Wellesley, determined to make the most of his independent command before Moore, Dalrymple and Burrard arrived, set off to march on Lisbon on 10 August. Junot had 26,000 French troops, but many of these men had to guard Lisbon and the forts on the Spanish frontier. He was therefore unable to muster more than 15,000 men to oppose Wellesley. On 17 August Wellesley won a victory at Rolica, driving 5000 French troops from a strong position. He continued his march south, reaching the village of Vimeiro, where his army was reinforced by 4000 troops landing at Maceira. On 20 August Sir Harry Burrard arrived off Maceira but decided to sleep on board ship. Later that night, Wellesley was informed that Junot was advancing towards him with 14,000 men.

While Burrard remained at sea, Wellesley prepared for battle, positioning his army on high ground. Junot resolved to attack. Wellesley's light infantry held Junot's *tirailleurs* at bay, protecting the British line. That line stood on the reverse slope of Vimeiro hill so that French artillery fire was less effective because enemy gunners could not see their target. On reaching the crest of the hill, the French columns were shot to pieces by musket fire and fled as British troops advanced, bayonets fixed. At this point Burrard arrived on the battlefield. Sensibly, he allowed Wellesley to continue in command. Further French attacks on Vimeiro hill, Vimeiro village and a ridge to the north were driven back. In less than three hours the battle was over. Wellesley begged Burrard to pursue the beaten French. Burrard refused, allowing Junot to retreat to Lisbon unmolested. Nevertheless, Vimeiro was a significant victory. The French lost some 2000 men; Britain 720.

The Convention of Cintra

The following day, Sir Hew Dalrymple arrived, superseding Burrard. Disdaining Wellesley's advice to march on Lisbon, Dalrymple accepted Junot's offer of an armistice, agreeing (by the Convention of Cintra) that the 24,000 French soldiers in Portugal should be transported back to France on British ships. The British public was horrified. It seemed that the British generals had snatched defeat from the jaws of victory. Wellesley, Dalrymple and Burrard became the subject of criticism and ridicule. In December 1808 a military inquiry into the Convention concluded that nothing had been done which called for the punishment of any of the parties concerned. It singled out Wellesley for praise, stating that his action in Portugal was 'highly honourable and successful, and such as might have been expected from a distinguished officer'. However, Burrard and Dalrymple never held command again.

Corunna 1809

Following Dalrymple and Burrard's recall to Britain, Sir John Moore took command of British forces in Portugal. Moore, aged 47, had fought in America, Corsica, the Caribbean, the Netherlands and Egypt, and was Britain's most respected soldier. Commanding a 35,000-strong army, his orders were to co-operate with the Spanish in expelling the French from Spain.

Moore marched into Spain with the bulk of his army in October 1808. Ten thousand men, most of whom were sick, were left in Lisbon. Meanwhile, another 10,000-strong force, commanded by Sir David Baird, landed at Corunna in mid-October. Moore's plan was that his and Baird's armies would combine at Salamanca.

By the time Moore reached Salamanca in late November, it was clear that his strategy was in ruins. Napoleon, with 200,000 troops, had crossed into Spain in November, determined to rectify matters. Spanish forces, which tried to resist the French, were defeated. Moore realised that his best option was to retreat to Portugal. However, the British ambassador in Spain put intense pressure on him to assist the Spaniards. For several days, Moore remained uncertain what to do. While he pondered marching to Madrid, Napoleon captured the Spanish capital.

Informed that Napoleon was marching south towards Andalusia and Lisbon, Moore decided to strike north-east towards Burgos. He hoped to force Napoleon to pull back from marching south in order to protect his communications. This might give the Spaniards breathing space to reorganise their armies. It was a huge gamble but Moore thought 'something must be risked for the honour of the Service'.

More's army left Salamanca on 12–13 December. The only French troops in Moore's vicinity were 20,000 men under Soult whom Moore hoped to defeat. On 20 December Moore and Baird joined forces at Mayorga. On 23 December, however, Moore, informed that Napoleon was hurrying forces northwards, had little option but to order a retreat through the Galician mountains to Corunna.

Confident that he had rectified the situation in Spain, Napoleon returned to Paris, leaving Soult to pursue Moore. Morale among the retreating British soldiers crumbled as the weather worsened, shoes and clothes wore out, and food supplies grew scarce. Nevertheless, the rear guard, which included the 95th rifles, prevented the French getting too close.

Moore reached Corunna on 11 January 1809, ahead of the troop transports that had been sent to meet him, most of which did not arrive until 15 January. By midday on 16 January most of the wounded and the artillery were on board the troop transports, but Moore was forced to fight the French vanguard outside Corunna. Some 15,000 British troops held their position against a similarly sized French force. Both sides lost 700–900 men. Moore was one of the fatalities. The battle enabled the British Army to embark and return to England. Some 26,000 men escaped; 7000 men had been lost on the retreat.

Many blamed Moore for the débâcle. He had certainly been indecisive at times. But at least his action had diverted French troops from attacking Portugal and southern Spain, and ensured that most of his troops had survived to fight another day.

Wellesley returns

Since Napoleon now controlled much of Spain, it seemed certain that the 10,000 British troops in Lisbon would have to be evacuated. Moore had declared that, 'If the French succeed in Spain it will be vain to attempt to resist them in Portugal.' Wellesley disagreed. 'I have always been of the opinion', wrote Wellesley to Castlereagh in March 1809, 'that Portugal might be defended whatever might be the result of the contest in Spain.' He stipulated that Portugal's defence must involve:

- the dispatch of at least 20,000 British troops to Portugal
- the Portuguese Army's reorganisation along British lines.

The Portuguese government now approached Wellesley with an offer of supreme command of their forces. He declined. General William Beresford – Wellesley's choice – was appointed instead. In April 1809 Wellesley was informed that he had been given command of the new British Army to be sent to Portugal.

Wellesley reached Lisbon on 22 April. The situation seemed desperate. Soult, with 20,000 men, had invaded Portugal from the north, capturing Oporto on 29 March. Marshal Victor, with 40,000 men, threatened Lisbon from the east. In overall command of the Portuguese Army as well as the British, Wellesley determined to defeat Soult and then turn on Victor. Leaving 12,000 men (mainly Portuguese) to defend Lisbon, he marched north with 16,000 British and 2400 Portuguese. Soult, in Oporto, believed Wellesley would be unable to cross the River Douro. But on 12 May Wellesley ferried men across the river in a few wine barges. By the time Soult realised the danger, some 600 British troops had occupied a seminary building. French efforts to capture the place were beaten back. Portuguese civilians now rushed down to the waterside and launched everything that would float, enabling more British troops to cross the Douro. Soult's army retreated from Oporto in disorder.

Pursued by Wellesley, Soult managed to escape back into Spain through difficult mountains. In so doing, he lost over 4000 men, most of his guns and masses of equipment. It would take weeks for his army to recover. Wellesley, who had sustained fewer than 200 casualties, was thus able to turn south to attack Victor.

Talavera

Lack of money, shoes and supplies slowed Wellesley's next move. But the situation seemed favourable:

- War between Austria and France broke out in April 1809. For several months there would be no reinforcements for French forces in Spain.
- The 280,000 French soldiers in Spain were widely dispersed.

In early July 1809, Wellesley's 20,000-strong army crossed into Spain, combined with 34,000 Spanish troops led by General Cuesta, and marched to attack Victor at Talavera, 70 miles (112 km) south-west of Madrid.

The Spanish proved appalling allies. Cuesta had no military ability and his men were barely disciplined. An opportunity to defeat Victor before he received reinforcements was wasted by Cuesta's last-minute refusal to carry out the agreed plan. Victor, strengthened with troops from Madrid, now led 50,000 men towards the Anglo-Spanish force. On 27 July, the armies engaged at Talavera. Two thousand Spaniards, frightened by the noise of their own guns, fled after firing a volley at distant French troops. The remaining Spanish forces were placed behind the walls of Talavera and improvised fortifications. British troops extended northwards from Talavera. Victor launched a night attack, which had some initial success before it was driven back by General **Rowland Hill**.

On 28 July, Victor launched a massive assault. Throughout the day, Wellesley's line held the French columns at bay. The French now retreated. They had suffered 7300 casualties, the British 5400. Wellesley had lost a quarter of his men but had beaten a numerically larger army.

The results of Talavera

As the French retreated, Cuesta proposed that the allied armies should march on Madrid. But Wellesley, who had lost all faith in Cuesta, refused. Learning that French forces were threatening his communications with Portugal, he retreated to the Spanish–Portuguese border. Elevated to the peerage for his victory at Talavera, Wellesley now became Viscount Wellington.

All Wellington could do was remain on the defensive, particularly after two Spanish armies were crushed by the French in November. In December he retreated into Portugal. There was no further fighting over the winter. This allowed Beresford time to train more Portuguese troops to British standards. By

 KEY FIGURE

Rowland Hill (1772–1842)

Served in the Peninsula from 1809 to 1814 and was one of the few generals whom Wellington trusted in an independent command. He was also popular with the men, who nicknamed him 'Daddy'.

mid-1810 some 25,000 Portuguese were ready for action, almost doubling the size of Wellington's force.

In January and February 1810 a French army of 60,000 men marched through Andalusia, capturing Seville. The Spanish Supreme Junta fled to Càdiz. Here, with British naval and military help, a new Spanish government managed to hold out against the French. Whilst most of Spain was under French occupation, Spanish guerrillas made the occupation difficult, forcing the French to keep thousands of men holding down territory.

Cuidad Rodrigo and Almeida

In 1810 Napoleon, having defeated Austria, was determined to invade Portugal. Rather than lead the invasion himself, he appointed Marshal Massena, one of his best soldiers, to command the 138,000-strong Portuguese Army. Wellington assured the British government that he could hold Lisbon. He was confident that Massena could not invade Portugal with a large army; there was simply not enough food to sustain it.

In May, French forces besieged Cuidad Rodrigo, a Spanish fortress town near the Portuguese frontier. Wellington, urged to march to its assistance, was not prepared to risk his army. The town held out valiantly but on 10 July surrendered. Massena now moved on Almeida, a Portuguese fortress town. Wellington hoped that the place would hold out until the autumn. But a lucky French shot blew up Almeida's gunpowder **magazine**, forcing the demoralised Portuguese garrison to surrender on 28 August.

Wellington prepared for further retreat. He issued drastic orders to local Portuguese authorities: the country was to be defended by a **scorched-earth policy** and by the activities of the *ordenanza*. People who lived in the area through which the French would march were to be evacuated.

Massena's invasion of Portugal

In September 1810 Massena, with 65,000 men, advanced towards Coimbra. Wellington, with 51,000 men, took up a strong position on Bussaco (Buçaco) ridge, blocking the main road. The French attack on 27 September failed. Massena suffered 4600 casualties, Wellington only 1252. The following day, Massena set about marching around Wellington's army, forcing him to retreat towards Lisbon.

Having occupied and looted Coimbra, Massena advanced south, confident that he was about to drive the British into the sea. Some 4500 sick and wounded Frenchmen, left inadequately guarded in Coimbra, were captured by Portuguese militia. Massena pressed on until, in mid-October, his forces reached the best kept secret of the war – the lines of Torres Vedras.

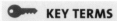 **KEY TERMS**

Magazine A military storehouse of weapons.

Scorched-earth policy This involves destroying all crops and animals in the path of the enemy, making it hard for them to find food.

Ordenanza A kind of Portuguese home guard, supposed to turn out in time of invasion.

The lines of Torres Vedras

Wellington had ordered the construction of the lines of Torres Vedras – a network of formidable defences some 20–30 miles (32–48 km) north of Lisbon – the previous year. Colonel Richard Fletcher, commanding the Royal Engineers, undertook the construction. He used Portuguese labour, supervised by 150 British soldiers and eighteen engineers. There were three defensive rings. The 26-mile (42-km) northern-most line, which ran from the Atlantic to the River Tagus, consisted of linked forts and earthworks covering the passes through to Lisbon. The Royal Navy protected the Atlantic flank and gunboats on the Tagus made it hard for the French to cross. A second – stronger – line of defences was built behind the first. A third line would protect the British Army if it was forced back to Lisbon and had to escape by sea from Portugal. A semaphore system enabled messages to be flagged from the Atlantic to the Tagus in seven minutes. Behind the lines there were 500 square miles (1300 km²) of safe territory for 200,000 Portuguese refugees. British ships provided enough supplies to feed Wellington's army, the people of Lisbon and the refugees.

The lines of Torres Vedras were manned by 25,000 Portuguese militia, 11,000 *ordenanza*, 8000 Spanish troops and 2500 British artillerymen and marines. Wellington's main army, nearly 60,000 strong, was deployed behind the lines, ready to concentrate against a French thrust, wherever it might come.

Massena thought the defences were too strong to attack but his pride would not allow him to retreat. Meanwhile his army grew desperately short of food. In mid-November, he finally withdrew 30 miles (48 km) to positions stretching between Santarem and Rio Maior, well protected by earthworks and marshes. Wellington followed and the besieged now became the besiegers. Massena was totally isolated. Portuguese militia and *ordenanza* prevented him communicating with Spain.

Confident that starvation and disease would damage the French more than a British attack, Wellington made no effort to dislodge the enemy. Both armies thus remained stationary over the winter. By February 1811 over 500 French soldiers were dying each week. In March Massena retreated back to Spain. He had lost between 20,000 and 30,000 men and immense quantities of guns and equipment. Except for Almeida, Portugal was now free from French control.

The war 1811–12

Wellington sent Beresford, with 20,000 men, to deal with Soult in the south and, if possible, recapture Badajoz. Wellington, with 35,000 troops, besieged Almeida.

Fuentes de Onoro

Massena, having quickly re-equipped his army, advanced towards Almeida with over 48,000 men. Allied troops repelled an attack on Fuentes de Onoro on 3 May 1811. Two days later Massena attacked again. Again, Fuentes de Onoro witnessed ferocious fighting, and again, allied troops held the village. Lacking ammunition, Massena retreated. French forces in Almeida escaped, to Wellington's chagrin, but at least he captured the town. Massena was now replaced as French commander by Marshal Marmont.

Albuera

In the south, Beresford besieged Badajoz. Soult, with 24,000 men, set out to relieve the fortress. The two armies met at Albuera on 16 May. Having outmanoeuvred Beresford, Soult looked set to triumph but at a critical moment 3700 allied troops held up 7800 French infantry. The close-range firefight was the most ferocious of the entire war. Carnage continued for almost an hour in a packed two acres of mud. 'There is no beating these British soldiers', said Soult later. 'They were completely beaten and the day was mine, but they did not know it and would not run away.' A British advance finally broke French resistance and Soult withdrew, having lost some 8000 men. But Beresford's army had suffered 5936 casualties. Wellington knew he could ill-afford another such 'victory'. Beresford was not given independent command again and Hill took over responsibility in the south. The arrival of French reinforcements forced the allies to abandon the siege of Badajoz.

Cuidad Rodrigo and Badajoz

In 1812 Wellington, equipped with siege guns from Britain, determined to capture Cuidad Rodrigo and Badajoz, the northern and southern gateways into Spain (see the map on page 47).

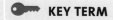

KEY TERM

Breaches Gaps or openings.

In early January 1812 Wellington besieged Cuidad Rodrigo, his guns making two **breaches** in the fortress's walls. On the night of 19–20 January Wellington's men stormed the town, capturing it in two hours. They then went on the rampage, drinking, looting and raping. Wellington and the French both lost about 500 men in the fighting. Two thousand French troops were taken prisoner.

Wellington now moved against Badajoz. Its defences and garrison were more formidable than those of Cuidad Rodrigo. Wellington, with 60,000 men, reached the fortress in mid-March. On 6 April, the walls of the town were breached in three places and he ordered an assault. Badajoz had to be taken quickly because Marmont was threatening Cuidad Rodrigo and Wellington needed to return north to protect the town. The British attackers lost nearly 5000 men but succeeded in capturing Badajoz. For nearly two days British soldiers ran amok as at Cuidad Rodrigo. Having at last brought his army under control, Wellington moved north to stop Marmont's advance on Cuidad Rodrigo.

The Battle of Salamanca

French forces in Spain were weakened by Napoleon's campaign against Russia in 1812. While 230,000 French troops remained in Spain, most were employed holding down the country. Thus, in mid-June 1812 Wellington advanced towards Salamanca with 48,500 men. Marmont's similar-sized army fell back. For several weeks the two forces, rarely more than a few miles apart, marched and counter-marched, both seeking to gain the initiative. On 22 July, Wellington struck at Marmont's over-extended army. The attack, spearheaded by British cavalry, was a triumph. Having lost some 14,000 men, the French army fled the field. Allied casualties numbered 5214. Wellington had won a major victory.

Advance and retreat

Wellington entered Madrid triumphantly on 12 August 1812. Hoping to push enemy troops back into France, he continued his advance northwards, reaching Burgos in mid-September. But the town's defences were stronger than he had expected and he failed to capture the place. Meanwhile, French armies under Soult, Joseph and Suchet threatened his rear. On 21 October, he abandoned Burgos and began to retreat. On several occasions the French threatened to crush his outnumbered army, but he managed to join forces with Hill at Salamanca in early November. Wellington admitted that he had got out of 'the worst scrape I ever was in'.

Wellington continued his retreat to Portugal, his army – wet, fatigued and hungry – harassed constantly by enemy cavalry. In late November, he reached Almeida and safety. Although the 1812 campaign ended in disappointment, Wellington had achieved a great deal:

- He had forced the French to abandon southern Spain.
- He had captured huge quantities of enemy material.

Morale among British troops quickly improved as new shoes, clothes and equipment arrived, as well as British and Portuguese reinforcements. As the British and French armies went into winter quarters, it was clear that Napoleon had suffered a disaster in Russia, losing tens of thousands of men on the retreat from Moscow. This meant it was unlikely that French forces in Spain would be reinforced.

The Battle of Vitoria

In May 1813 Wellington, now in command of Spanish as well as British and Portuguese forces, determined to strike out for the Pyrenees. His 80,000-strong army advanced 300 miles (480 km) in less than 30 days through parts of Spain that the French thought impassable for a large army. French forces fell back in confusion. Spanish guerrillas ensured that Wellington knew more about the whereabouts of the French armies than the French did themselves.

On 21 June Wellington attacked Joseph Bonaparte's 66,000-strong army at Vitoria. The assault went much to plan and the French, having lost 8000 men, retreated in panic. Joseph Bonaparte abandoned 3000 convoy wagons, carriages and carts and all but two of his 153 guns. The ransack of the French baggage train, coupled with heavy rain, made any pursuit of the French impossible. News of Wellington's victory resounded across Europe, ensuring that the coalition of Russia, Prussia and Sweden against Napoleon remained firm. Austria joined the coalition in August.

The Pyrenees

By the end of June 1813 Wellington had driven most French forces back across the Pyrenees. Only three enemy pockets remained in north-eastern Spain: the town of Vera and the fortresses at San Sebastian and Pamplona. Vera fell by mid-July. As Wellington prepared to storm San Sebastian, Soult moved against him with some 80,000 men. Given that Wellington's forces were besieging two fortresses 40 miles (64 km) apart, he was in a weak position. The ensuing campaign took place in mountainous terrain. Outnumbered allied forces held up the French at Maya on 25 July. At Sorauren, on 28 July, Wellington's 18,000 men stood firm against 30,000 French, blocking their efforts to relieve Pamplona. A second battle in the Sorauren area on 30 July ended in British victory. Soult retreated into France. His nine-day offensive had cost him 13,500 men; Wellington had lost only 7100.

On 31 August allied troops stormed San Sebastian, suffering 3700 casualties. There was then a lull in the fighting:

- Pamplona continued to hold out, the French finally surrendering on 25 October.
- Wellington had problems with the Spanish government, who quibbled at his control of Spanish troops while he quibbled at the Spanish government's inability to provide its soldiers with pay and supplies.
- Wellington was reluctant to invade France until he was certain of the situation in Germany, where Napoleon was fighting against Russia, Prussia and Austria.

The invasion of France

On 7 October allied troops crossed the River Bidasoa, breaking the French line of defence and establishing a bridgehead in France. The news from central Europe was also excellent. At the Battle of the Nations, fought at Leipzig on 16–19 October 1813, Napoleon was decisively defeated and forced to retreat to the River Rhine.

On 10 November British troops took strong French positions and crossed the River Nivelle. Allied casualties were 2625; French losses 4350. Wellington considered this action 'my best work' in the Peninsular War. Wellington now sent most of his Spanish battalions back over the Pyrenees. He knew that if Spanish troops marched deep into France, they would be certain to plunder and seek revenge for French atrocities in Spain. This might antagonise French civilians, setting them against the allies, a situation Wellington wished to avoid at all costs. On 9 December allied troops forced their way across the River Nive. Winter weather, rather than Soult's forces, halted Wellington's advance for the next nine weeks.

In February 1814 Wellington pressed north as Soult retreated. In April allied and French troops fought a needless battle at Toulouse. Unbeknown to Wellington, Prussian, Russian and Austrian forces had entered Paris on 31 March and Napoleon had abdicated a week later. The war was seemingly over.

Wellington had fought a remarkable campaign. His army, with Britain's contribution never exceeding 40,000 men, had killed, wounded or captured 200,000 enemy troops, losing only 36,000 men in the process. (The reasons for Wellington's success are examined on pages 61–3.)

The War of 1812

In 1812 war broke out between the USA and Britain (see page 19). For two years a small number of British units and Canadian militia repulsed American incursions into Canada. After Napoleon's abdication, more British troops were sent to North America and British forces captured and burned Washington, the American capital. The Treaty of Ghent, signed in October 1814, ended the war. Before news of the peace reached America, British forces, led by Sir Edward Pakenham, sustained heavy casualties attacking strongly fortified positions at New Orleans in January 1815.

The Hundred Days

In February 1815, Napoleon, who had been exiled on the Italian island of Elba, escaped. Landing in France with a small force, he set about gathering recruits and marched towards Paris. Louis XVIII, the newly restored French king, fled and Napoleon entered the French capital in March. Opposed by Britain, Russia, Austria and Prussia, he sought to win a major victory that would shatter his adversaries' morale. Thus, while the bulk of the Austrian and Russian forces were still massing on France's eastern frontier, he advanced northwards towards the British and Prussian armies, hoping to annihilate each separately.

Ligny and Quatre Bras

Wellington commanded an Anglo–Belgian–Dutch–Hanoverian army, some 90,000 strong. Unfortunately for him, many of Britain's Peninsular War veterans were still crossing the Atlantic after fighting in America. Marshal Blucher commanded a Prussian force of similar size to Wellington's. The two forces occupied southern Belgium, with Wellington's troops in the west and Blucher's further east.

On 15 June 1815, the 120,000-strong French army thrust northwards, taking Wellington and Blucher by surprise. On 16 June Napoleon defeated the Prussians at Ligny. Wellington's army, attacked by Marshal Ney, clung on to

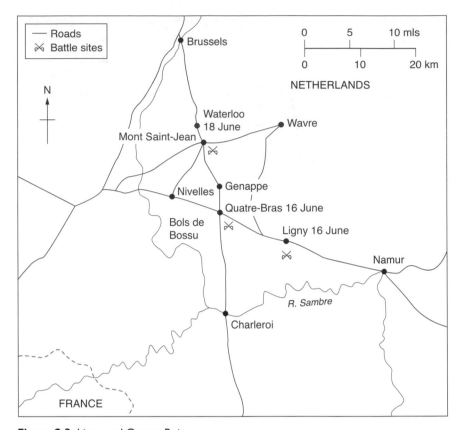

Figure 2.3 Ligny and Quatre Bois.

the crossroads at Quatre Bras. While Blucher had been badly mauled, Napoleon had failed to crush either of his adversaries. Sending a third of his army, under Marshal Grouchy, to pursue the Prussians, Napoleon marched against Wellington.

The Battle of Waterloo

On 17 June 1815 Wellington's army retreated towards Brussels. Assured that Blucher would march to his assistance, he positioned his army on a low ridge south of Waterloo. The French pursuit was hampered by heavy rain, which continued throughout the night of 17–18 June. As the rain abated on the morning of 18 June, French troops squelched into position. Aware that the wet ground would hinder the effect of artillery fire, Napoleon postponed his attack until 11.30a.m. to give the earth time to dry. Unfortunately for Napoleon, this also gave the 72,000 Prussians, advancing on his right flank, more time to reach the battlefield. But for a few hours 75,000 French confronted Wellington's hybrid force of 68,000 men. French attacks failed to capture the chateau of Hougemont on Wellington's right flank or drive his army from the ridge.

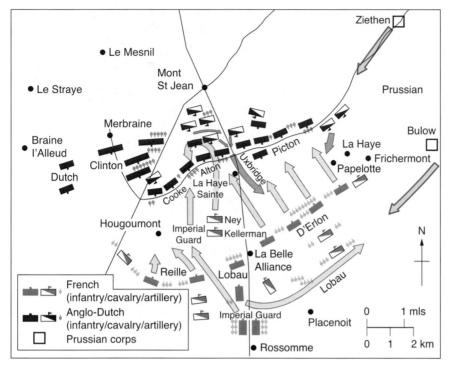

Figure 2.4 The Battle of Waterloo.

By 1.30p.m. Blucher's troops had begun arriving on the battlefield, forcing Napoleon to divert the bulk of his reserves to stave off the threat. Ney led the dwindling balance of the French Army in a succession of uncoordinated assaults on the ridge. French cavalry, unsupported by infantry, failed to break Wellington's centre in a series of reckless charges. The last French attack came from the infantry of the **Imperial Guard**. This unit was similarly repulsed. With the Prussians advancing, Wellington ordered his own army forward. The French army fled the field. Within days Napoleon abdicated for the second time.

The Battle of Waterloo, as Wellington conceded, had been 'a close run thing'. His army had suffered over 15,000 casualties and Blucher's another 7000. Some 25,000 French were slain or wounded. Fittingly pitted against Napoleon in both men's final battle, Wellington (assisted greatly by Blucher) had triumphed.

The situation in 1815

On 15 July 1815 Napoleon surrendered on board HMS *Bellerophon*. It was symbolic that he should do so on a British ship of the line. While the army won national plaudits in the final stages of the Napoleonic War, Britain's victory was largely the result of the Royal Navy, which had enabled Britain to escape invasion, expand its trade and continue to fight France. 'If anyone wishes to know the history of this war', said Wellington, 'I will tell them it is our maritime supremacy.'

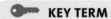 **KEY TERM**

Imperial Guard Napoleon's bravest and most loyal soldiers.

In 1815 Britain's economy was powerful and growing. So was its empire. Its military and diplomatic prestige was at an all-time high. Its army had defeated Napoleon. Its navy had as many large ships as the combined fleets of France, Russia, the Netherlands, Spain, Portugal and the USA.

The British armed forces soon suffered severe cuts as Parliament tried to reduce both taxation and the national debt. Warships in commission fell from 713 in 1814 to 121 in 1818. By 1817 nearly 90 per cent of commissioned naval officers were on 'half-pay'. The army, needed for policing both Britain and its empire, was reduced at a slower rate, from 240,000 soldiers in 1815 to 103,000 in 1828.

Summary diagram: Wellington's role in the defeat of the French	
1807	French takeover of Portugal and Spain
1808	Spanish and Portuguese people rebelled British forces sent to Portugal Battle of Vimeiro – Convention of Cintra
1800	Retreat to Corunna Wellesley returned to Portugal French capture of Oporto – French invasion of Spain Battle of Talavera – Wellesley became Wellington
1810	Wellington retreated to Portugal French captured Cuidad Rodrigo and Almeida Massena invaded Portugal Battle of Busaco – Wellington victorious but forced to retreat Lines of Torres Vedras
1811	Massena forced to retreat Battle of Fuentes de Onoro – Wellington captured Almeida Battle of Albuera
1812	Wellington captured Cuidad Rodrigo and Badajoz Battle of Salamanca – Wellington marched into Madrid Wellington forced to retreat to Portugal
1813	Wellington invaded Spain Battle of Vitoria – French forces abandoned most of Spain Battles in the Pyrenees Wellington invaded France
1814	Wellington pushed into France Napoleon abdicated British troops sent to fight in USA
1815	Napoleon returned from exile Battles of Ligny and Quatre Bras Battle of Waterloo The situation in 1815

Key debate

▶ *To what extent was Wellington's leadership responsible for British success in the Peninsular War?*

Napoleon was confident that his forces would drive British troops in the Peninsula into the sea. That did not happen. Instead, the Peninsular War was the most successful campaign in the British Army's long history. Was this simply due to Wellington?

The leadership of Wellington

EXTRACT 1

From Jac Weller, *Wellington in the Peninsula*, Greenhill Books, 1992, pp. 376–7.

The contributions to Allied success made by Wellington personally fall into three classes: his military system, his grand strategy, and his combat manoeuvres and tactics. In all three, the changes he made in previous British standards and procedures were startling … Wellington was coldly efficient, confident of his own ability, and sure of the army he created. He might not be greatly loved by his men, but when it came to fighting, they wanted him to lead them, and no one else … he never failed them, nor asked them to do anything beyond their strength on any field.

'In war', said Napoleon, 'men are nothing: it is the man who is everything'. One man stands tall as the architect of allied victory in the Peninsula. That man was Wellington. In a six-year campaign, he barely lost a gun, let alone a battle. He did make some miscalculations, for example, underestimating the capacity of the French to rally and return to the fray as soon as they did after their retreat from Portugal in 1811 or in the wake of their defeats at Salamanca and Vitoria. But overall, Wellington proved himself a military genius. Napoleon sent a succession of tried and tested marshals against him – Soult, Victor, Massena, Marmont – and Wellington defeated them all.

Wellington put his success down to his emphasis on supply. 'No troops can serve to any good purpose', he said, 'unless they are regularly fed. A starving army is worse than none.' French armies in Spain and Portugal **requisitioned** food. This alienated the Spanish and Portuguese and helped to swell the ranks of the guerrillas. Given that Britain needed to retain Spanish and Portuguese goodwill, Wellington's army had to be supplied by a system of magazines. Vast trains of bullock carts and riverboats brought supplies to the magazines, drawing food not only from the Peninsula but from Britain, the USA and the Mediterranean. To move rations forward from the magazines to the troops, a multitude of mules and wagons and their drivers were hired. While the French Army was always hunting for its supplies, Wellington ensured that his supplies were always hunting for him.

 KEY TERM

Requisitioned Forcefully acquired – without paying.

Other factors

While Wellington's leadership was important, British victory was also the result of other factors.

The British Army

By 1813 it was clear that the British Army surpassed the French Army in every way – except numbers. Wellington was wholly justified in claiming that his army was 'the most complete machine for its numbers now existing in Europe'.

Portuguese and Spanish troops

In the Peninsula British troops fought side by side with Portuguese and Spanish troops. Initially the Portuguese and Spanish armies were poor: untrained, ill-supplied and deplorably led. Wellington's eldest brother, while briefly ambassador at Seville, remarked that he 'would not entrust the protection of a favourite dog to the whole Spanish Army'. But once Portuguese and Spanish troops were put under British command, they showed great courage and endurance.

The Spanish and Portuguese people

The Spanish and Portuguese people's stubborn resistance to French rule was crucially important. Guerrillas tied down masses of French troops, harried French lines of communication, and provided Wellington with intelligence of enemy movements.

The Royal Navy

The navy supported the army, conveying supplies and transporting troops. Without naval dominance, Britain would not have been able to conduct the Peninsular War.

The geography of the Peninsula

Bounded on three sides by the sea, the Iberian Peninsula enabled Britain to use its maritime power to enormous effect. The barren terrain also made it hard for French armies to live off the land.

The British government

The Tory administrations of Portland, Perceval and Liverpool had the will and found the means to support Wellington's army.

EXTRACT 2

From R. Muir *et al.*, *Inside Wellington's Army 1808–1814*, Pen & Sword Books, 2006, p. 35.

The advantages of the Peninsula as a theatre for British operations are much more obvious in retrospect than they were at the time, and in the wake of the Spanish defeats of late 1808 and Sir John Moore's retreat to Corunna many politicians and leading soldiers in Britain despaired of the cause. Nonetheless, the British government maintained its commitment to the Peninsula … Canning's urgency ensured that Portugal was not forgotten, that reinforcements were sent to Lisbon, and that Beresford was dispatched to reform the Portuguese army. Crucially, the ministers entrusted Wellington with command of the army and gave him broad discretion to act as he thought best.

The strength of the British economy

The strength of the British economy underpinned the entire British war effort.

EXTRACT 3

From Roger Knight, *Britain Against Napoleon*, Penguin, 2014, p. 166.

… the foundations of military victory lay in the industrial capacity of cannon-founders, the expertise of gunsmiths in their machine shops, the diligence of shipbuilders and the makers of ropes, uniforms, gun-carriages and gunpowder, the hard work of those who toiled in the increasingly efficient agricultural sector, the merchant seamen whose ships transported vital stores and food, and the crews of packet ships who provided the means of communication throughout the year … They were all needed as much as the tens of thousands of young soldiers and seamen who resisted, survived and finally overcame the threat from Napoleon.

> **?** Which of Extracts 1–3 provides the most convincing explanation for Britain's success in the Peninsular War?

Coalition support

Without the military assistance of Russia, Prussia and Austria, it is hard to see how Britain could have won the Peninsular War.

Chapter summary

The British Army was not well prepared for war in 1793. It was small in number and had recruitment problems. However, the army was well trained and useful reforms were introduced by the Duke of York. The army, ultimately, was brilliantly led by Wellington, who established his military reputation in India. He went on to display his genius in the Peninsular War (1808–14) and at Waterloo (1815), never losing a battle. But British success in the Peninsular War was not just the result of Wellington's leadership. The fighting qualities of the British Army, including Portuguese and Spanish troops, was vital. Wellington was also massively assisted by the Spanish and Portuguese people, who refused to accept French rule.

Refresher questions

Use these questions to remind yourself of the key material covered in this chapter.

1 What were the strengths and weaknesses of the British Army in the years 1793–1815?

2 How great a reformer was the Duke of York?

3 How successful was the British Army between 1793 and 1809?

4 Why was Wellesley (Wellington) blamed after the Battle of Vimeiro?

5 Was the Corunna campaign a total disaster?

6 Why were the French unable to drive the British from Portugal in 1810?

7 Why were Cuidad Rodrigo and Badajoz so important from 1810 to 1812?

8 Which was Wellington's greatest victory in the Peninsular War?

9 Why were British forces so successful in the Peninsular War?

10 Why did allied forces win the Battle of Waterloo in 1815?

 Question practice

ESSAY QUESTIONS

1 How far do you agree that the British Army was composed of the 'scum of the earth' during the French Wars in the years 1793–1815?

2 How far can Wellington's success in the Peninsular War in the years 1809–14 be attributed to the lines of Torres Vedras?

3 How accurate is it to say that Wellington's success in the Peninsular War in the years 1808–14 was the result of his emphasis on supplies?

4 To what extent was Wellington responsible for allied victory at Waterloo in 1815?

SOURCE ANALYSIS QUESTION

1 Assess the value of Source 1 for revealing the nature of the warfare in Portugal in October 1810 and for explaining the reasons for Wellington's success not just in 1810 but throughout the Peninsular War. Explain your answer, using the source, the information given about its origin and your own knowledge about the historical context.

SOURCE 1

From Sergeant William Lawrence's *The Autobiography of Sergeant William Lawrence*, published in London in 1886 (but written much earlier). Lawrence, a sergeant in the 40th Foot, describes the retreat towards Lisbon in early October 1810.

Lord Wellington had indeed issued a proclamation ordering all the inhabitants to fall back on the approach of the enemy, and destroy any articles that they might possess and were not able to carry with them, that were at all likely to be of any use to the enemy; and so thousands of the population of the country that seemed about to fall within the bounds of the enemy's marches were to be seen flying from their dwellings, and our army during its retreat was accompanied by crowds of miserable men, women and children, all eager to reach the capital, as they knew that if they fell in with the French, they would be treated as some had been before, with all the barbarities of an atrocious enemy …

From Leiria we went on further to Torres Vedras, which we gained after a long, tedious and impressive march; and there we took up our position at some fine breastworks which Lord Wellington had for some time previous ordered to be thrown up by the Portuguese peasantry in case of the retreat of our army. Now we found how much we needed them, for on the 10th of October the French came in sight of our strong position, where we had drawn up, determined that they should not proceed one step farther towards Lisbon. Massena was rather surprised at our strength, which was quite unexpected by him. He had thought of driving the English into the sea, but he now found his mistake, so encamped about a mile and a half from our position.

CHAPTER 3

The Crimean War 1854–6

In Britain the Crimean War is best remembered for the Charge of the Light Brigade, for Florence Nightingale, and for popularising the cardigan and the balaclava. In some respects this trivialises a major war, the only conflict between 1815 and 1914 involving more than two of Europe's great powers and a war in which over 500,000 men died. This chapter will consider the war and its impact on Britain by exploring the following themes:

★ The situation in 1854

★ The war 1854–6

★ The war's impact on Britain

★ Florence Nightingale, Mary Seacole and nursing

★ Military reform

The key debate on *page 100* of this chapter asks the question: To what extent did the Crimean War lead to a change of attitude towards the army?

Key dates

1854	March	Britain and France declared war on Russia	1855		Palmerston became prime minister
	Sept.	Battle of Alma	1856		Treaty of Paris
	Oct.	Battle of Balaclava			
	Nov.	Battle of Inkerman	1868–74		Cardwell's military reforms

1 The situation in 1854

▶ *What were the British Army's main weaknesses in 1854?*

The causes of the Crimean War

After the Treaty of Vienna (1815) Europe's great powers – Austria, Russia, Britain, Prussia and France – enjoyed nearly four decades of international peace. But Russian territorial designs on the ramshackle Ottoman (or Turkish) Empire, which included much of the Balkans and the Middle East, led to a political crisis.

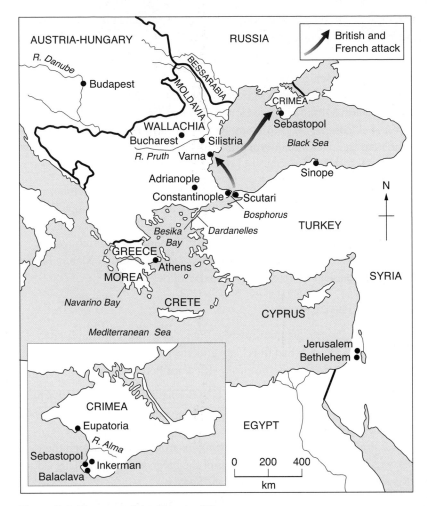

Figure 3.1 The start of the Crimean War.

The British government, led by **Lord Aberdeen**, a **Peelite**, feared that if Russia seized Constantinople (present-day Istanbul), its Black Sea fleet would be able to sail through **the Straits** and threaten British naval supremacy in the East Mediterranean.

Emperor Napoleon III of France, a nephew of Napoleon Bonaparte, hoped to destroy the 1815 peace settlement which endeavoured to contain France. He was thus keen to challenge Russia, the country most associated with ensuring that France did not again dominate Europe.

In June 1853 British ships were sent to Besika Bay just outside the Dardanelles (see the map above) as a gesture of support for the Ottomans. They were soon joined by a French fleet. By opposing Russia, Britain could not escape co-operation with France, even though Aberdeen did not trust Napoleon III. The possibility of a French attack on Britain had been taken seriously between 1851 and 1853. It was therefore ironic that the Royal Navy, recently strengthened

KEY FIGURE

Lord Aberdeen (1784–1860)

Became head of a coalition government in Britain in 1852. His government comprised Liberals, Whigs, Radicals and fellow Peelites.

KEY TERMS

Peelites Supporters of Sir Robert Peel who split with the Conservative (Tory) Party in 1846 over the Repeal of the Corn Laws.

The Straits The Bosphorus and the Dardanelles, which link the Black Sea to the Mediterranean.

to protect Britain from French attack, was now allied with the power it was primarily designed to fight.

In July, Tsar Nicholas I of Russia ordered his troops into the Ottoman provinces of Moldavia and Wallachia. Attempts to reach a peaceful solution to the crisis failed. Divisions within Aberdeen's government did not help: the prime minister was pacific and anti-Ottoman while Home Secretary Lord Palmerston (see page 89) was bellicose and anti-Russian. Palmerston, who insisted that Britain must stand firm against Russian expansion, was in alignment with the majority of Britons.

In October the Ottoman Empire declared war on Russia. On 30 November the Russian Black Sea Fleet annihilated an Ottoman squadron at Sinope. In January 1854 the British and French fleets sailed into the Black Sea. A British and French joint note, sent to the tsar on 27 February, demanding a withdrawal of Russian troops from Moldavia and Wallachia, was ignored. On 27 March, France declared war on Russia. Britain did the same the following day.

Diplomatic initiatives

In July 1854, following threats from Austria, Russia evacuated Moldavia and Wallachia. The Balkan issue had thus been effectively solved. Austria now made diplomatic efforts to end the war, proposing the Four Points:

- Russia was to renounce any special rights in Serbia, Moldavia and Wallachia, whose protection would be guaranteed by all the European powers.
- The navigation of the Danube was to be free to all commerce.
- The 1841 Straits Convention, banning warships from sailing through the Straits, was to be revised 'in the interests of the balance of power'. This would end Russian naval domination of the Black Sea.
- The Christian subjects of the Ottoman Empire were to be placed under general European (rather than just Russian) protection.

Accepted by Britain and France, the Four Points were rejected by Russia in September. This left Britain and France with little option but to fight.

The choice of the Crimea

Allied forces, sent to Varna (see the map on page 67) to raise the siege of Silistria, arrived to find the Russians in the process of withdrawing. Still determined to strike a blow against Russia, the Duke of Newcastle, secretary of state for war, urged Lord Raglan, the head of the British expeditionary force, to attack the Crimean port of Sebastopol (also called Sevastopol). Raglan, despite some misgivings, agreed.

The British Army

The 26,000-strong British Army that sailed for the Crimea in September 1854, comprising five infantry **divisions** and one cavalry division, was described by

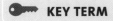 **KEY TERM**

Division A formation usually comprising 4000–5000 soldiers.

The Times as 'the finest army that has ever left these shores'. But its dashing appearance served only to camouflage problems in command and organisation. In many respects the army had been neglected since 1815, not altogether surprisingly given four decades of European peace.

The influence of Wellington

The army after 1815 was essentially run by the military high command without government interference. The fact that the army had triumphed in the Peninsular War and at Waterloo, and also performed well in campaigns against non-European forces, strengthened the forces of conservatism and complacency – both within the army and politically. Wellington was commander-in-chief in 1827–8 and again in 1842–52. Even when not in that position he exercised massive authority over military affairs. Although not entirely opposed to new ideas, he took the view that what had served the army well in the past was the surest guarantee of continuing success. He also believed that calls for reform were really no more than demands for further cuts in military spending. (The army budget had declined from £43 million in 1815 to £9.5 million in the 1840s.)

Lord Raglan

Sixty-five-year old Lord Raglan was appointed to command the British expeditionary force. He had served on Wellington's staff in the Peninsula and had subsequently been Wellington's military secretary. No one doubted Raglan's administrative ability or bravery. At Waterloo, his right elbow had been shattered by a musket-ball and he had let the surgeon amputate his damaged arm without a murmur. He also had many personal qualities: diplomacy, loyalty to subordinates and devotion to duty. Unfortunately, he had not seen active service since 1815, and had never commanded an army.

Divisional command

The quality of British military command was a cause for some concern. Only one of Raglan's five infantry divisional commanders was under 60, and he, the Duke of Cambridge, was the queen's 37-year-old cousin who had not seen action before. The chief engineer, Sir John Burgoyne, was 72. Only two of the infantry divisional commanders had led anything larger than a battalion into action.

British officers

While there were signs of growing professionalism among sections of the officer corps, actual experience of command was necessarily confined to colonial wars and many officers had seen no active service at all. The system of buying commissions ensured that wealth often triumphed over ability. In 1814–15, the greatly enlarged British Army had been led by men mainly from the professional classes (see page 36). However, by 1854, the much smaller army was led by officers drawn principally from the landed gentry, and from families with a military tradition. While most had a high sense of honour and duty, some joined the army because it provided them with a fashionable and not too strenuous existence.

Military administration

Military administration in 1854 was a shambles:

- The secretary of state for war and the colonies was theoretically responsible for military policy and for political oversight of all troops outside Britain.
- The secretary at war looked after military financial and legal matters.
- The commander-in-chief saw to discipline, appointments, promotions and the army's general state of readiness.
- The adjutant-general dealt with recruiting, discipline, pay, arms and clothing.
- The quartermaster-general was responsible for movement, barracks, camps and transport.
- The Board of General Officers advised the adjutant-general on clothing and equipment.
- The home secretary administered the **yeomanry** and the militia and the distribution of regular troops in Britain.
- The Ordnance Board controlled the engineers and the artillery as well as the army's ammunition needs.
- The Commissariat, a Treasury department, was responsible for food, fuel and transport.

Such a cumbersome structure produced rivalries, procrastination and inertia. Periodically, ministers discussed plans for reform. But successive cabinets were too timid to override the hostility of Wellington and other senior officers to any change that would diminish the commander-in-chief's authority or subject the army to greater political control.

The problem of manpower

The army rarely had more than 115,000 men. Soldiers served 21 years in the infantry or 24 years in the cavalry. Long service overseas exacted a heavy toll in human life and health, particularly in tropical stations. Between 1839 and 1853 there were 58,139 deaths, the vast majority from disease. The army also had difficulty attracting sufficient recruits. This was largely because of poor conditions of service:

- Most barracks, whether in Britain or abroad, were overcrowded and insanitary.
- A soldier's basic pay was poor, **1s.** a day for infantry. A deduction of 6d. a day was made for food.
- The families of married soldiers were expected to live in the same barrack rooms as the rest of the men.
- The army disciplinary code remained severe. Soldiers could be flogged for a variety of crimes and misdemeanours, although in 1846 the maximum number of lashes was reduced to 50.
- Army routine was monotonous: drill, drill and more drill.

 **KEY TERMS**

Yeomanry Volunteer cavalry who served in Britain.

1s. (one shilling) Twelve old pence (12d.) or 5 pence in modern money.

SOURCE A

Louis Noir, a French veteran soldier, describing the British Army in 1854, quoted in Orlando Figes, *Crimea*, Penguin, 2011, p. 178.

The English recruiters seemed to have brought out the dregs of their society, the lower classes being more susceptible to their offers of money. If the sons of the better-off had been conscripted, the beatings given to the English soldiers by their officers would have been outlawed by the military code … In England, the soldier is really just a serf – he is no more than the property of the government. It drives him by two contradictory impulses. The first is the stick. The second is material well-being. The English have a developed instinct for comfort; to live well in a comfortable tent with a nice big side of roast beef, a flagon of red wine and a plentiful supply of rum – that is … the essential precondition of his bravery … But if these supplies do not arrive on time, if he has to sleep out in the mud, find his firewood, and go without his beef and grog, the English become battle-shy, and demoralization spreads through the ranks.

> According to Source A, what were the main weaknesses of the British Army?

The situation by 1854

Since 1815 no one in Britain had seriously considered the possibility of troops being called on to fight a major European war. As a result, little thought had been given to **staff work** and large-scale administrative co-ordination. Yet in 1854, the army was expected to achieve a quick and comprehensive victory over Russia. In the circumstances, it is a tribute to the professionalism and bravery of many of its officers and men that the army fought as well as it did. The fact that the infantry were armed with the **minié rifle** (soon to be replaced by the lighter **Enfield rifle**) gave British troops an undoubted advantage over Russians still armed with smoothbore muskets (see page 39).

The French Army

The French expeditionary force, which initially consisted of 40,000 infantry, plus artillery and cavalry, soon grew to 120,000. French divisional commanders were notably younger than their British equivalents. Promotion from the ranks was commonplace and the officers were more professional than their British equivalents. The most striking area of French superiority was in organisation and supply.

The Russian Army

In 1854, the Russian Army was over a million strong. Its conscripted rank and file suffered worse conditions of service than their British counterparts. Most Russian officers were from the landowning class and many took their military duties lightly.

KEY TERMS

Staff work Preparatory planning and administrative work undertaken by the commanding officer's personal team.

Minié rifle A minié rifle fired the minié ball, an inch-long (2.5 cm) lead bullet that expanded into the groove of the rifle-musket's barrel. The minié rifle was accurate at over 400 yards (366 m); the smoothbore musket had an effective range of less than 100 yards.

Enfield rifle An improved version of the minié rifle.

The Ottoman Army

On paper, the Ottoman army was 700,000 strong. In reality, it was probably only half that number. Ottoman forces were poorly led, poorly equipped, poorly trained and poorly supplied.

The Royal Navy

While the Royal Navy had been greatly reduced in size after 1815, it remained the world's strongest navy. The main battle fleet was stationed in European waters. The captains of some 130 frigates and gunboats, scattered around the world defended the growing British Empire. The threat posed by the navy to flatten major coastal cities and cut trade gave Britain the power to intervene on the world stage as the British government saw fit.

The navy kept up with new developments, not least the coming of steam. Paddle steamers proved their worth, for example, negotiating inlets and rivers during the First Opium War with China (1839–42). Nevertheless, their twin paddles occupied too much room to mount an effective broadside. Accordingly, the navy relied mainly on sail throughout the 1830s and 1840s.

The development of the screw propeller in the late 1830s had a major impact on naval developments. Given that it was placed under water on the **stern** and did not interfere with the broadside, the screw had obvious advantages. In 1845 HMS *Ajax* was the first battleship to be fitted with an engine that turned a screw propeller. In 1847 the French Navy ordered the world's first purpose-built steam-powered battleship. The Royal Navy quickly responded, building more steam battleships than the French to retain Britain's naval dominance. HMS *Duke of Wellington*, launched in 1853, was twice the size of HMS *Victory* (see page 13), carried 131 guns and had a speed of 10 knots (19 km/hour), making it the world's most powerful battleship. Nevertheless, given the limitations of engines and the problem of carrying sufficient coal, steam remained an auxiliary to sail in the 1850s.

KEY TERMS

Stern The back of a ship.

Nepotism Undue favouritism to one's relations and close friends.

> ## Sir James Graham's reforms
>
> Sir James Graham, a Whig politician, was first lord of the admiralty from 1830 to 1834. He introduced a number of naval reforms:
>
> - He improved the navy's administration, amalgamating the Admiralty and the Navy Board, and ensuring there was less **nepotism**, bribery and corruption.
> - He made some improvements in seamen's conditions.

Summary diagram: The situation in 1854

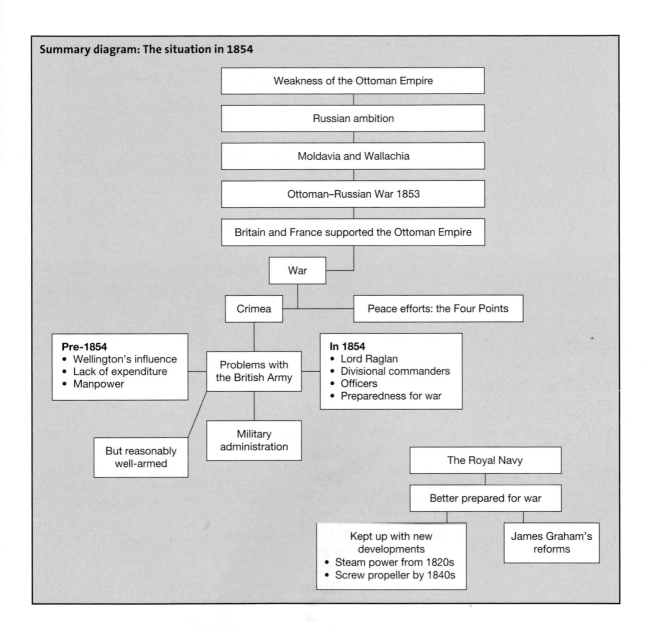

2 The war 1854–6

▶ *To what extent was Lord Raglan to blame for the British Army's suffering in 1854–5?*

On 14 September 1854, allied troops began landing at Kalamita Bay, north of Sebastopol. St Arnaud, the French commander, wanted to march immediately on Sebastopol but Raglan insisted on rounding up wagons, baggage animals and supplies from the surrounding countryside. On 19 September, the allied

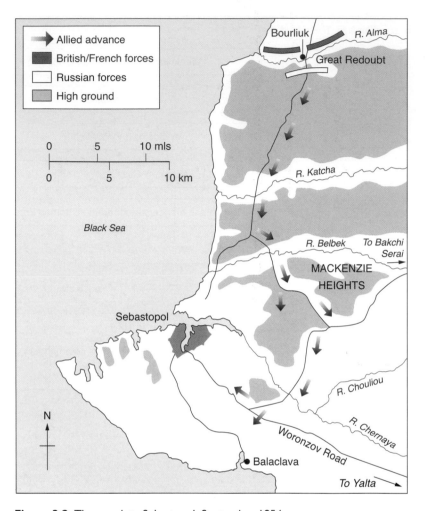

Figure 3.2 The march to Sebastopol, September 1854.

army – 63,000 strong – moved south. The Russian commander-in-chief, Prince Menshikov, with only 33,000 men, withdrew to a strong position behind the River Alma.

The Battle of Alma

St Arnaud proposed that the French forces attack on the right, next to the sea. Protected by the fleet's guns, they would roll up the Russian left flank while British troops advanced against the Russian centre and right. Raglan considered that the French commander had underestimated Russian strength, but not wishing to cause an unseemly altercation, he assured St Arnaud that he could rely on his 'vigorous co-operation'.

On 20 September the British infantry moved forward. Coming under artillery fire, the troops halted and lay patiently for 90 minutes, waiting to see how the

French attack developed. Informed that St Arnaud needed support, Raglan ordered his men to advance. The Light Division led the way, crossing the Alma and capturing the Great Redoubt. Exposed to enemy artillery fire and infantry attack, the Light Division fell back, but a general British advance resulted in the Grenadier Guards recapturing the Great Redoubt while the Highland Brigade drove back twelve Russian battalions.

The Russians now began to withdraw. Lord Lucan, who led the British cavalry, was desperate to pursue the Russians and turn the retreat into a rout. But Raglan, aware that Russian cavalry were lurking to his left, disagreed. Instead, he ordered his men to bivouac for the night. The Battle of Alma, the first full-scale battle between European nations since Waterloo, was over. The Russians had lost 5700 men and been driven from a strong position. The British had suffered 1500 casualties, the French under 1000.

The Siege of Sebastopol

On 23 September, the allied army advanced on Sebastopol. Raglan favoured an immediate attack. Had the allies done this, there would have been little to stop them marching into the town. However, Raglan's chief engineer, Sir John Burgoyne, believed the Russian defences posed a serious obstacle. St Arnaud, who was fatally ill, agreed. He advocated attacking Sebastopol from the south. Raglan, anxious to preserve allied accord, deferred to the French. This decision was one of the most crucial of the war.

On 26 September, British forces entered Balaclava, a fishing port too small to serve as a supply base for both armies. Raglan, poorly advised by Admiral Lyons, chose to remain at Balaclava. Consequently, the French, now led by General Canrobert, went to bays further west. Raglan's decision to stay at Balaclava was to place an enormous strain on his army. It was committed to defending the allied flank from Russian attack as well as laying siege to Sebastopol.

Raglan continued to press for an assault on Sebastopol. But Canrobert insisted that the city's defences must first be reduced by artillery bombardment. Given allied inaction, the Russians had time to improve Sebastopol's defences.

By 17 October the allies had dragged 126 siege guns into position and the cannonade finally began. Facing them on the landward side of Sebastopol were 341 Russian guns; double the number of three weeks earlier. An allied naval bombardment, coinciding with the land cannonade, resulted in damage to several warships and 500 allied casualties. The allied land bombardment was more effective, so much so that had the allies attacked they would probably have captured Sebastopol. But Canrobert opposed such a move, allowing the Russians time to patch up their defences. This pattern was repeated over several days: a successful bombardment, a failure to attack and Russian repairs carried out under cover of darkness.

The Battle of Balaclava

On 25 October, a Russian army of 25,000 infantry, 6000 cavalry and 78 guns advanced towards Balaclava. After overrunning Ottoman outposts along the Causeway Heights, several thousand Russian cavalry charged the 93rd Highland Regiment. Its 550 men, in two lines (standard infantry practice was to face cavalry attack in squares), turned aside the cavalry but could not check the Russian assault single-handed. This task fell to the British cavalry. The 800-strong Heavy Brigade, led by General Scarlett, charged the enemy. After a few minutes of desperate fighting, the Russian cavalry fled. The Heavy Brigade, charging uphill, had won an amazing victory, losing only ten men.

The Charge of the Light Brigade

The Earl of Cardigan, head of the 664-strong Light Brigade, watched the triumph of the Heavy Brigade with some envy. An arrogant snob, Cardigan was Lord Lucan's brother-in-law but the two men had long hated each other. Cardigan's officers wanted to launch themselves against the fleeing enemy. But Cardigan, having no orders from Lucan, refused to attack.

Raglan's order

Raglan was positioned on the Sapoune Heights. Annoyed by the loss of initiative, he sent a message to Lucan requesting him to occupy the ground the Russians were vacating. Without infantry to assist him, Lucan declined to regard the message as an order. Taking advantage of the respite, the Russians set about removing the guns from the Ottoman redoubts on the Causeway Heights. The exasperated Raglan composed a new order for Lucan: 'Lord Raglan wishes the cavalry to advance rapidly to the front, follow the enemy and try to prevent the enemy carrying away the guns.'

Nolan's role

Captain Louis Nolan was the staff officer chosen to deliver the message. He was selected probably because he was an excellent horseman who could ride rapidly down the steep slope into the valley below. But excitable, conceited and scornful of both Lucan and Cardigan, he was far from the ideal messenger. Nolan handed Lucan the order. Having read its contents, Lucan announced that such an attack would be 'useless'. Nolan replied that Raglan's orders were that the cavalry should attack immediately.

'Attack, sir!' said Lucan. 'Attack what? What guns, sir? Where and what to do?' Nolan waved his arm in a contemptuous gesture down the valley. 'There, my Lord. There is the enemy! There are your guns!'

Lucan's role

Lucan, who lacked Raglan's high vantage point, could not see the guns on the far side of the Causeway Heights. Nolan's angry wave gave Lucan the

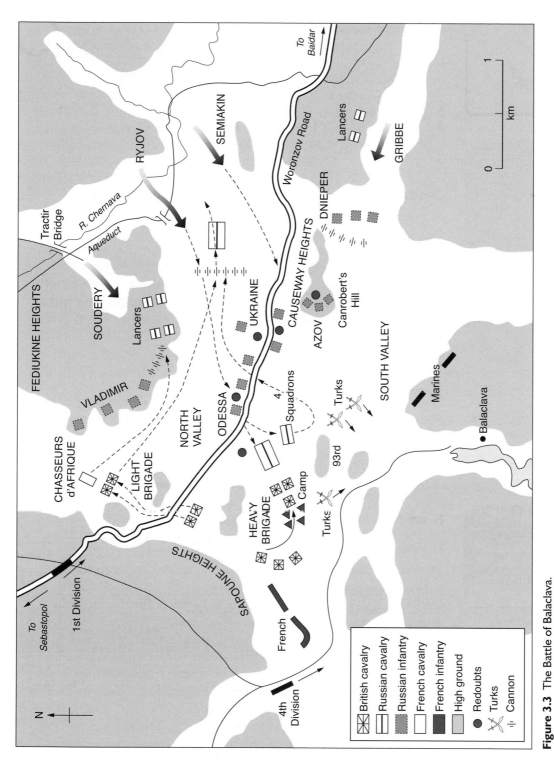

Figure 3.3 The Battle of Balaclava.

impression that he had been ordered to attack the mass of Russian guns at the far end of the valley some 2000 metres away. Realising that such an attack would be suicidal, Lucan rode over to Cardigan and ordered him to advance towards the main Russian army. 'Certainly, sir', Cardigan replied. 'But allow me to point out to you that the Russians have a battery in the valley in our front, and batteries and riflemen on each flank.' 'I know it', said Lucan. 'But Lord Raglan will have it. We have no choice but to obey.' Cardigan turned away murmuring, 'Well, here goes the last of the Brudenells!' (Brudenell was Cardigan's family name.)

Cardigan's role

Cardigan gave the order for the Light Brigade to advance in three lines. Ahead were twenty battalions of Russian infantry, supported by over 50 guns. These forces were deployed on both sides, and at the opposite end, of the valley. It would take the Light Brigade some seven minutes to reach the main Russian batteries. As the horsemen trotted down the valley, Nolan suddenly dashed before Cardigan who led the charge, waving his sword and shrieking at him. Nolan probably realised that the cavalry were heading in the wrong direction and was trying to avert disaster. But at this very moment a splinter from an exploding shell tore into his chest and killed him. Cardigan's men therefore continued their charge.

Artillery and musket fire soon poured into the Light Brigade from three sides. Reaching the Russian guns, the cavalry hacked at the gunners. Then, seeing Russian cavalry drawn up behind the guns, Cardigan turned and trotted back down the valley. His men followed, running the same gauntlet of fire as they retreated. The whole incident lasted barely 20 minutes. Of the 664 men who charged, 110 were killed, 130 wounded and 58 taken prisoner. Making no effort to rally or find out what had happened to his men, Cardigan left the battlefield, boarded his private yacht and drank champagne.

The aftermath of the charge

The futility of the Light Brigade's action and its reckless bravery prompted French General Bosquet to declare: 'It is magnificent but it is not war.' He continued: 'It is madness.' In his dispatches, Raglan blamed Lucan. While accepting that he might have misunderstood the order, Raglan believed that Lucan should have exercised his discretion. Lucan responded by claiming that throughout the campaign Raglan had allowed him no independence and required that his orders be followed to the letter. Lucan's criticism of his superior was not tolerated and in March 1855 he was recalled to Britain, where he continued to defend himself, blaming Raglan and Nolan. Cardigan, who had merely – indeed bravely – obeyed orders, blamed Lucan for giving him those orders. Leaving the Crimea at his own request, he returned home a hero and was promoted to inspector-general of the cavalry.

The charge is usually seen as a classic example of military ineptitude. In reality, it was an accident, and accidents happen in most wars. Moreover, it had some success, the Light Brigade inflicting more casualties on the Russians than it suffered. But the notion of a tragic blunder, redeemed by heroic sacrifice, was immortalised by Alfred, Lord Tennyson, the **Poet Laureate**.

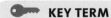

> **KEY TERM**
>
> **Poet Laureate** A title bestowed by the monarch on a poet whose duties include writing poems to celebrate important occasions.

How does Source B glorify the Charge of the Light Brigade? **?**

SOURCE B

After reading William Russell's account glorifying the British valour shown during the Charge in *The Times*, Alfred Lord Tennyson wrote the poem *The Charge of the Light Brigade* in a few minutes. It was published in December 1854.

Half a league, half a league,
Half a league onward,
All in the valley of Death
Rode the six hundred.
'Forward, the Light Brigade!
'Charge for the guns!' he said:
Into the valley of Death
Rode the six hundred.

'Forward, the Light Brigade!'
Was there a man dismay'd?
Not tho' the soldier knew
Someone had blunder'd:
Theirs not to make reply,
Theirs not to reason why,
Theirs but to do and die:
Into the valley of Death
Rode the six hundred.

Cannon to right of them,
Cannon to left of them,
Cannon in front of them
Volley'd and thunder'd;
Storm'd at with shot and shell,
Boldly they rode and well,
Into the jaws of Death,
Into the mouth of Hell
Rode the six hundred.

Flash'd all their sabres bare,
Flash'd as they turn'd in air,
Sabring the gunners there,
Charging an army, while
All the world wonder'd:
Plunged in the battery-smoke
Right thro' the line they broke;
Cossack and Russian
Reel'd from the sabre stroke
Shatter'd and sunder'd.
Then they rode back, but not
Not the six hundred.

Cannon to right of them,
Cannon to left of them,
Cannon behind them
Volley'd and thunder'd;
Storm'd at with shot and shell,
While horse and hero fell,
They that had fought so well
Came thro' the jaws of Death
Back from the mouth of Hell,
All that was left of them,
Left of six hundred.

When can their glory fade?
O the wild charge they made!
All the world wonder'd.
Honour the charge they made,
Honour the Light Brigade,
Noble six hundred.

The results of the Battle of Balaclava

The Battle of Balaclava, coupled with the driving back of a Russian attack on 26 October, ensured that the Russian advance was halted. The siege of

Sebastopol thus continued. However, the Russians confined the British to a narrow area between Balaclava and Sebastopol. British positions guarding the approaches to Balaclava were vulnerable. Moreover, by November Menshikov commanded 120,000 men. Raglan had only 25,000 troops and the French just 40,000.

The Battle of Inkerman

Early on 5 November, the Russians attacked Inkerman Ridge. Their manoeuvrings were hidden, first by rain and then by fog. The fighting quickly broke up into a series of encounters which were impossible to direct or co-ordinate. All over the battlefield, small units of British infantry fought much larger numbers of Russians. Around 9.00a.m., as the mist began to clear, it seemed that the outnumbered British forces must be driven back. The arrival of French troops, however, helped to turn the tide of battle. Soon after noon, the Russians retreated, having suffered 11,000 casualties. The British lost 597 killed and 1860 wounded, the French lost 130 killed and 750 wounded.

Although the allied armies had fought magnificently, they were still no nearer capturing Sebastopol. Raglan, aware of the army's administrative shortcomings, warned the Duke of Newcastle of the dangers of wintering in the Crimea. In reply, Newcastle declared that Crimean winters were among the mildest in the world.

The winter of 1854–5

The winter 1854–5 was one of the worst Crimean winters in living memory, sometimes so cold that icicles formed on the men's moustaches at night. While such cold spells were rarely prolonged, the weather was also wet. Given the shortage of tents and the lack of firewood, men were unable to cook or stay dry and warm.

The problem of supply

SOURCE C

James Filder, the commissary-general, writing to the Treasury on 13 November 1854, quoted in Christopher Hibbert, *The Destruction of Lord Raglan*, Penguin, 1963, p. 251.

I am full of apprehension as to our power of keeping this army supplied during the coming winter … In this crowded little harbour [Balaclava] only a proportion of our vessels can be admitted at a time … With all the siege and other stores which are being disembarked, we can do little more than land sufficient supplies to keep pace with the daily consumption of the troops; and to add to our difficulties, the road from the harbour to the camp, not being a made one, is impassable after heavy rains; our obstacles in these respects will increase as the winter comes. We shall have many more stores to convey than we have hitherto had – fuel, for instance.

? Why, according to Source C, was Filder 'full of apprehension'?

On 14 November a terrible storm resulted in the loss of more than twenty ships carrying much-needed stores. The *Progress*, for example, had been carrying enough hay to feed all the horses in the British Army for three weeks. On land, scores of tents were blown to shreds. The storm was in part to blame for what now occurred. However, in Balaclava there never was a lack of stores. The problem lay in the inefficient way they were organised.

Congestion in Balaclava harbour

Over the winter, Balaclava became a place of nightmarish chaos. Much of the blame rested with Admiral Boxer, who was in charge of transport arrangements. His inefficiency led to ships arriving at Balaclava without notice and with nobody sure what supplies they carried. On the port's crowded quayside, there was total confusion. Everything was piled together, consumables often rotting in the open air.

The problem of transport

Transporting supplies from Britain to Balaclava, 4000 miles (6500 km) away, was easy. It was the transport from Balaclava to the siege lines, just six miles (9.5 km) away, that was the problem. Russian control of the Worontsov Road (see the map on page 74) initially deprived the army of the only metalled road up the Sapoune Ridge. However, the Russians abandoned their position on 6 December, before the worst of the winter set in, so the Commissariat could not use this as an excuse. Freezing or muddy tracks were less of a problem than the lack of forage to feed the pack animals, which in turn prevented more transport animals being brought in to improve the situation. The Commissariat thus found it impossible to provide the troops above Balaclava with basic necessities: food, fuel, tents and clothing. Eventually, in January 1855, a railway contractor, Samuel Peto, was brought in to lay a track from Balaclava to the heights above the port.

Administrative incompetence

Army administrators in Britain found themselves entangled in a bureaucratic mesh. Departmental jealousies cut across the path to efficiency. Even when the appalling state of the army was common knowledge, no one, it seemed, was able to act.

The medical situation

As more and more men went down with **cholera**, scurvy, gangrene, **typhus**, **typhoid** and dysentery, the medical situation became dire. Little money had been spent in planning for the soldiers' medical care, and hospital tents and medicines were scarce. The filthy, verminous and overcrowded hospital at Balaclava provided little comfort. Those men who were shipped off to the hospitals at Scutari fared no better. Soon letters reached relatives in Britain describing the dreadful conditions, conditions confirmed and denounced by *The Times* and other newspapers. It was at Scutari that Florence Nightingale battled

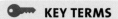

KEY TERMS

Cholera An infection of the intestine caused by bacteria transmitted in contaminated water. This causes severe vomiting and diarrhoea, which leads to dehydration that can be fatal.

Typhus A dangerous fever transmitted by lice, fleas, mites or ticks.

Typhoid A disease contracted by drinking infected water.

to improve matters (see pages 92–5). When she arrived she found men piled up in corridors. More than 1000 patients were suffering from acute diarrhoea and there were only twenty chamber pots to go round. An inch of liquid filth floated over the floor. Men died in dreadful numbers.

Dr Blake, surgeon of the 55th battalion, kept a medical history. He treated:

- 640 men for fever, including typhus: 57 died
- 368 cases of respiratory diseases, including pneumonia: 17 died
- 1256 cases of infections of the bowels and stomach, including dysentery: 76 died
- 96 cases of cholera: 47 died.

Six men died from frostbite, three from scurvy, four from diseases of the brain and 21 from 'unknown causes'.

In total, Blake treated 3025 cases of sickness, compared with 564 men treated for wounds. 'The hospital accommodation through the greater part of the winter', he wrote, 'was so limited that it was necessary to fill the few tents literally as full as they could hold'.

Raglan's role

Raglan was deeply concerned by the situation and worked hard, as did many officers, to remedy matters. But he did not do enough to inform the government of his worries or appeal for more help. Nor did he do much to rouse the mood of his men. His reluctance to show himself to the troops or even to say a few words of encouragement further damaged morale. His manner gave the impression that he was unaware of, or unconcerned about, the men's welfare. Accordingly, many men blamed him for their distress.

The result

The Crimean winter was a battle waged against disease, cold, incompetence, mismanagement and the absence of foresight. It was a battle lost. Consequently, many men died. By the end of January 1855, the British Army was only 11,000 strong. The sick and wounded totalled 23,000. The French Army coped with the rigours of the winter far more efficiently. Britons, informed of the suffering and bureaucratic muddle by William Russell and other war correspondents, were appalled. It seemed inconceivable that the richest country in the world could not provide its army with basic necessities. Aberdeen was blamed. He fell from power and was replaced as prime minister by Palmerston in February 1855 (see page 89).

The war 1855–6

As spring approached, the administrative chaos in the Crimea lessened. Provisions were located in separate depots on the plateau above Balaclava, the railway line was completed, more Ottoman labour was recruited and the confusion in Balaclava was tackled. After the third week of February, there was a marked decline in the deaths of soldiers in the military hospitals: 3168 died in January; 1409 in March; 582 in April. By March 1855, as troops received plentiful supplies of food and clothing, the morale of the army improved.

The diplomatic situation

- In December 1854, Austria signed a treaty with Britain and France. Although it was called an alliance, the treaty did not mean that Austria had to fight Russia.
- In January 1855, **Piedmont**, hoping to win support for its Italian ambitions, allied with Britain and France.
- The death of Tsar Nicholas in March 1855 offered some hope of peace. His successor, Alexander II, did not have the same commitment to the war.

 **KEY TERM**

Piedmont A kingdom in northern Italy.

Sebastopol

Over the winter of 1854–5 allied operations against Sebastopol virtually ceased. However, by March 1855 the allies were ready to try again. By the late spring there were some 175,000 allied troops in the Crimea, only 32,000 of whom were British. Some 20,000 Ottomans arrived in April and 15,000 Piedmontese in May. There were also 10,000 foreign mercenaries: Germans, Swiss and Poles. The rest of the troops were French.

The allies still faced problems:

- Sebastopol was not encircled and could thus be easily supplied and reinforced.
- Sebastopol's defences – a series of earthwork fortresses – remained strong.

However, Russian problems were greater than those of the allies:

- There were no railway lines south of Moscow. It took three months for men and supplies to get from Moscow and St Petersburg to the Crimea.
- The corrupt Russian administrative system made supply a lottery.
- Fearing and facing attacks on a number of fronts, Russia failed to concentrate its military effort in the Crimea. Instead, it stationed many troops on the Austrian border to guard against a 100,000-strong Austrian Army of 'observation'.

On 9 April 1855 the allies began a second great bombardment of Sebastopol. Five hundred and twenty allied guns poured 165,000 rounds into the town. The bombardment continued for ten days. The Russians sustained heavy casualties but maintained their defences. Raglan was keen to attack but the French were less enthusiastic. As the alliance's junior partner, Raglan had to go along with Canrobert's decision.

The death of Raglan

In May 1855 Canrobert was replaced by General Pelissier, who determined to attack Sebastopol. On 7 June, the French captured the Mamelon fortress while British forces took the Quarries. On 18 June British forces attacked the Redan while the French attacked the Malakhov fortifications: the key to Sebastopol's defensive system. Both assaults failed, Raglan losing 1500 men and Pelissier 3500. The defeat widened divisions between allied forces, the British blaming the French and the French the British for the débâcle.

On 28 June, Raglan, overworked and dispirited, died of dysentery. Sir James Simpson, who had little recent military experience, replaced him. Simpson had no wish to command and resigned four months later.

The capture of Sebastopol

On 16 August 1855, an attack by 60,000 Russians across the River Chernya was decisively defeated by French and Piedmontese troops. This was the Russians' last effort to break the allied siege. On 8 September, French forces captured the

SOURCE D

? How useful is Source D for the historian studying the Crimean War?

A photograph by Roger Fenton showing officers of the 4th Light Dragoons in February 1856.

Malakhov fortifications (losing 7500 casualties in the process). A British attack on the Redan failed, with a loss of 2500 casualties. However, the Russians now abandoned Sebastopol. Its loss, while a serious setback for Russia, was not a total disaster. Russian guns to the north still dominated the city, preventing the allies from occupying it in safety.

The war in the Baltic

While a considerable part of the fleet was sent to the Black Sea to support allied land forces, the Royal Navy waged a wider war against Russia. In 1854, 68-year-old Sir Charles Napier was given command of a Baltic Fleet. Although his fleet was initially smaller than that of the enemy, he succeeded in blockading the Russian coast until the end of October 1854. Back in Britain, Napier faced a

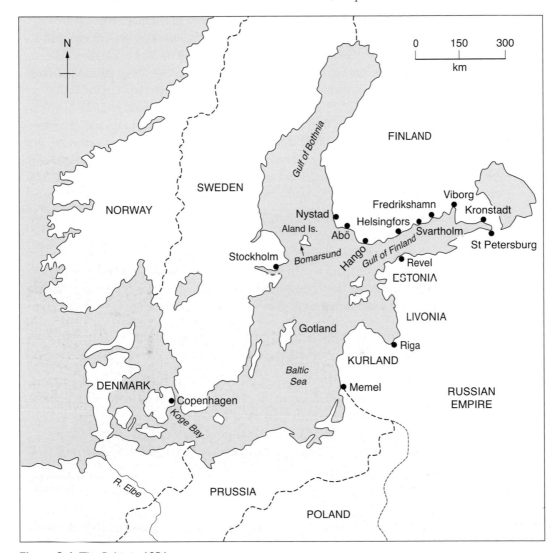

Figure 3.4 The Baltic in 1854.

grilling from an Admiralty unimpressed with his performance. In fact, he had been remarkably successful, bottling up the Russian fleet, tying down 30,000 Russian soldiers and capturing the fortress of Bomarsund.

In 1855, Admiral Dundas replaced Napier and continued his good work, blocking Russia's ports and destroying the forts at Svastholm and Fredrikshamn. By 1856, the allies had some 250 ships in the Baltic. Palmerston hoped that this 'Great Armament' would be strong enough to threaten St Petersburg.

The end of the war

With Sebastopol's fall, the Crimea campaign petered out. The winter of 1855–6 was an odd contrast to the year before. As a result of lessons learned, British troops were well supplied. The French Army, by contrast, had a far worse winter, thousands of soldiers dying of disease. Napoleon III felt that Sebastopol's capture satisfied France's honour and wanted an end to the war. In contrast, Palmerston, confident of thrashing Russia, wanted the war to continue. His hopes did not come to fruition. In December 1855, Austria issued an ultimatum threatening Russia with war if it did not negotiate on the basis of the Four Points (see page 68). The Russians were aware that this was bluff; the Austrian Army was actually in the process of demobilising. Russia's main concern was the Baltic, where the allied naval blockade was damaging Russia's economy and threatening St Petersburg. Therefore, Tsar Alexander II agreed to peace talks. Palmerston had little choice but to agree to an **armistice** in February 1856. The Treaty of Paris, signed in March 1856, essentially confirmed the Four Points.

The allies could claim that they had achieved most of their objectives. The Ottoman Empire had survived. More importantly, Russia was seriously weakened, its Balkan ambitions checked and its navy kept out of the Mediterranean. Britain had emerged victorious. If its army had not covered itself in glory, the Royal Navy had performed well. No other navy could rival it in size, modernity and technical skill.

The military implications of the Crimean War

In many respects the Crimean War was a midway point between Waterloo and the First World War. Generally, the armies wore Napoleonic uniforms and employed Napoleonic tactics but fought with improved weapons. Wellington would have felt at home with most of the means and methods of fighting. The war emphasised the overriding importance of logistics, entrenchments and firepower, anticipating the experience of the American Civil War (1861–5).

The Crimean War involved far heavier casualties than any other European war fought between 1815 and 1914. Some 22,000 British soldiers died (98,000 Britons fought in the Crimea). France lost 95,000, the Ottoman Empire 150,000 and Russia at least half a million dead. Most died of disease; less than one in five was killed in battle.

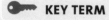 **KEY TERM**

Armistice An agreement to suspend fighting.

Summary diagram: The war 1854–6

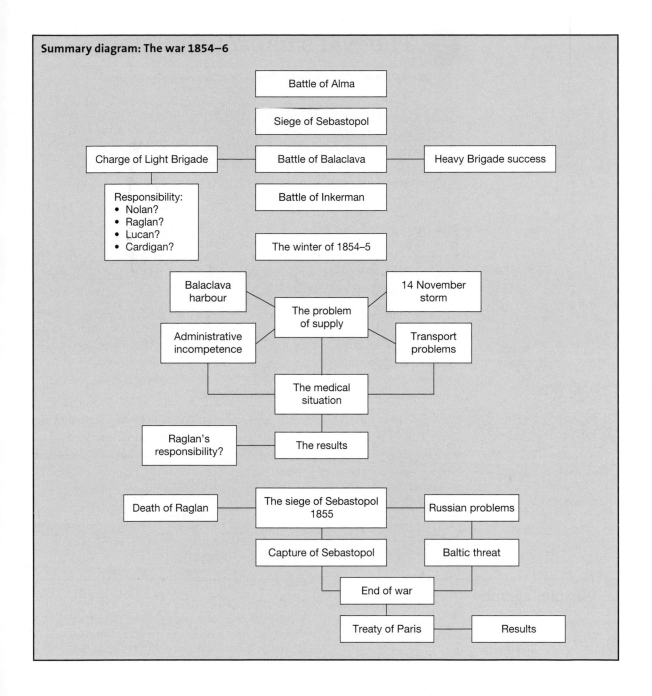

3 The war's impact on Britain

> ▶ *To what extent did the Crimean War impact on Britain?*

From a British perspective, the Crimean War was a limited war. Britain relied on naval power, an economic blockade, allies, a relatively small army and industrial output to secure its aims. The war had a minimal impact on civilian life. Nevertheless, it did have some important results. It revealed the power of the press and led to calls for greater efficiency in military and government management.

The impact of the press

Newspaper coverage of the war, aided by the electric telegraph, ensured that the public was able to read about the reality of warfare with immediacy for the first time. Thanks to new technology and the abolition of various taxes, the cost of newspapers was falling. That said, newspapers remained too expensive for most of the population and many Britons were unable to read one, even if they could afford to buy one. Daily newspapers in the 1850s largely catered for the literate middle and upper classes.

The impact of William Howard Russell

The single most influential reporter was Irishman William Howard Russell of *The Times*. His reports – sharp, clear, sometimes funny, often moving, always vivid – were hugely significant. They were 'eagerly awaited and avidly read by almost the entire literate population of London', according to historian Christopher Hibbert. Russell invariably paid credit to the bravery of the British troops. Although he initially avoided criticising Raglan, he asked awkward questions and when he saw problems, he wrote about them. Russell was not the only influential reporter. Thomas Chenery, *The Times*' correspondent in Constantinople, was the first to report the dreadful conditions in the hospitals at Scutari.

War photography

Roger Fenton went to the Crimea in February 1855 as the first official war photographer, at the insistence of Prince Albert, Queen Victoria's husband. It was hoped that his photographs might counteract the (perceived) anti-war reporting of *The Times*. Location photography in 1855 was no easy matter. Fenton carried his bulky equipment in a converted wine-wagon. Given the primitive photographic technology, he was unable to take action shots. Thus, most of his 350 photographs were either carefully posed pictures of men or images of the landscape. He avoided making pictures of dead or injured soldiers. On returning from the Crimea, his prints were displayed in a London gallery and also published in bound volumes.

Fenton was not the only photographer in the Crimea. James Robertson and Frenchman Jean-Charles Langlois also took photographs.

Newspapers in the 1850s lacked the technology to print photographs. However, the *Illustrated London News* sent several artists to the Crimea to sketch events. Their sketches were then converted into engravings for the paper.

The press attack on Raglan

The army's plight in 1854 stirred John Delane, *The Times'* editor, to attack Raglan and his staff for gross incompetence.

SOURCE E

On 23 December 1854, *The Times* informed its readers that:

The noblest army ever sent from these shores has been sacrificed to the grossest mismanagement. Incompetency, lethargy, aristocratic hauteur, official indifference, favour, routine, perverseness, and stupidity reign, revel and riot in the Camp before Sevastopol … We say it with extreme reluctance, no one sees or hears anything of the Commander-in-Chief.

The Times maintained its attack on both Raglan specifically and the army's aristocratic and privileged leadership in general. The horrors brought so vividly to light by *The Times* and other papers led to a bitter outcry and a search for scapegoats. From Britain's point of view there was probably no greater inefficiency than there had been at the beginning of past wars but thanks to newspaper correspondents it appeared as though there was.

Raglan, who had a poor opinion of the press, considered the personal attacks on him as unworthy of response. His main concern was that press's reporting might give the Russians useful information about the army's plans. Nevertheless, Raglan made no efforts to get rid of the correspondents. Nor did the British government impose press censorship. It feared that if it did so this might be interpreted as a means of hiding from public view its responsibility for what was happening in the Crimea.

Palmerston

On 29 January 1855, the **Radical** MP John Arthur Roebuck's motion to set up a committee to inquire into the conduct of the war was carried by 305 votes to 148. The vote stunned Aberdeen, who resigned the following day. Palmerston, at 71 years old, now became prime minister. Benjamin Disraeli, the Conservative leader in the Commons, remarked: 'He [Palmerston] is really an imposter, utterly exhausted, and at best only ginger-beer, and not champagne.' But that was not the way most Britons saw things. As a highly visible foreign secretary (1830–41 and 1846–51), Palmerston had never been shy to lecture **autocratic regimes**. With his progressive rhetoric abroad and his support for moderate reform at home, Palmerston embodied a wide spectrum of opinion both within and outside the restricted government circles of the time.

Palmerston's leadership 1855–6

While Palmerston was popular with the public, his position in Parliament was far from secure. He survived partly because of his own political skills and partly because his opponents were disunited. Within a month, the main Peelites in

Why, according to Source E, was *The Times* critical of Raglan? **?**

⚷ KEY TERMS

Radical(s) Supporters of profound economic and social change.

Autocratic regimes Governments where one (unelected) ruler has total power.

his cabinet resigned. The ostensible reason was Palmerston's refusal to veto the appointment of a committee of inquiry into the war. In reality, the Peelites had no wish to work with Palmerston, whom they disliked. Their departure ensured that Palmerston's administration no longer looked like Aberdeen's coalition.

Lord Panmure, who replaced Newcastle as secretary of state for war, sent General Sir James Simpson to report on Raglan's staff. Simpson reported that they were doing a good job. While injecting some energy into the war effort, Panmure and Palmerston benefited from the fact that much had already been done to remedy matters. Palmerston's administration made only modest changes to the war effort:

- A Sanitary Commission (see page 95) helped to improve conditions both at Scutari and in the Crimea.
- A special transport department was established, improving the supply situation.
- Some of the most inefficient administrators were sacked.
- The bureaucratic structure was simplified. The military duties of the colonial secretary were transferred to the War Office, which also took over the Commissariat from the Treasury. The Ordnance Board was abolished and its responsibilities were shared between the secretary of state for war and the commander-in-chief.

Administrative reform

As criticisms in Parliament and the press of military mismanagement increased, there were demands for reform of the Civil Service. Many assumed that the problems stemmed from the aristocracy's monopoly of power in all areas of government. In 1855, the Administrative Reform Association mounted an intensive campaign:

- contrasting aristocratic administrative bungling with the triumphs of commerce
- urging that business-like procedures be applied to government and administration
- claiming that competitive exams would allow the middle classes to take over the running of the state.

Palmerston pointed out that the most serious breakdowns had taken place 'not where the gentry were, not where the aristocracy were, but where there were persons belonging to other classes of the community – in the medical department, the Commissariat department, the transport service, which have not been filled by the aristocracy or the gentry'.

The much-vaunted Civil Service reforms of 1855 were not particularly significant. Nor had they much to do with the Crimean War. Sir Stafford Northcote and Sir Charles Trevelyan's report recommending changes to the Civil Service had been presented in 1853 – before the war. Its main recommendations, for competition in recruitment and promotion by merit, were only partially implemented. A Civil Service Commission was established but departments continued to arrange their own standards for entry. Those with power still came from the aristocracy.

Financing the war

Given that the Crimean War was relatively short and limited in scope, and Britain was at the height of its economic power, paying for the war was not a serious problem. William Gladstone, chancellor of the exchequer in 1854, believed in balancing the budget and reducing taxes. However, the military costs of the war led to him increasing taxation. Income tax rates were doubled and additional revenue was raised from increases in stamp duty and in duties on spirits, sugar and malt. Although he had hoped to pay for the war without recourse to borrowing, Gladstone was soon forced to increase the national debt by offering **government bonds** for sale.

Sir George Cornewall Lewis replaced the Peelite Gladstone as chancellor in 1855. By 1855 war expenditure had risen sharply as both the army and navy had more than doubled in size. Unlike Gladstone, Lewis was not particularly concerned about balancing the budget. Convinced that heavy taxation was more damaging to the economy than borrowing, he borrowed. Just under half of the war's cost was ultimately met by government borrowing.

The war's economic impact

By 1850, Britain had become the home of the world's first urban industrialised economy. With only two per cent of the world's population, it accounted for 50 per cent of the world's trade in coal, cotton and iron. By the mid-nineteenth century, Britain was both the workshop of the world and the world's banking house. Overall, the Crimean War had little impact on the economy.

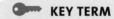 **KEY TERM**

Government bonds
Securities issued by the government, allowing it to borrow money. Those who bought the bonds were guaranteed to receive their money back in the future.

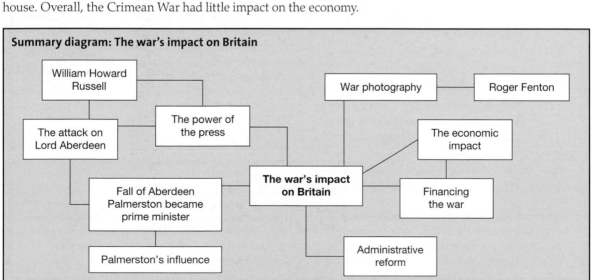

Summary diagram: The war's impact on Britain

④ Florence Nightingale, Mary Seacole and nursing

▶ *How successful were Florence Nightingale and Mary Seacole in the Crimean War?*

Florence Nightingale's work in the Crimean War has long been recognised. Mary Seacole's role has more recently been emphasised. However, there was nothing new in women helping wounded and sick soldiers. Soldiers' wives had long tended soldiers and nuns had often acted as nurses. Nor were Nightingale and Seacole the only women to serve in the Crimea:

- Russian women cared for Russian sick and wounded.
- French nuns served as nurses.
- Irish nuns, led by Mother Francis Bridgeman, aided the British Army in the Crimea.
- Mary Stanley took out a group of nurses to work at the hospital at Koulali.

Florence Nightingale

1820	Born into an upper-class British family in Florence, Italy
1844	In spite of family opposition, she decided to enter nursing
1847	Met MP Sidney Herbert. They became lifelong friends
1854	Went to help the Crimean army, largely as a result of Herbert's influence
1855	Made hospital inspections in the Crimea
1857	Suffered from depression. Despite being intermittently bedridden, she continued to promote the development of nursing and hospital reform
1860	Set up the Nightingale Training School
1910	Died

Nightingale is usually seen as the saviour of sick and wounded soldiers in the Crimea. Until recently it was often asserted that she massively reduced the death rate in the hospitals at Scutari. Unfortunately, the truth is different. Despite the unstinting efforts of Nightingale and her team, death rates did not drop; on the contrary, they continued to rise. Indeed, the death count at Nightingale's hospital at Scutari was the highest of all the hospitals in the region. Over the winter of 1854–5 over 4000 soldiers died at Scutari. According to historian Hugh Small, she effectively presided over 'a death camp'. While she helped her patients to die in greater comfort, she did not save their lives.

Not until a Sanitary Commission was sent out by the government in March 1855 was there a marked improvement. The Sanitary Commission effected the flushing out of the sewers and improvements to ventilation. Thereafter, death rates were sharply reduced.

During the war Nightingale believed that the high death rates were due to poor nutrition and supplies rather than poor hygiene. Once she realised her mistake, she worked incessantly to improve matters in army and civilian hospitals.

Nightingale's work during the Crimean War

Convinced she was doing God's work, Florence Nightingale devoted her life to nursing. Her decision to do so was remarkable. Women of her wealthy background were expected to marry and bear children. They did not become nurses. Florence never married and had no children. She was fortunate that her father:

- believed women should be educated and personally taught her a range of subjects
- gave her a large income, allowing her to live comfortably while pursuing her vocation.

When reports began to filter back to Britain about the horrific hospital conditions in the Ottoman Empire and the Crimea, she volunteered to help. On 21 October, she and 38 volunteer female nurses were sent, under the authorisation of the Secretary of State for War Sidney Herbert, to the Black Sea. Arriving in November at Selimiye Barracks in Scutari (modern-day Uskudar in Istanbul), they found sick and wounded soldiers being badly cared for by overworked medical staff – all male. Medicines were in short supply and hygiene was neglected.

In the army, there was a deep prejudice against women's involvement in medicine. Dr John Hall, the inspector general of hospitals and Raglan's principal medical officer, tried to have Nightingale shipped back to Britain. Although he failed, Hall and his doctors initially allowed her nurses to undertake only menial duties. But the flood of men pouring into the hospitals forced officialdom's hand and Nightingale's influence grew accordingly, particularly as she managed a fund of £30,000 – money raised in Britain to help the soldiers. This enabled her to purchase some of the necessities so badly needed. She also worked with energy, ensuring that wards were cleaned, fresh bed linen was available and special diets were prepared.

For all Nightingale's zeal, 52 per cent of patients at Scutari died in February 1855. At this stage, she had no better understanding of the hazards of polluted water, lack of ventilation and poor hygiene than army doctors. There was no concept of germ theory in the 1850s. Nevertheless, she became a national heroine and gained the nickname 'The Lady with the Lamp', derived from a phrase in *The Times*. In many ways Nightingale was – and is – wrongly depicted. Rather than the caring 'Lady with the Lamp', she was more a tough-minded administrator.

SOURCE F

From a report by John MacDonald published in *The Times*, February 1855. At the time, MacDonald was in the Crimea, administering the fund collected by *The Times* to support sick and wounded soldiers.

Wherever there is disease in its most dangerous form, and the hand of the spoiler distressingly nigh, there is that incomparable woman [Nightingale] sure to be seen; her benign presence is an influence for good comfort even amid the

Why, according to Source F, did Nightingale have an important influence?

struggles of expiring nature. She is a 'ministering angel' without any exaggeration in these hospitals, and as her slender form glides quietly along each corridor, every poor fellow's face softens with gratitude at the sight of her. When all the medical officers have retired for the night and silence and darkness have settled down upon those miles of prostrate sick, she may be observed alone, with a little lamp in her hand, making her solitary rounds.

The Royal Commission on the Health of the Army

Nightingale's Crimea experience was only the prelude to her more important post-war career. On returning to Britain, she was determined to improve the health of British troops. Through her efforts, a Royal Commission on the Health of the Army was appointed in 1857. When she began collecting evidence for the

SOURCE G

? How useful is Source G to a historian?

'The Lady with the Lamp.' The public image of Florence Nightingale, doing her rounds at Scutari. A painting by Henrietta Rae created between 1879 and 1928, long after the Crimean War.

Commission, Nightingale realised that most of the soldiers at Scutari died as a result of poor hygiene and sanitation. Henceforward, she promoted the thorough overhaul of the health of the army in general and the improvement of sanitary conditions in particular. Shrewd and forceful, she manipulated her fame to masterly effect. As a result of the Royal Commission's findings and Nightingale's pressure, sanitation and diet in army barracks and military hospitals were improved.

Hospital design

Nightingale made extensive efforts to identify the best types of hospitals and to improve hospital design. Her book *Notes on Hospitals* (1859), which addressed many issues with regard to hospital construction, provision and management, had considerable effect on hospital design, not just in Britain but across Europe.

The Nightingale Training School

In November 1855, while Nightingale was still in the Crimea, a public meeting to give recognition to her work led to the establishment of the Nightingale Fund for the training of nurses. With £45,000 at her disposal, she was able to set up the Nightingale Training School at St Thomas' Hospital in London in 1860, the first secular nursing school in the world. The first trained Nightingale nurses began work in 1865 at the Liverpool Workhouse Infirmary.

Nightingale's influence in India

In 1858–9 Nightingale successfully lobbied for the establishment of a Royal Commission into the health of soldiers in India. It completed its study in 1863. Thereafter, as a result of sanitary reform, mortality among soldiers in India declined considerably. She later made a comprehensive statistical study of sanitation in Indian rural life and helped to improve medical care in India generally.

Nightingale's influence as a role model

Nightingale's achievements are all the more impressive when they are considered against the background of social restraints on women in Victorian England. Few women pursued professional careers. Interestingly, she did not assist and was not interested in the cause of equal rights. In fact, she opposed women's suffrage. She seems to have had little respect for women in general, preferring the friendship of powerful men. Nevertheless, she undoubtedly inspired many women to devote their lives to nursing. The pioneer of modern nursing, she set an example of compassion, commitment to patient care and diligent hospital administration.

Mary Seacole

Mary Seacole (1805–81), daughter of a Scottish army officer and a Jamaican woman, has recently become almost as well known as Nightingale for her work in the Crimea. Taught herbal remedies by her mother, she helped to treat cholera victims in Jamaica and Panama in the 1840s and 1850s. Hearing of the poor medical provision for British soldiers, she travelled to London and applied to the War Office, hoping to be sent as an assistant to the Crimea. Her application was rejected.

Borrowing money, she went out to the Ottoman Empire. When Nightingale declined her offer of help, she sailed to Balaclava. Building a 'hotel' from salvaged materials, she provided a canteen business at the same time as nursing sick soldiers. Nightingale was ambivalent about Seacole. She wrote that Seacole 'kept – I will not call it a "bad house" – but something not very unlike it … She was very kind to the men and, what is more, to the officers – and did some good – and made many more drunk'. Russell in *The Times* was more complimentary, writing in September 1855 that she was a 'warm and successful physician, who doctors and cures all manner of men with extraordinary success. She is always in attendance near the battle-field to aid the wounded and has earned many a poor fellow's blessing'.

In 1856, Seacole returned to Britain, in poor health and bankrupt. Her plight was highlighted in the press and a Testimonial Fund was set up for her, to which many prominent people contributed, including Nightingale, indicating the regard in which she was held. She is generally praised today for her achievements in overcoming the racial and gender prejudices of many sections of Victorian society. It should be said, however, that her nursing achievements were far less considerable than those of Nightingale.

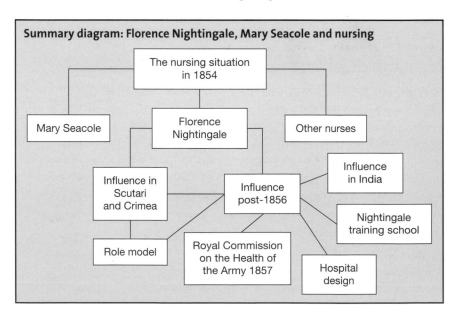

Summary diagram: Florence Nightingale, Mary Seacole and nursing

Military reform

▶ *How successful were Cardwell's army reforms?*

During the Crimean War, army affairs commanded unprecedented public and parliamentary interest. Nevertheless, and despite being found wanting in many respects, the army survived the war largely unchanged and after 1856 the progress of military reform resumed its former unhurried pace.

Administrative reform 1854–6

The select committee to investigate the conditions of the army, secured by Roebuck (see page 89), reported in June 1855. It criticised the arrangements for transport, provisioning and hospital care, and condemned ministers for having sanctioned an expedition which was ill-prepared for a protracted war. By the time the report came out, however, feelings of indignation had cooled and little resulted from the committee's censure.

The McNeill–Tulloch report

The final surge of parliamentary interest in Crimean mismanagement came in January 1856 with the report of a commission, headed by Sir John McNeill (a Scottish surgeon and diplomat) and Colonel Alexander Tulloch (an administrative expert at the War Office). The two men had been sent to the Crimea in February 1855 to inquire into the working of the Commissariat and the causes of delays in distributing stores sent to Balaclava. Their report, which sharply criticised Raglan's personal staff and Commissary-General Filder, provoked heated exchanges in the Commons. An ensuing commission of inquiry undertaken by the army exonerated all concerned. Nevertheless, the McNeill–Tulloch report did lead to reform of the Commissariat in 1858.

Lack of impetus for military change

In the period 1856–68 no fewer than seventeen royal commissions, eighteen select committees, nineteen internal War Office inquiries and 35 committees of officers dealt in some manner with military administration. But little was actually done. Military success in India (and elsewhere) and the waning of public disquiet over army affairs undermined the cause of reform. Parliament, once more preoccupied with the economy, gave only sporadic attention to the army. The Duke of Cambridge, commander-in-chief from 1856 to 1895, was sceptical of most aspects of change, fearing it might damage the *esprit de corps* of the army.

The American Civil War provoked a good deal of interest in British military circles but little effective analysis. Most experts dismissed the novel tactics and techniques developed in the USA as aberrations arising from unique circumstances. While Prussia's success against Austria (1866) and France

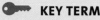 **KEY TERM**

Esprit de corps Morale.

(1870–1) left a deep impression on some British officers, few politicians looked to Germany as a model for reform. Most Britons assumed they would never again be involved in a major continental war.

Military reform 1856–68

There were some reforms in the dozen years after 1856:

- Nightingale and her disciples kept up a vigorous campaign to improve soldiers' health.
- A major programme of barrack construction was launched in 1859–60.
- Military authorities set up a Staff College at Camberley to raise officers' training standards.
- The army was generally provided with the best available weapons.

Armstrong's artillery

In the late 1850s the industrialist William Armstrong produced a breech-loading and rifled artillery piece. Rather than profit from his design, he surrendered his patent of the gun to the British government. Armstrong's gun, which was more accurate than muzzle-loading, smoothbore artillery pieces, was adopted by the army in 1859–60. This seemed to inaugurate a new era in artillery technology. However, in 1863 the army decided that the old guns were superior to Armstrong's guns in range, accuracy, ease of working, endurance and cost. The British government, therefore, ceased ordering from Armstrong. For seventeen years, it purchased muzzle-loading artillery. Given that Britain was only involved in colonial wars in this period – wars in which it easily outgunned the enemy – this had only a minimal effect.

The problem of recruitment

Army authorities and successive governments did little to enhance the appeal of service life:

- Soldiers remained poorly paid.
- Scant provision was made for recreation.
- Military discipline remained harsh. Flogging was not abolished until 1881.

Consequently, the army rarely met its recruitment targets.

Cardwell's reforms 1868–74

In 1868, Edward Cardwell was appointed secretary of state for war in Gladstone's first ministry. Cardwell, who retained his post until 1874, undertook comprehensive reform of the army's organisation:

- He reorganised the War Office, establishing clear divisions of duties.
- Short-term enlistments were introduced. Infantry had an initial engagement of six (later seven) years and then joined the army reserve. Although soldiers

could extend their period of service to 21 years, it was expected that most would quit the army at the end of the minimum period. Cardwell hoped that short-term enlistments would reduce the pension list, help to form a reserve, ensure that the army contained men in the prime of life, induce a better class of man to enlist, enhance the appeal of service life and improve recruitment.

- Cardwell determined to abolish the purchase system, whereby officers bought their commissions. Although he managed to push the measure through the Commons in July 1871, he failed to secure the passage of the bill through the Lords. The government resolved the impasse by announcing the abolition of purchase by Royal Warrant from 1 November 1871.
- The Localisation Act of 1872 divided the country into 66 territorial districts, and based two regular battalions, two militia battalions and a quota of volunteers in each district with a depot to receive recruits. The scheme was designed to foster local connections, to improve the efficiency of the auxiliary forces and to induce men from the militia to enter the regular army. One of the two regular battalions was to be based at home while the other served abroad. The home-based battalion was to train recruits and to supply drafts and reliefs for the battalion overseas.

How effective were Cardwell's reforms?

The desire for economy underlay most of Cardwell's measures. His reforms promised far more than they delivered:

- Despite the reorganisation of the War Office, no planning department was established and no chief of staff appointed to set out the strategy of the army as a whole.
- The army lost more men than it gained with the introduction of short-service enlistments. Recruitment remained a major problem.
- The abolition of the purchase of commissions did little to alter the social composition of the officer corps. Officers came from broadly the same classes in 1900 as they had done in 1870. Without a large private income, few officers could survive financially, so poor was their army pay.
- The localisation of forces did not transform the army. The constant need for men to serve overseas put great strain on home battalions. By the Zulu War (1879), there were only 59 battalions at home supporting 82 abroad. For the rest of the century, the home battalions were essentially 'squeezed lemons', supplying men for a larger number of battalions abroad.

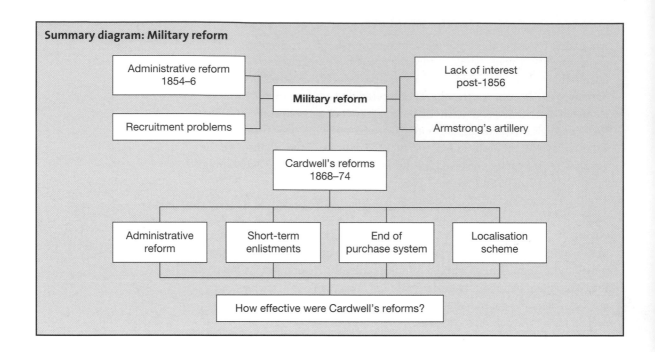

Summary diagram: Military reform

- Administrative reform 1854–6
- Recruitment problems
- **Military reform**
- Lack of interest post-1856
- Armstrong's artillery
- Cardwell's reforms 1868–74
  - Administrative reform
  - Short-term enlistments
  - End of purchase system
  - Localisation scheme
- How effective were Cardwell's reforms?

 Key debate

▶ *To what extent did the Crimean War lead to a change of attitude towards the army?*

A case has recently been made by Orlando Figes that the Crimean War led to a change of attitude among the British to the army.

EXTRACT 1

From Orlando Figes, *Crimea: The Last Crusade*, Penguin, 2011, p. 468.

The Crimean War brought about a sea change in Britain's attitudes towards its fighting men. It laid the basis of the modern national myth built on the idea of the soldier defending the nation's honour, right and liberty. Before the war the idea of military honour was defined by aristocracy. Gallantry and valour were attained by high-born martial leaders like the Duke of York, the son of George III and commander of the British army against Napoleon, whose column was erected in 1833 ... But the common soldier was ignored. Placing the Guards Memorial [to commemorate the Crimean War] opposite the Duke of York's column was symbolic of a fundamental shift in Victorian values. It represented a challenge to the leadership of the aristocracy, which had been so discredited by the military blunders in the Crimea. If the British military hero had previously been a gentleman ..., now he was a trooper ... who fought courageously and won Britain's wars in spite of the blunders of the generals.

Not all historians agree.

EXTRACT 2

From Denis Judd, *The Crimean War*, Book Club Associates, 1975, pp. 183–4.

For the British common soldier who had achieved and endured so much, there were some short-term benefits. The national conscience was aroused by the endurance of the troops, and this stimulated a demand for military reform. But the impact of the Crimean War in this respect should not be exaggerated. Reforms only trickled out for the rest of the Victorian age. Nor did the public reputation of the red-coated rank and file change for good overnight … Nor were the officers, who had demonstrated their bravery and spontaneity as well as their lack of professionalism in the Crimea, transformed at a stroke into first-rate tacticians and sound strategists. The Victorian officer class remained blue-blooded and, at times, distinctly bone-headed.

> Extracts 1 and 2 differ in emphasis. Which provides the more convincing explanation?

Did the war bring about a change in Britain's attitudes towards its soldiers?

The argument for:

- Previously military heroes had invariably been generals. The heroes who returned from the Crimea were the common troops. Their deeds were recognised for the first time in 1856 with the introduction of the Victoria Cross, awarded to gallant servicemen regardless of class or rank.
- In 1861, the Crimean War was commemorated with the unveiling of a Guards Memorial in London. The three bronze guardsmen symbolised a fundamental shift in values. Britain's military heroes were no longer only dukes but also ordinary soldiers.
- The military blunders by the army's aristocratic leadership appalled most Britons. The mismanagement stimulated a new assertiveness in the middle classes, which rallied round the principles of professional competence and meritocracy in opposition to the privilege of birth.
- It was a sign of middle-class triumph that in the decades after the war, Conservative and Liberal governments alike introduced reforms promoting middle-class ideals: the opening of the Civil Service to talent and a new system of merit-based promotion in the armed services.

The argument against:

- Generals remained the heroes of most wars. British cities have statues to colonial generals who won campaigns in India and Africa after 1856, not statues to the ordinary soldiers who fought the battles.
- After 1856, few people put ordinary soldiers on a pedestal. Despite the popularising of the army's imperial role, many families regarded it as a disgrace if any of their members enlisted.

- The landed classes continued to exert huge power for decades after the mid-1850s, maintaining their grip on Parliament, the army and most other citadels of power.
- The system of purchase of commissions did not end until Cardwell's reforms in 1871 (see page 99), and even then these reforms did not change the nature of the officer class.
- The fact that the Crimean War ended in victory sustained a belief that the heart of the British system was sound.
- As soon as peace was restored, the army was starved of money.
- Cardwell's reforms had more to do with the Franco-Prussian War than the Crimean War.

Chapter summary

The British Army was not best prepared for a war in 1854. It was small in number and there had been few changes since 1815. Despite this, the army fought well in the first battles in the Crimea, defeating the Russians at Alma, Balaclava (famous for the Charge of the Light Brigade) and Inkerman. Failing to capture Sebastopol, the army suffered terribly over the winter of 1854–5. Administrative incompetence led to a shortage of supplies and the army's medical provisions were unable to cope with the number of sick men. Florence Nightingale, Mary Seacole and a number of other women tried to improve matters. War correspondents, like William Russell, exposed the army's failures. Newspaper criticism helped bring about the fall of Aberdeen in 1855 and the coming to power of Palmerston. The capture of Sebastopol and the threat posed by the Royal Navy in the Baltic led to the Treaty of Paris in 1856. Despite the failings revealed in the Crimean War, there were no major changes to the army until Cardwell's reforms between 1868 and 1874. These reforms led to the end of the purchase system. It is debatable whether the Crimean War brought about a change of British attitude towards its soldiers.

Refresher questions

Use these questions to remind yourself of the key material covered in this chapter.

1 What were the main weaknesses of the British Army in 1854?

2 What were Raglan's main mistakes in 1854?

3 Who was most to blame for the Charge of the Light Brigade?

4 Who was responsible for the British Army's suffering during the winter of 1854–5?

5 Why did it take the allies so long to capture Sebastopol?

6 What was the Royal Navy's role in the Crimean War?

7 Why did the press have such an impact on political opinion?

8 How did Britain pay for the Crimean War?

9 How important was Florence Nightingale?

10 How important was Mary Seacole?

11 How significant were Cardwell's reforms?

Question practice

ESSAY QUESTIONS

1 How far was aristocratic blundering in the years 1854–6 responsible for British problems in the Crimean War?

2 To what extent was Britain successful in the Crimean War in the years 1854–6?

3 How far do you agree with the opinion that, in the years 1854–6, Florence Nightingale presided over 'a death camp' at the hospital in which she worked at Scutari?

4 To what extent did Cardwell's reforms in the years 1868–74 overhaul the British Army?

SOURCE ANALYSIS QUESTION

1 Assess the value of Source 1 for revealing the difficulties provisioning the British Army and the attitudes of British officers in the Crimean War. Explain your answer, using the source, the information given about its origin and your own knowledge about the historical context.

SOURCE I

From the draft of a letter from Colonel George Bell of the 1st (Royal) Regiment to *The Times* on 28 November 1854, quoted in Orlando Figes, *Crimea*, Penguin, 2011, pp. 291–2.

All the elements of destruction are against us, sickness & death, & nakedness, & uncertain ration of salt meat. Not a drop of Rum for two days, the only stand by to keep the soldier on his legs at all. If this fails we are done. The Communication to Balaclava impossible, knee deep all the way for 6 miles. Wheels can't move, & the poor wretched starved baggage animals have not strength to wade through the mud without a load. Horses – cavalry, artillery, officers' chargers & Baggage Animals die by the score every night at their peg from cold & starvation. Worse than this, the men are dropping down fearfully. I saw nine men of 1st Battalion Royal Regiment lying dead in one tent today, and 15 more dying! All cases of Cholera … The poor men's backs are never dry, their one suit of rags hang in tatters about them, they go down to the Trenches at night wet to the skin, lie there in water, mud & slush till morning, come back with cramps to a crowded Hospital Marquee tattered by the storm, lie down in a fetid atmosphere, quite enough of itself to breed contagion, & die there in agony. This is no romance, it is my duty as a C.O. [Commanding Officer] to see & endeavour to alleviate the sufferings & privations of my humble but gallant comrades. I can't do it. I have no power. Everything almost is wanting in this Hospital department, so badly put together from the start. No people complain so much of it as the Medical officers of regiments & many of the Staff doctors too.

CHAPTER 4

The Second Boer War 1899–1902

The Second Boer War was fought between Britain and two Boer republics: the Transvaal and the Orange Free State. Britain was to be seriously embarrassed, first by Boer success and then by tenacious Boer resistance. The war led to a serious debate about Britain's imperial role, national efficiency and military reform. This chapter will consider the key issues of the war by examining the following:

★ The situation in 1899

★ The war: October 1899 to September 1900

★ Guerrilla war: September 1900 to May 1902

★ The war's impact on Britain

★ Reorganisation of imperial defence

Key dates

1899	Oct.	Start of Second Boer War	1900	May	Relief of Mafeking	
	Dec.	Black Week		Sept.	Khaki election	
1900	Jan.	Roberts took command of British forces	1901		Concentration camp scandal	
	Jan.	Battle of Spion Kop	1902		Treaty of Vereeniging	
	Feb.	Relief of Kimberley and Ladysmith	1907		Territorial Army created	

 ## 1 The situation in 1899

▶ *To what extent was Britain prepared for war in 1899?*

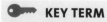 **KEY TERM**

Boer The Dutch word for farmer.

In 1815, Britain formally acquired Cape Colony from the Netherlands. Most of the Dutch colonists – or **Boers** – were fiercely independent farmers. In the 1830s some 5000 Boers, who disliked many aspects of British rule, especially the decision to abolish slavery, migrated northwards. Their Great Trek was initially towards Natal. But, after Britain annexed Natal in 1843, they headed into the interior where they founded the Orange Free State and the Transvaal. The Boers' desire for land created antagonism with black Africans, especially the Zulus. In 1877, Britain, hoping to unite its southern African colonies with the Boer republics, took control of the Transvaal and proceeded to defeat the Zulus in 1879.

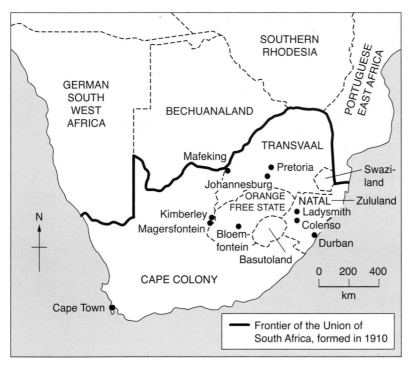

Figure 4.1 Southern Africa in the late nineteenth century.

The causes of the war

Soon after the Zulu defeat, the Transvaal asked Britain to restore its independence. When Britain refused, the Boers rebelled. In the First Boer War (1880–1) British forces were defeated, most heavily at Majuba Hill. Gladstone's government agreed to recognise the Transvaal and the Orange Free State as self-governing nations under the **suzerainty** of the British Crown. It was not altogether clear what this meant or what powers Britain retained over the republics.

The discovery of gold in 1886 made the Transvaal the richest nation in southern Africa. This situation threatened to tilt the economic balance of power in the Boers' favour. Conceivably, the Transvaal might try to take over the whole of southern Africa, a feasible proposition given that thousands of Boers still lived in Cape Colony and Natal.

The problem of the *uitlanders*

The Transvaal lacked the manpower and the industrial base to develop its goldmines. Consequently, waves of immigrants – *uitlanders* – mainly from Britain poured into the Transvaal hoping to make their fortune. By the mid-1890s:

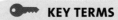

KEY TERMS

Suzerainty Overlordship; ultimate power.

Uitlanders White foreigners living in the Transvaal and the Orange Free State.

- much of the Transvaal's new wealth was in the hands of a few British and German mine owners
- *uitlanders* outnumbered the Boer inhabitants.

Determined to maintain Boer supremacy, the Transvaal government, led by President Kruger, insisted that *uitlanders* had to reside for fourteen years in the Transvaal before they could apply for naturalisation. Kruger's denial of voting rights to the *uitlanders* gave the British government a pretext for interference in the Transvaal.

Lord Salisbury and Joseph Chamberlain

In 1895 **Salisbury** became Conservative prime minister. He was also foreign secretary. His aims were to protect Britain's essential interests – security, India and the rest of the Empire, the sea lanes – by preserving peace. Salisbury appointed **Joseph Chamberlain** as colonial secretary. Chamberlain had long advocated forging a more cohesive Empire, bound together by economic interest and with a viable imperial Parliament. His aggressive defence of British interests sometimes collided with Salisbury's quieter conduct of policy.

Cecil Rhodes

Cecil Rhodes played a crucial role in southern Africa. Arriving in Cape Colony in 1870, aged seventeen, he made a fortune from diamond mining. In 1887 he established a powerful gold-mining company in the Transvaal and in 1890 became prime minister of Cape Colony. Convinced that the British were 'the first race in the world and that the more of the world we inhabit the better it is for the human race', he dreamed of expanding Britain's African empire. Standing in the way of Rhodes' ambitions were the two Boer republics.

The Jameson raid

In 1895, having encouraged *uitlanders* to agitate for voting rights, Rhodes hatched a scheme to seize control of the Transvaal. Men, mainly from his Chartered Company, would seize Johannesburg, trigger an uprising by *uitlanders* and overthrow Kruger. In December 1895, Dr Jameson, a key administrator of the Chartered Company, led 600 armed men into the Transvaal. But after a brief skirmish with Boer militia, Jameson surrendered. As a result of Jameson's raid:

- Rhodes was forced to resign as prime minister of Cape Colony.
- Transvaal, led by President Kruger, and the Orange Free State, led by President Steyn, drew closer together in opposition to the British threat, signing a military pact in 1897.
- Convinced that war with Britain was highly likely, Kruger purchased the best European weapons for Transvaal's armed forces.

🔑 KEY FIGURES

Lord Salisbury (1830–1903)

Prime minister 1886–92 and 1895–1902. His premiership is usually associated with 'splendid isolation'; the idea that Britain did not need to make binding alliances with any other power.

Joseph Chamberlain (1836–1914)

The son of a successful manufacturer, elected Liberal MP for Birmingham in 1876 and became president of the Board of Trade in 1880. After resigning from the cabinet over the issue of Irish Home Rule in 1886, he became leader of the Liberal Unionists in the Commons.

Alfred Milner

In 1897, the British government sent out Alfred Milner as high commissioner of southern Africa. A passionate imperialist, Milner believed that there was 'a greater issue than the grievances of the *uitlanders* at stake … our supremacy in South Africa … and our existence as a great power in the world is involved'. In his dealings with Kruger, Milner took an uncompromising stance: *uitlanders* must be granted full citizenship.

The coming of war

In an effort to resolve Anglo-Transvaal problems, Milner and Kruger attended a conference in Bloemfontein, capital of the Orange Free State, on 31 May 1899. Milner demanded that Transvaal enact a law that would immediately give *uitlanders* the right to vote. When Kruger rejected the demand, Milner walked out of the meeting on 5 June. He was confident that Kruger would 'bluff up to the cannon's mouth' and then accept Britain's demands.

Salisbury had misgivings about Milner's 'forward policy', believing that war with the Transvaal, 'unless upon the utmost and clearest provocation', would be 'entirely unpopular in the country'. As tension mounted, Salisbury's government did not send substantial reinforcements to southern Africa. The secretary of state for war, Lord Lansdowne, feared that such action might encourage a Boer attack rather than help to bring about a negotiated settlement.

While few Britons wanted war, the cabinet, most MPs and the British press agreed with Milner that the Boers needed 'teaching a lesson'. In September, Chamberlain sent an ultimatum demanding full equality for British citizens resident in the Transvaal. On 9 October Kruger issued his own ultimatum. This gave Britain 48 hours to withdraw all its troops from the Transvaal border, otherwise the Transvaal and the Orange Free State would declare war. Most newspaper editorials shared the sentiment of the *Daily Telegraph*, which declared: 'there can only be one answer to this grotesque challenge. Kruger has asked for war and war he must have.' The Boers declared war on 11 October. Kruger's actions, as Salisbury said, 'liberated us from the necessity of explaining to the people of England why we are at war'.

The British Army in 1899

Most Britons expected an easy victory. Salisbury was more realistic. He told Queen Victoria that, 'We have no army capable of meeting even a second-class Continental Power.'

Problems of military reform

The British Army remained small, with fewer than 135,000 men (excluding those in India). In the last two decades of the nineteenth century the main aim of military reformers was not so much to boost numbers as to bring the army up to a higher level of professionalism. There were formidable obstacles in their way:

- The government was not anxious to spend money on the army.
- The army generally performed well in colonial wars in the 1880s and 1890s. There was thus little pressure for change.
- The Duke of Cambridge, commander-in-chief of the army from 1856 to 1895, was a defender of traditional practices.

In 1895, Cambridge was replaced by Lord Wolseley. Wolseley, and the young officers whom he favoured, realised the need for reform. But, deprived of money by Salisbury's economically minded government, there was not much they could do.

British preparedness

George Wyndham, under-secretary at the War Office, claimed in October 1899 that the army was 'more efficient than at any time since Waterloo'. There was some truth in this view:

- Many officers and men had been hardened in a number of successful colonial wars. This success had been due in part to the fact that military leaders had responded well to scientific and technological innovation.
- Wolseley had emphasised the importance of supply and transportation. Once war was declared in 1899, mobilisation went remarkably well, with the Admiralty transporting men and supplies over a distance of 6000 miles (9500 km) without a hitch.

Nevertheless, there were problems:

- There was a shortage of ammunition.
- The army had plenty of red, white and blue uniforms, which were unsuitable for action on the **veldt**, but an inadequate supply of **khaki**.
- Several auxiliary departments, for example, the Royal Army Medical Corps, were understaffed.
- Intelligence and staff work were inadequate.
- British officers failed to recognise the impact of fire from trench positions and the mobility of cavalry raids, both of which had been demonstrated during the American Civil War.

The Boer Army

On paper, the Boer Army looked no match for the British:

- The Boers could put fewer than 60,000 men in the field. The total white population of the two republics, women and children included, was only 300,000.
- The Boer Army, apart from a few artillery troops, was essentially a civilian militia. When danger loomed, all adult male citizens (aged 16–60) in a district were expected to form a **commando**, which elected officers. Each man brought his own weapon and his own horse. Those who could not afford a rifle were given one by the authorities.

KEY TERMS

Veldt Open grass-country.

Khaki A dull-brownish cloth used for military uniforms. It provided better camouflage than red tunics.

Commando An armed group of Boers, varying in size from a few dozen men to several hundred.

SOURCE A

A photograph of Boer civilian-soldiers, taken in 1900.

But the Boers should not have been underestimated:

- The First Boer War suggested that the Boers, excellent horsemen and hunters, were likely to be tough opponents.
- The Boers were armed with Europe's best weapons, including smokeless Mauser rifles from Germany and Creusot siege guns from France.
- They had a greater familiarity with the terrain than British officers.
- Boer morale was strong. It was sustained by the belief that they were engaged in a life-and-death struggle to preserve their distinctive culture.
- Many Boers in Cape Colony and Natal sympathised with the two republics.

> Look at Source A and comment on the Boers' military appearance.

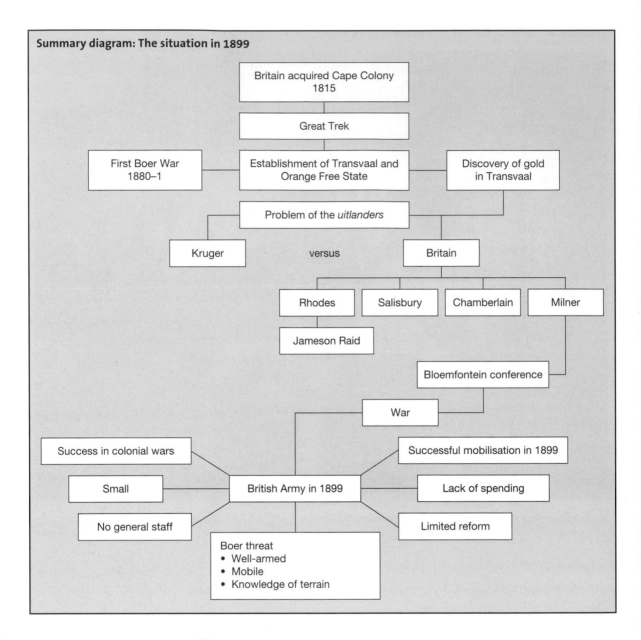

Summary diagram: The situation in 1899

Britain acquired Cape Colony 1815

Great Trek

First Boer War 1880–1 — Establishment of Transvaal and Orange Free State — Discovery of gold in Transvaal

Problem of the *uitlanders*

Kruger   versus   Britain

Rhodes   Salisbury   Chamberlain   Milner

Jameson Raid

Bloemfontein conference

War

Success in colonial wars   Successful mobilisation in 1899

Small   British Army in 1899   Lack of spending

No general staff   Limited reform

Boer threat
- Well-armed
- Mobile
- Knowledge of terrain

② The war: October 1899 to September 1900

▶ *Why were British forces so unsuccessful from October 1899 to January 1900 and so successful from February to August 1900?*

Fortunately for Britain, Sir George White, with 10,000 men from the Indian Army, had been shipped over to Natal. He arrived on 7 October 1899, in time to prevent the Boers marching unimpeded on Durban. Nevertheless, the Boers, with some 35,000 men in the field, decisively outnumbered British forces in the region. Britain's First Army Corps, earmarked for service in southern Africa, did not sail from Southampton until 12 October.

Ladysmith

White, establishing his main base at Ladysmith, allowed General Penn-Symons to send a brigade forward to Dundee. This became the site of the war's first battle. Boer guns began shelling the British camp on 20 October. Penn-Symons counterattacked. His men drove the Boers from Talana Hill but at a cost of 446 British casualties. Penn-Symons himself was fatally wounded. Fearing that more Boers were about to attack, White retreated to Ladysmith. The town was surrounded by Boers who bombarded it with siege guns. White ordered a major sortie against enemy artillery positions. The result – the Battle of Modderspruit – was a British disaster, with 140 men killed and over 1000 captured. White was now trapped in Ladysmith.

Mafeking and Kimberley

Colonel Robert Baden-Powell had raised some 1200 local men at Mafeking, hoping to lead raids against the enemy. But, instead of being the aggressor, Baden-Powell found himself the defender when 7000 Boers commanded by Piet Cronje attacked Mafeking. The town held out but the Boers besieged the place, hoping to starve it into surrender.

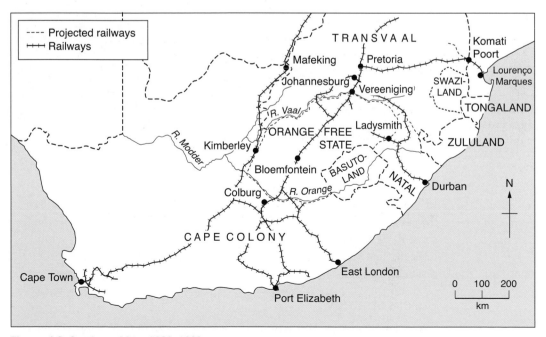

Figure 4.2 Southern Africa 1899–1902.

In early November, 7500 Boers laid siege to the diamond-mining town of Kimberley, defended by 5000 men. The town, which had some 40,000 inhabitants, was well stocked with provisions.

The Boers' decision to commit themselves to sieges handed the initiative back to the British, who were given time to recover. Other than a single attempt to storm Ladysmith, the Boers made no attempt to capture the besieged towns.

SOURCE B

What features in Source B suggest that the photograph was taken during the course of real fighting?

A photograph of British soldiers in southern Africa in 1900.

The situation in Cape Colony

In November, Boers crossed into Cape Colony, defended by only 7000 British troops. The government of Cape Colony adopted a neutral stance. Even when some 10,000 Cape Dutch joined the invading commandos, it was only with difficulty that Milner secured permission to declare martial law in the most disaffected districts.

Buller's strategy

General Sir Redvers Buller, Wolseley's protégé, arrived in Cape Town on 31 October 1899, followed on 18 November by the first contingent of the First

Army Corps. This changed the balance of power in Britain's favour. Buller initially intended to launch an offensive straight up the railway line from Cape Town via Bloemfontein to Pretoria, the Transvaal capital. But fearing the political repercussions of abandoning White to his fate and losing Kimberley, Buller split his army into three widely spread detachments:

- General Lord Methuen, with 20,000 men, set out to relieve Kimberley and Mafeking.
- General Gatacre, with 3000 men, headed towards Stormberg to secure the northern Cape from Boer raids and rebellion by Boer inhabitants.
- Buller led the main force to relieve Ladysmith.

Black Week

Methuen won two small but costly victories at Belmont (23 November) and at Graspan (25 November). He then walked into a trap set for him by the Boer commander de la Rey at the Modder River on 28 November, losing 500 casualties before the Boers retreated to Magersfontein.

In 'Black Week' – 10–15 December 1899 – the British suffered a series of defeats:

- On 10 December, Gatacre's attempt to take Stormberg ended in defeat, with over 700 casualties.
- On 11 December, Methuen launched an ill-judged attack at Magersfontein. The Highland Brigade, pinned down by accurate Boer fire, broke in ill-disciplined retreat. Methuen lost 900 men and failed to relieve Kimberley.
- On 15 December, Buller, with 21,000 men, tried to cross the Tugela River at Colenso to relieve Ladysmith. Eight thousand Boers, led by Louis Botha, repelled all British efforts to cross the river. Buller suffered nearly 1400 casualties. Eight Boers died.

The Boers, fighting on the defensive, had the advantage of prepared positions. Adept at siting trenches, their marksmanship was also superior to that of the British. British troops experienced the difficulties of crossing battlefields swept by smokeless, **magazine rifles** which could kill at 2000 yards (1830 m). The Boers were helped, too, by unimaginative British command.

The situation in December 1899

After his defeat at Colenso, Buller signalled by **heliograph** to White in Ladysmith that he should surrender. This action convinced the British government that Buller must be replaced. Lord Roberts, hero of the 1880 Afghan War, was sent to command the British forces with Kitchener, hero of the 1898 Sudan campaign, as his chief of staff.

To meet the emergency, Britons rushed to join the army. By January 1900, 180,000 troops, the largest force Britain had ever sent overseas, were in southern Africa. Some 30,000 men from British-controlled southern Africa came forward as volunteers, as did men from Australia, Canada and New Zealand in a display

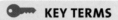

KEY TERMS

Magazine rifles Rifles which can fire a succession of shots without reloading.

Heliograph An apparatus for signalling by reflecting the sun's rays.

of imperial solidarity. By 1902, 16,310 Australians, 6051 Canadians and 6416 New Zealanders had seen service in Africa. Even so, it should be noted that volunteers who fought in southern Africa comprised only 0.76 per cent of British men of military age.

Lord Roberts

Lord Roberts (known affectionately as 'Bobs') arrived at the Cape in January 1900. He issued new tactical guidelines, insisting on careful reconnaissance before an attack, the avoidance of frontal attacks in mass formations, and more use of cover by infantry and artillery. Like Buller, Roberts decided he must relieve the beleaguered garrisons. Leaving Buller in command in Natal, Roberts massed his main force near the Orange River behind Methuen's force at the Modder River and prepared to make an outflanking move designed to relieve Kimberley and then take Bloemfontein. Kitchener improvised a transport system of wagons, unshackling British troops from dependence on the railway lines.

Spion Kop

With fresh reinforcements, Buller made another bid to relieve Ladysmith. General Warren successfully crossed the Tugela west of Colenso, but then faced a Boer defensive position centred on a hill known as Spion Kop. In the resulting battle, British troops captured the summit during the early hours of 24 January 1900. But as the morning fog lifted they realised that they were overlooked by Boer gun emplacements on surrounding hills. The rest of the day was a disaster for the British Army, largely caused by poor communications between Buller and his commanders. Contradictory orders were issued, some ordering men off the hill, others ordering reinforcements to defend it. The result was 1350 casualties and a retreat back across the Tugela. Widely publicised photographs of dead soldiers strewn across Spion Kop's ridge brought home to the British public the reality of war. On 5 February, Buller attacked Botha at Vaal Krantz and was again defeated.

Kimberley relieved

Further west, Roberts and Kitchener launched their offensive on 10 February, intending to outflank the Boers defending Magersfontein. To ensure greater mobility, they doubled the number of their mounted infantry but skimped on the supplies needed to sustain them – a problem aggravated by the loss of the ox-wagon convoy containing medicines and food at Waterval Drift on 15 February. This setback was overlooked when, on the same day, news came through that John French's cavalry had made a successful dash to relieve Kimberley, ending its 124-day siege.

Roberts, pursuing Cronje, who had abandoned Magersfontein, succeeded in trapping the Boer army at Paardeberg. On 17 February, a pincer movement, involving French's cavalry and Robert's main force, failed to take the entrenched Boer position. Roberts now resorted to bombarding Cronje into submission. On 28 February, the Boer leader surrendered with 4000 men.

Ladysmith relieved

On 14 February, Buller made a fourth attempt to relieve Ladysmith. His progress was slow. But on 26 February Buller, using all his forces in one all-out attack, succeeded in crossing the Tugela and defeating Botha north of Colenso. After a siege lasting 118 days, Ladysmith was relieved.

Mafeking relieved

Roberts advanced into the Orange Free State from the west, putting the Boers to flight at Poplar Grove on 7 March and capturing Bloemfontein unopposed on 13 March. Roberts was then forced to delay for six weeks:

- His army was short of supplies.
- There was an outbreak of typhoid, partly caused by troops drinking from the Modder River at Paardeberg, which had been polluted by the corpses of men and horses. Almost 1000 troops died in the epidemic. The Hospital Field Service was unable to cope with the situation.

Despite these problems, Roberts was able to send a small force towards Mafeking, which was relieved on 17 May after a 217-day siege, provoking huge celebrations in Britain. Its defender, Baden-Powell, became a national hero – with good cause. He had tied down 7000 Boers, almost a fifth of their total forces, at a crucial period in the war when Cape Colony was almost denuded of defenders.

British success

In May, Roberts continued his advance. Given the overwhelming superiority of British numbers, the Boers could only retreat. On 28 May, the Orange Free State was annexed. Meeting little Boer resistance, Roberts captured Johannesburg on 31 May and Pretoria on 5 June.

General Hunter, meanwhile, set out to mop up the last major Boer force in the Orange Free State. Although he failed to capture President Steyn, Hunter trapped the main Boer army, led by Pretorius, forcing 4500 men to surrender.

Kruger and what remained of his government retreated to eastern Transvaal. Roberts, joined by Buller, advanced down the railway line leading to **Portuguese East Africa**, reaching Komati Poort on 21 July, cutting the Boers off from the outside world. Roberts finally broke the Boers' defensive position at Bergendal on 26 August. Kruger fled to Europe, dying in exile in 1904. Botha led the remains of the Boer Army through the Drakensberg mountains into the Transvaal high veldt.

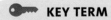 **KEY TERM**

Portuguese East Africa
Present-day Mozambique.

The end of the war?

After the capture of Bloemfontein, Johannesburg and Pretoria, and Kruger's flight, most British observers believed the war was effectively over. On 3 September 1900, the Transvaal was formally annexed. Many troops returned home to a heroes' welcome. In November 1900, after handing over to Kitchener, Roberts set sail for England, where he replaced Wolseley as commander-in-chief and was voted £100,000 as a reward for his work by a grateful Parliament. All that remained to be done in southern Africa, it seemed, was to mop up small pockets of resistance.

Summary diagram: The war: October 1899 to September 1900

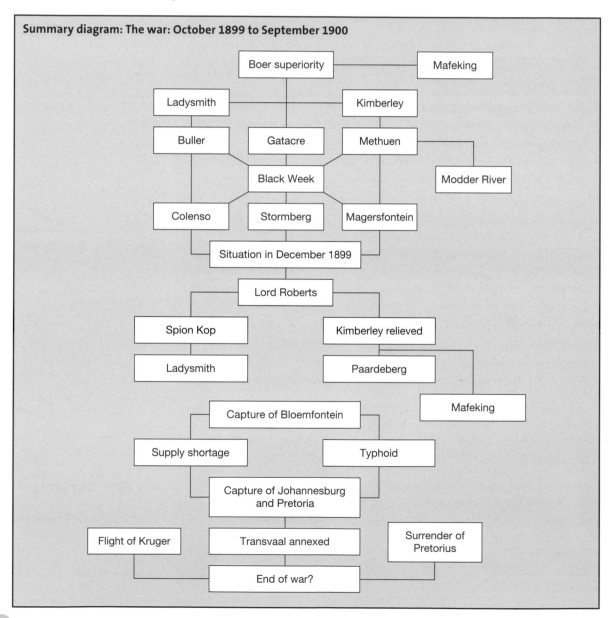

3 Guerrilla war: September 1900 to May 1902

▶ *How successful were the British in dealing with the continued Boer challenge from 1900 to 1902?*

By September 1900 British forces were nominally in control of both Boer republics. But some 20,000 Boers and their most determined leaders remained at large.

Boer tactics

Boer commandos were sent to their home districts, where they could rely on local support and had personal knowledge of the terrain. Ordered to act against the British whenever possible, their tactics were to strike fast and hard, causing as much damage as they could, and then to withdraw and vanish before British reinforcements could arrive. This resulted in a disorganised pattern of scattered engagements. The vast size of the republics made it difficult for the 250,000 British troops to control territory effectively. As soon as troops left a district, British authority faded away. Skilled Boer leaders – De Wet, de la Rey, Smuts, Botha – continued to be troublesome, not only in the Orange Free State and the Transvaal but also in Cape Colony.

Blockhouses

Kitchener, endeavouring to restrict the movement of Boer raiders and to protect his supply routes, built 8000 fortified blockhouses, each housing six to eight soldiers. The blockhouses were eventually linked with barbed wire fences, stretching over 4000 miles (6400 km) and parcelling the veldt into small areas. British troops were then able to conduct a series of 'sweeps' across these areas in an attempt to trap the enemy. British forces deployed the latest technology, maintaining communications through the telephone and the telegraph cable.

Raiding columns

Kitchener established mounted raiding columns in support of the larger sweeper columns. These were used to rapidly follow and harass the Boers, hoping to delay them or cut off their escape, while the main columns caught up. The British also used armoured trains to deliver rapid reaction forces to incidents or to drop men off ahead of retreating commandos.

Scorched earth

Before leaving southern Africa, Roberts initiated a policy of burning farms thought to be giving support to commandos. Kitchener continued this scorched-earth policy, targeting everything that could give sustenance to Boer guerrillas. As British troops swept the countryside, they destroyed property and crops, salted fields and poisoned wells.

Concentration camps

Concentration camps were set up as refugee camps for families who had been forced to quit their homes. Moving Boer women and children into camps was also intended to prevent civilians assisting the commandos. In military terms the concentration camp policy may have been a mistake. Although in the long run it perhaps undermined the Boers' will to resist, in the short term it freed them from responsibility for their families and thus had the opposite effect to that intended. In humanitarian terms the policy was disastrous. Inadequate food, poor shelter, bad hygiene and sanitation, shortage of medical facilities and overcrowding led to diseases such as measles, typhoid and dysentery, to which children were particularly vulnerable. Over 20,000 Boer women and children died in the 40 camps; about one in four of the inmates.

Tens of thousands of black Africans were also forcibly removed from Boer areas and placed in separate camps. Conditions in these camps were probably worse than in the Boer camps. Few records were kept but over 12,000 black inmates probably died.

The high death rate in the camps was the result of incompetence and lack of foresight on the part of British military authorities. It was not a deliberate policy of extermination. Kitchener argued that to turn the people held in the camps out on to the ransacked veldt would have been even more cruel.

Criticism of the camps

In early 1901, Radical Liberals, led by David Lloyd George, denounced the concentration camps. The war secretary, St John Broderick, defended the policy by claiming that the camps were 'voluntary' and that the interned Boers were 'contented and comfortable'. When this claim proved untenable, he resorted to the 'military necessity' argument.

Liberal leader Henry Campbell-Bannerman did not initially support the Radicals:

- He saw it as his duty to support the government in time of war.
- The Radicals only made up about a third of Liberal MPs. Aware that many Liberals supported the war, Campbell-Bannerman was reluctant to press a matter which was certain to divide his party.

SOURCE C

From a letter by Emily Hobhouse to a family member in 1901. Hobhouse, an opponent of the war, is writing about her visit to the camp for civilians at Bloemfontein in January 1901.

The authorities are at their wits' end and have no more idea how to cope with the difficulty of providing clothes for the people than the man in the moon. Crass male ignorance, stupidity, helplessness and muddling. I rub as much salt into the sore places of their minds as I possibly can, because it is good for them; but I can't help melting a little when they are very humble and confess that the whole thing is a grievous mistake and gigantic blunder and presents an almost insoluble problem and they don't know how to face it.

However, **Emily Hobhouse**'s description of camp conditions in June 1901 created an international outcry. German Chancellor von Bülow denounced Britain's treatment of the Boers as 'brutal and inhuman'. Campbell-Bannerman now attacked 'the methods of barbarism' being used in southern Africa.

The Fawcett Commission

Concerned by the public outcry, the government called on Kitchener for a detailed report. His statistical returns confirmed that death rates in the camps were very high. The government responded by appointing, uniquely, an all-woman commission, headed by Millicent Fawcett, a Liberal Unionist. Between August and December 1901, the commission conducted its own tour of the camps, confirming everything that Hobhouse had said. It recommended a long list of measures, including the need for increased rations and more nurses.

In November 1901, Chamberlain ordered Milner to ensure that 'all possible steps are being taken to reduce the rate of mortality'. Civil authorities now took over the running of the camps. By early 1902, the death rate for white inmates dropped to two per cent, a lower rate than was found in many British cities during the same period. But by then the damage had been done.

A change of policy

Given the uproar over the camp conditions, in December 1901 Kitchener instructed all column commanders not to bring in women and children when they 'cleared' the country. This was a shrewd move. While seeming to appease his critics, it also handicapped the guerrillas, who now had to care for their desperate families.

To what extent does Source C blame the authorities for the conditions in the camps?

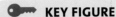

KEY FIGURE

Emily Hobhouse (1860–1926)

Sister of a leader-writer for the *Manchester Guardian*, Hobhouse visited some of the concentration camps in early 1901.

A white man's war?

At first there was an unwritten agreement that the war would be a 'white man's war'. The memories of the Zulu War were still fresh and Boers and British alike feared the consequences of a mass militarisation of the black population. But, as the conflict continued, Britain increasingly recruited black men as scouts, watchmen in blockhouses and auxiliaries. By 1902, some 30,000 black people had served in the British Army. Black Africans, almost without exception, were pro-British.

The end of the war

So successful were Kitchener's tactics of containment and harassment that many Boer 'joiners' threw in their lot with British authorities in 1901. By early 1902, it was obvious, even to Boer 'bitter-enders', that further resistance was futile.

The war ended with the Treaty of Vereeniging, signed on 31 May 1902. Boer commandos, except for a few 'irreconcilables', pledged their allegiance to Britain and recognised Britain's annexation of the two republics. Britain, in return, was generous:

- Boers were given £3 million for reconstruction purposes.
- Britain agreed to restore Boer self-government at the earliest opportunity.

Post-war reconstruction was presided over by Milner. His attempts to destroy Boer influence were unsuccessful. Britain, for all its sacrifices, had not secured total predominance in southern Africa. In 1906–7, Britain restored self-government and free elections for whites to the Transvaal and the Orange Free State. In 1910 the Transvaal, the Orange Free State, Cape Colony and Natal formed the Union of South Africa.

The cost of the war

The war cost around 60,000 lives: 22,000 British soldiers died (7792 were killed in battle, the rest though disease, especially typhoid) and 100,000 British troops were wounded or incapacitated by disease. Some 7000 Boer soldiers died. Over 20,000 Boer civilians and 12,000 black Africans died in the concentration camps.

The scale of the war exceeded all expectations. It required the services of 450,000 British and colonial troops and cost the British taxpayer £217 million. By 1901 it was costing the Treasury £140 to knock out a single Boer combatant.

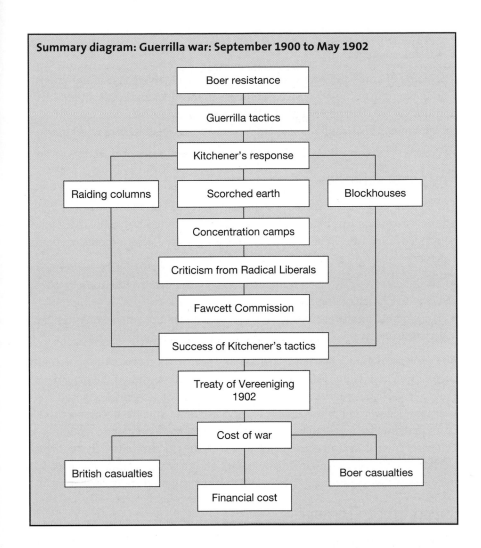

Summary diagram: Guerrilla war: September 1900 to May 1902

- Boer resistance
- Guerrilla tactics
- Kitchener's response
  - Raiding columns
  - Scorched earth
  - Blockhouses
- Concentration camps
- Criticism from Radical Liberals
- Fawcett Commission
- Success of Kitchener's tactics
- Treaty of Vereeniging 1902
- Cost of war
  - British casualties
  - Financial cost
  - Boer casualties

4 The war's impact on Britain

▶ *What were the main political, financial and social results of the war?*

In 1899, most Britons supported the war. However, the fact that it initially went badly, and then dragged on for three years, led people to become increasingly concerned.

British 'democracy'

Britain was more democratic in 1899 than it had been in the mid-nineteenth century. The 1867 and 1884 Parliamentary Reform Acts had increased the franchise. However:

- Only 60 per cent of adult males had the vote.
- Women could not vote.

The House of Lords still had considerable power, while the House of Commons was drawn from a similar social constituency to the House of Lords. In the 1880s and 1890s more than half of British MPs came from aristocratic and landed backgrounds. This class dominated ministerial posts, regardless of which party was in power.

The political parties

The Liberals and the Conservative-Unionists were the two main parties in 1899. The only exception was in Ireland, where Catholics elected Nationalist MPs who demanded home rule. Religion and class were important determinants of voting behaviour:

- The Liberal Party was closely aligned with nonconformity, the Conservatives with the Church of England.
- Working-class voters tended to vote Liberal while middle-class voters tended to vote Conservative. As yet, there was no strong Labour Party.

The key issue dividing the main parties in the last two decades of the nineteenth century was Irish Home Rule. By 1886 Gladstone had committed the Liberal Party to establishing an Irish Parliament, which the Conservatives opposed. Gladstone's government was unable to carry its Home Rule Bill because a third of the parliamentary Liberal Party voted against the measure. These Liberal Unionists entered into an electoral alliance with the Conservatives. In the 1895 election, the Conservative-Unionists, led by Salisbury, won a landslide victory, the Conservatives winning 341 seats and the Liberal Unionists 70 seats.

Support for the Empire

In the 1890s most Britons felt a sense of pride in the Empire, deriving satisfaction from the thought that they constituted a successful imperial 'race'. Most regarded the superiority of whites over non-whites as self-evident. They also placed Britons in the vanguard of the white races. However, the 'Anglo-Saxon' race was not usually thought of in purely biological terms. It was envisaged more as a carrier of a distinct set of values and institutions. In fact, the most common justification of Empire rested less on race and more on the concept of 'mission'. There was a strong belief that British rule improved the quality of life of 'lower races'.

Support for the war

Most MPs supported the war in 1899. In all likelihood, so did most Britons (although this cannot be quantified). There was undoubtedly a strong sense of patriotism among the general population, reflected in the pride people had in the Empire.

The impact of the press

The press, as well as encouraging support for both the imperial idea and the war, reflected the support of the general public. By the 1890s, more Britons could afford to buy daily newspapers, the costs of which were falling as a result of technical improvements and advertising revenue. Some 150 daily papers catered for the tastes of an expanding reading public, and the dailies were supplemented by a plethora of weekly papers and monthly periodicals. In the absence of other methods of mass communication, the press was the main medium for politicians to put their views to the people and for people to keep themselves informed about public affairs.

The *Daily Mail*

In 1896, **Alfred Harmsworth** launched the *Daily Mail*, selling his paper for a halfpenny when most established papers cost a penny. By 1900, the *Mail* had built up a circulation of nearly a million, far more than its rivals. This had two effects:

- Other papers had to drop their prices to stay competitive.
- New papers appeared in imitation of the *Daily Mail*.

The *Mail* was fiercely imperialist. Marketing itself as the voice of Empire, it devoted huge amounts of space to imperial topics.

War correspondents

Many newspapers sent war correspondents to southern Africa to report on the war at first hand. War reporting throughout the 1890s had been popular with the public and had helped to sell newspapers. Some Boer War correspondents, like George Stevens of the *Daily Mail*, became 'stars'. Winston Churchill, who filed reports for the *Morning Post,* used his experiences in southern Africa to launch his political career (see page 124).

War correspondents exercised huge political influence through their access to news and their control over its dissemination. Image could be as potent as reality, particularly when it came to military reputations. General Buller's contempt for the press and his heavy-handed methods of censorship cost him dear. Unable to present his own side of the story, he was widely depicted by journalists as a blundering buffoon. Roberts, by contrast, went out of his way to butter up the correspondents. He also took care to keep them away from unpleasant scenes such as the typhoid epidemic. Baden-Powell provides a striking example of how heroic status could be achieved through press manipulation. His exploits at Mafeking, although not inconsiderable, became magnified in the public's imagination as a result of the newspaper coverage they received.

 KEY FIGURE

Alfred Harmsworth (1865–1922)

A great newspaper magnate, Harmsworth launched the *Daily Mail* and the *Daily Mirror* and acquired the *Observer* and *The Times*. He was made Viscount Northcliffe in 1905.

Winston Churchill

1874	Born, the son of Lord Randolph Churchill and his American wife Jenny
1893–4	Trained as a cavalry officer at Sandhurst
1897	Campaigned on the North West Frontier of India; wrote articles for *The Pioneer* and *Daily Telegraph*
1898	Fought in the Sudan; also worked as a war correspondent for the *Morning Post*
1900	Elected Conservative MP for Oldham
1904	Joined the Liberal Party because he opposed tariff reform (see page 128)
1911–15	First lord of the admiralty
1917	Minister of munitions
1924–9	Conservative chancellor of the exchequer
1940–5	Prime minister
1951–5	Returned as prime minister
1965	Died

Churchill, at the forefront of the political scene for over 50 years, is best known for his leadership during the Second World War. The Boer War was an important step in his rise to political power. In 1899 he obtained a commission to act as war correspondent for the *Morning Post*. Rushing out to southern Africa, he tried to get as close to the action as possible. Accompanying a scouting expedition in an armoured train, he was captured by Boers and held in a prisoner-of-war camp in Pretoria. Escaping from the camp, he travelled almost 300 miles (480 km) to Portuguese Lourenço Marques (present-day Maputo, Mozambique). This exploit made him a national hero. Continuing as a war correspondent, he also gained a commission in the South African Light Horse. He was among the first British troops into both Ladysmith and Pretoria. Returning to England in 1900, he published two books about his Boer War experiences and was elected as a Conservative MP in 1900.

The impact of other media

Britons were vicariously caught up in the conflict in two other ways:

- The war was vividly captured through photographs. Troops, as well as journalists, had access to cartridge film first used in the Pocket and Bullet Kodaks of 1896, supplemented from 1900 by the cheap Brownie camera.
- As a result of the **bioscope**, invented in 1895, audiences could see moving pictures from southern Africa. However 'staged' much of the footage was, it gave the war a sharper immediacy.

KEY TERM

Bioscope The first moving film apparatus.

The commercial world was quick to exploit the war's drama. Soldiers, throughout the late nineteenth century, had featured prominently in advertisements but during the war they were used to promote every conceivable kind of product (see Source D).

'Khaki fever'

In 1899–1900, 'khaki fever' raged throughout Britain. Labour leader John Burns thought his fellow countrymen to be 'khaki clad, khaki mad and khaki bad':

- Half a million people cheered the First Army Corps as it left Southampton.
- Men rushed to volunteer for the army.
- Hysterical fervour greeted news of the lifting of the siege of Ladysmith and the relief of Mafeking.

SOURCE D

An advertisement from the *Illustrated London News* in 1900.

> According to Source D, how did Bovril help the troops and the troops help Bovril?

- Prominent 'pro-Boers' who tried to hold public meetings were given a rough ride. When Lloyd George addressed a pro-Boer rally in Birmingham, disorder broke out. One man was left dead, others were injured and Lloyd George had to be smuggled out of the town hall disguised as a policeman.

Opposition to imperialism

Not all Britons supported imperialism:

- In 1881 historian J.R. Seeley noted that some Britons loathed the Empire because it exposed them to 'wars and quarrels in every part of the globe'.
- Some writers and politicians insisted that imperial ambitions, and expense, served to distract attention from social problems at home.
- Some attacked the Empire for its exploitation of native races.

- Critics of imperialism saw greed as the motivating force in overseas expansion.
- Imperial issues had driven a wedge between Liberal Imperialists and Radical Liberals throughout the 1880s and 1890s.

Opposition to the war

A sizeable minority of the population – Liberals, socialists, Irish Nationalists – vehemently opposed the war from the start. They were backed by C.P. Scott's *Manchester Guardian*, the *Morning Star*, the *Daily News* (from 1901) and assorted socialist journals. There were also a number of influential anti-war groups, including the Stop the War Committee and the League against Aggression and Militarism.

The opposition's case

The opposition's case was stated, at its simplest, in a resolution drafted by Lloyd George in 1900 in which the war was denounced as 'a crime and a blunder, committed at the instigation of irresponsible capitalists'. Opposition to government policy was often accompanied by an idealisation of the enemy, who were seen as living a simple pastoral life, devoted to family and farm.

Religious opposition?

Radical Liberals attacked the war simply because they considered it to be morally wrong. In taking this stand, they received little backing from the churches. Most Anglican and Methodist clergymen supported the war. Nonconformists prevaricated. In 1900, the organising committee of the National Council of Free Churches banned all discussion of the war. While some prominent Quakers denounced the war, a significant minority declined to follow this lead.

Labour opposition?

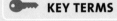

KEY TERMS

TUC The Trades Union Congress.

Independent Labour Party (ILP) Formed in 1893, it hoped to unite various socialist groups. In the 1895 election it fielded 28 candidates, all of whom finished bottom of the poll.

Social Democratic Federation (SDF) The SDF advocated violent revolution to overthrow the capitalist system.

Organised labour took a cautious approach. The **TUC** officially maintained a position of neutrality, partly because of the assumption that questions of foreign policy and imperial defence lay outside the TUC's remit, partly because the leadership did not wish to pick a quarrel with the numerous trade unionists who had rushed to join the army. The **Independent Labour Party (ILP)** and the **Social Democratic Federation (SDF)** stood by their anti-war convictions. Their members believed that the conflict was a capitalist war. But other labour leaders announced that in a national emergency they were Britons first and socialists second. Socialists' criticism of the war was muted by their unwillingness to rock the boat while engaged in constructing the Labour Representation Committee (LRC), which sought to bring together the main socialist groups and interested trade unions.

Irish Nationalist opposition

The most outspoken opponents of the war were the Irish Nationalists, who empathised with the Boers as fellow victims of imperialist aggression.

Political divisions

Anger at government mismanagement in 1899 gave the Liberals much to exploit. Salisbury's failure to provide decisive leadership meant that Arthur Balfour, the **Leader of the Commons**, found himself playing a key role. But badly judged speeches in November 1899, when he said he had no more idea than 'the man in the street' of the Boers' military preparedness, led to much criticism. Secretary of State for War Lansdowne was so discredited that some newspapers demanded he be put on trial.

The Liberal leader, Campbell-Bannerman, accused Chamberlain of precipitating an unnecessary war through a reckless policy of bluff. However, he could not defend the Boers, particularly while they were occupying British territory and when the war was going so badly. His 'middle-of-the-road' policy did not satisfy either the Radical or Imperialist factions within his party.

The 'Khaki election'

In September 1900 Salisbury called a general election. During the campaign Chamberlain declared that 'every vote given against the government is a vote given to the Boers'. The Conservative-Unionists were returned with a majority of 134, much the same as in 1895. Historians struggle to make sense of the so-called 'Khaki election'. In some constituencies the election was dominated by the war. Elsewhere the war took second place to other issues. Arguably, the election results reflected Liberal disorganisation rather than a vote in support of the war. The Liberals had difficulty fielding candidates because the party was in dire financial straits as many of its wealthy backers, disliking the anti-imperialist stance of some party members, deserted it.

Salisbury, responding to press pressure, reshuffled his cabinet. Lansdowne took over the role of foreign secretary, while St John Brodrick became the secretary of state for war. Lord Selborne, Salisbury's son-in-law, became first lord of the admiralty. Chamberlain remained at the Colonial Office. In 1902 Salisbury stepped down and was replaced as prime minister by his nephew Balfour.

Liberal problems

Emily Hobhouse's revelations of conditions in the concentration camps (see pages 118–19) brought Liberal tensions to a head. In June 1901 Campbell-Bannerman moved closer towards the pro-Boer MPs by using the phrase 'methods of barbarism' to describe Britain's pacification policy. Liberal Imperialists, shocked at this attack on the army and hopeful of reconciliation

KEY TERM

Leader of the Commons
The prime minister, Salisbury, was a peer and sat in the Lords. Therefore, Balfour led the Conservatives in the Commons.

with the Liberal Unionists, plotted to replace their leader. But Campbell-Bannerman retained the support of most Liberal MPs and the Liberal Imperialists' efforts were in vain.

The financial impact of the war

The Boer War cost £217 million. This led to divisive debate about how the cost should be met.

Raising money 1899–1902

In 1901 Chancellor of the Exchequer Michael Hicks Beach:

- put a tax on refined sugar
- imposed a levy of 1s. on exported coal
- raised income tax by 2d. to 1s. 2d. in the pound.

But only a third of the war's cost was met by taxation. The government also resorted to borrowing.

Joseph Chamberlain and tariff reform 1903–5

Charles Ritchie, Hicks Beach's successor as chancellor in 1902, favoured retrenchment rather than raising taxation. Joseph Chamberlain, by contrast, campaigned for tariff reform, proposing, in 1903, that protective duties should be levied on corn and on manufactured goods imported from countries outside the Empire. Given his main concern – imperial unity – he argued that there should be no tariffs on colonial imports. In Chamberlain's view, tariff reform would:

- raise money
- strengthen the Empire
- protect British industry from foreign competition
- safeguard British jobs
- pay for much-needed social reform.

Opposition to tariff reform

Chamberlain's support for tariff reform split the Conservative-Unionist coalition wide open. Free traders opposed his proposals, claiming:

- duties on corn would raise food prices
- high duties would simply protect inefficient British industries
- free trade, by keeping food and other costs low, helped to reduce labour costs. Thus, many industries derived a competitive edge over their foreign rivals, which generated further profits and employment.

The 1906 election

With the Conservative-Unionists bitterly divided over tariff reform, Balfour resigned in late 1905. Campbell-Bannerman, who formed a minority government, called a general election in January 1906. The Liberals, with 400 seats, won an overwhelming victory. The Conservative-Unionists retained only 157 seats. The Boer War hardly featured in the election. Conservative-Unionists did not want to remind voters of their mismanagement of the war while Liberals wished to forget their past divisions.

Imperial sentiment

Historians disagree about the extent to which the war led to a decline in imperial sentiment in Britain.

Decline of imperial sentiment?

- Before 1899, imperialism had generally been seen as a 'positive mission' designed to bring 'civilisation' to underdeveloped societies. After the war, imperialism became more synonymous with 'capitalist cliques' and 'methods of barbarism'.
- Before 1899, imperialism had attracted supporters from both major political parties. After 1902, it was associated mainly with the Conservative-Unionists, who were heavily defeated in the 1906 and 1910 elections.
- Chamberlain failed to persuade the British public to support his schemes for imperial unity.
- The Liberal governments of Campbell-Bannerman (1905–8) and Asquith (1908–16) accorded low priority to imperial affairs.

Continuing strength of imperial sentiment?

- Popular newspapers like the *Daily Mail* and the *Daily Express* continued to adopt a stridently imperialistic tone.
- Britons continued to be bombarded with imperial imagery, from newspaper advertisements, hoardings and commercial packaging. Arguably, businessmen would not have marketed their wares in this way had the Empire not been popular.
- Millions of Britons were directly involved in the imperial process, emigrating to Canada, Australia, New Zealand and South Africa. First generation emigrants retained close links with Britain. This helped to keep alive the sense that Britain was the centre of a 'Greater Britain', which reached out to all corners of the globe.
- British patriotism, of which pride in Empire was an important element, remained strong. A number of patriotic leagues continued to be influential.

- Young Britons were inculcated with imperial pride. Many public schools prepared their pupils for future careers as colonial administrators or army officers. School textbooks stressed the achievements of Britons who helped to establish the Empire. The success of the scout and guide movements, fostered by Baden-Powell, the hero of Mafeking, stressed the obligations and rewards of imperial citizenship.

The social impact of the war

The Boer War's immediate effect was to divert political attention and potential economic resources from several areas of activity, including old-age pensions, for which there had been some pressure in the 1890s. However, the national efficiency movement, arising from the war, encouraged social reform.

National inequality

In Britain in 1900 there were huge inequalities of wealth. A tenth of the population owned 92 per cent of the nation's wealth. By contrast, nearly nine-tenths of the population fell below the income tax threshold of £160 a year. Living standards were rising: between 1882 and 1899 average real wages rose by over a third and people, generally, had better diets, better health and more leisure time. Nevertheless:

- **Charles Booth**'s and **Seebohm Rowntree**'s research suggested that nearly a third of people were living in poverty, largely due to unemployment, old age and sickness.
- Infant mortality remained high, at around 150 per 1000. Mortality for infants, and for adults, was affected by class. The poor died young.
- Given the marked differences in height between children from rich and poor backgrounds, it almost seemed as though Britain's social classes constituted separate races.
- Urbanisation was seen as contributing to the nation's physical and moral decay.
- There was evidence that differences in the number of babies born to people of different social classes was bringing about a situation in which, according to **eugenics** supporter Karl Pearson, 'the fertile, but unfit, one sixth' of the population was about to reproduce one half of the next generation, a trend which would lead to 'race suicide'.
- Many Britons believed in **Social Darwinism**. They were convinced that the 'fittest' nations would dominate the rest. Thus, imperial needs legitimised government and voluntary action on welfare issues, not least ensuring the survival of healthy babies and the care of children to ensure that the next generation was fit for the challenges ahead.

Many groups – including politicians, trade unionists and Christian organisations – wished to do something to alleviate both poverty and the inequality of wealth. But there was no agreement about the best way to do this.

KEY FIGURES

Charles Booth (1840–1916)

A Liverpool ship-owner and manufacturer, Booth carried out a series of investigations into poverty in London between 1886 and 1903.

Seebohm Rowntree (1871–1954)

A Quaker and a member of the York chocolate and cocoa manufacturing family, Rowntree carried out a survey of poverty in York. His findings were published in 1901.

KEY TERMS

Eugenics The idea that there should be 'scientific' breeding. The 'fit' should be encouraged to have large numbers of children while the 'unfit' should be discouraged from reproducing.

Social Darwinism Social Darwinists believed that only the fittest nations and social systems could thrive and prosper.

National efficiency

The fact that it took an imperial army of 450,000 men 32 months to defeat 60,000 Boers shattered national complacency and helped to create a sense of danger. Many believed that the British Empire might be brought down – like the Roman Empire – by decadence and incompetence. Analysis of society's problems preoccupied the political class under the guiding rule of national efficiency. The national efficiency movement, held together by an informal network of friends and acquaintances, wanted to:

- shame the existing elite into modernising itself before it was swept away
- institute a career system open to talent
- ensure that all children received a good education
- modernise Britain's secondary schooling and higher education systems, particularly by taking science and technology seriously, so that the country retained its economic competitiveness.

National efficiency appealed to many different groups:

- Some socialists supported it, hoping it would lead to social reform.
- Many Liberals and Conservatives welcomed it on the grounds that it seemed both progressive and patriotic.

National efficiency supporters insisted that the old battles between Conservatism and Liberalism, even those between capitalism and socialism, meant little compared with the more serious battle taking place between the forces of competence and incompetence. Germany was seen as a model to emulate but also as a rival whose efficiency threatened Britain.

Obsession with national efficiency fostered a view of people as a resource; a resource that was being squandered through neglect. In 1901, journalist Arnold White claimed that at the Manchester recruiting station three out of five recruits in 1899 had to be rejected because they failed to meet the army's physical standards. In reality, 33 per cent of men were rejected in 1899, 28 per cent in 1900 and 29 per cent in 1901. Anxieties about physical deterioration influenced policy debates long after the Boer War had ended.

Social reform

National efficiency boosted demands for social reform. The Conservative-Unionist government (1900–5) introduced some reforms. The 1902 Education Act, for example, led to a dramatic improvement in the provision of secondary education. The Liberal government after 1905 introduced many more reforms, including mother and infant clinics (1907), old-age pensions (1908) and a National Insurance scheme (1911).

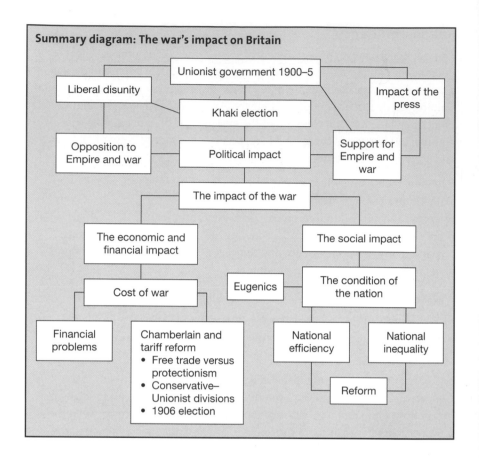

Summary diagram: The war's impact on Britain

5 Reorganisation of imperial defence

▶ *How effective were Britain's efforts to improve its armed forces after 1899?*

The humiliations suffered early in the Boer War indicated that the British Army needed to be reformed, despite the fact that the army had waged war very professionally after 1899. The war led to full-scale government investigations into military planning, recruitment, army and navy organisation, and home defence.

Broderick's proposed reform

In 1901, St John Broderick, secretary of state for war, proposed the creation of six self-contained army corps: three, composed of regulars, would be ready to fight abroad; the other three, consisting of both regular and auxiliary units, would form a home defence force. Broderick's reforms never really got off the ground, incurring criticism from the press and Parliament. His army corps seemed too small to fight in a European war but needlessly large for the colonial conflicts they were more likely to face. In 1903 Broderick was replaced by Hugh Arnold-Forster, who immediately appointed a small committee, headed by Lord Esher, to report on reform of the War Office.

The Esher Committee

Esher's committee, which reported in 1904, recommended that:

- There should be a 'clean sweep' of the War Office, including removing Lord Roberts from his position as commander-in-chief.
- The commander-in-chief should be replaced by an inspector-general of the forces.
- An Army Council should be created. Modelled on the Board of Admiralty, War Office ministers would be joined by four military members, the First Military Member heading a newly formed General Staff.
- The centre of defence planning should be the Committee of Imperial Defence (CID), a body created in 1902 after the service ministers Selborne (navy) and Broderick (army) had approached Balfour, declaring their inability to resolve strategic difficulties between their respective departments.

Balfour accepted these proposals, which were consequently implemented.

Arnold-Forster's changes

Meanwhile, Arnold-Forster submitted new proposals on army reform; reforms influenced by the need to cut spending and to offset a recruiting crisis. Abandoning both Broderick's army corps scheme and the Cardwellian system of linked battalions (see page 99), the army was to be divided between a short-term (three-year) home defence force of 30 battalions and a long-service (nine-year) army of 112 battalions for overseas operations. Convinced of the navy's ability to defend Britain against invasion, Arnold-Forster saw little need for large auxiliary forces. Thus, he sought substantial economies by reducing the **volunteers**, disbanding half of the militia and absorbing the remainder into the home army.

Arnold-Forster's proposals encountered such fierce opposition – from the CID, the cabinet, the new Army Council and Parliament – that he had to abandon his auxiliary forces' proposals. Although he gained cabinet approval for long-service enlistments in 1904 and an experiment in short-service recruiting in 1905, his scheme had too little time to take effect as Balfour's government fell from office in December 1905.

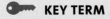

KEY TERM

Volunteers Men with some basic military training who could be called on to fight if Britain was invaded.

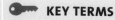
The German threat

British defence thinking was dependent on the international situation. By 1905 Germany was increasingly seen as a potential enemy. In response to the German threat, Britain had signed an ***entente*** with France in 1904.

As Anglo-German relations deteriorated, the rivalry between Britain's armed services intensified. Should Britain spend money on its army or the navy? And what role precisely should the army have? **Navalists** argued that in the event of war with Germany, land fighting should be left to France while Britain maintained control of the seas. Money spent on a large army, they thought, would be subtracted from the navy, on which Britain's safety ultimately depended. But many army officers believed that British troops could make a difference on the continent. In 1905, military talks between Britain and France began in earnest, talks which assumed, but did not specify or commit, that, in the event of war with Germany, British troops would reinforce the French left flank. If Britain was to send an army to the continent, it would clearly need a different type of army from the one it possessed.

The National Service League

The National Service League (NSL), established in 1902, campaigned for compulsory military service, claiming that this would toughen the physique and character of the urban masses. In 1905, Lord Roberts resigned from the Committee of Imperial Defence so that he could support the NSL. Membership of the NSL rose from 10,000 in 1907 to 96,500 in 1913. However, compulsion had few supporters in Parliament. MPs from all parties realised that calls for conscription would be electoral suicide.

Haldane's reforms

After 1905, the Liberal government was committed to reducing military expenditure. Given the financial constraints, Secretary of State for War Richard Haldane resolved to reduce the draft estimates of £30 million bequeathed by Arnold-Forster, and determined that any reorganised army had to operate within a budget of £28 million per year. This figure, rather than any true strategy, dictated the size of the force he set about creating. Haldane envisaged a two-line army:

- an expeditionary force of three army corps (150,000 men)
- a territorial force, created from the volunteers, the militia and the yeomanry, which could support and expand the expeditionary force.

Although Haldane was aware of the need to plan for a continental war, he could not reform the army purely to meet the demands of such a war. His first priority was the provision of drafts for the battalions overseas. Hence, he restored the Cardwellian system by reverting to the old terms of service (seven or eight years' service in the colours, followed by five or four years in the reserve), and rectified the imbalance between the 71 battalions at home and 85 abroad, withdrawing or disbanding some of the overseas units to leave a balance of 74 battalions at home and abroad.

Unlike Arnold-Forster, Haldane ensured that he had support of the Army Council and cabinet before he presented his proposals to Parliament. He had little difficulty in reducing the regular forces. Vehement Conservative opposition merely rallied the support of Liberals behind him.

The expeditionary force was initially seen as a 'general purpose' army which could be employed as a strike force anywhere in the world. But increasingly it was assumed by most politicians and army leaders that it was likely to be used against Germany.

The Territorials

Following the Territorial and Reserve Forces Act of 1907, the territorial force was successfully launched. While recruiting was initially brisk, the force never met its full establishment of 312,000 men. It had 236,389 men by September 1913. Most regular army officers viewed the part-time territorial soldiers with derision. Nevertheless, the territorial force, with artillery, engineers and medical and supply services, was more complete in its arms and equipment than the old volunteer force. Haldane had thus provided the framework for a reserve that could be used in the event of war.

The Officer Training Corps

By comparison with most European countries, Britain remained an unmilitaristic society. Nevertheless, one consequence of the Boer War and the German threat was the spread of cadet corps, especially in public schools. In 1908, Haldane organised these bodies into the Officer Training Corps (OTC), giving them a War Office subsidy and attaching them to the appropriate territorial division. Thus, Haldane used upper-middle class patriotism to reinforce his army reform scheme. By 1914, some 20,000 schoolboys and 5000 undergraduates were enrolled in the OTC.

The army in 1914

Haldane relied on army officers to implement the details of military reform:

- General Douglas Haig, as director of military training, sought to improve efficiency and preparedness by devising training schemes and holding regular large-scale manoeuvres.
- General Henry Wilson, director of military operations, formulated mobilisation plans, especially the preparation of railway timetables and shipping arrangements. The alacrity with which the British Expeditionary Force (BEF) was transported to France in August 1914 (see page 147) owed much to Wilson's work.

By 1914, while its social composition had not changed significantly since the Crimean War, the army had improved professionally. Learning lessons from the Boer War, it had developed tactical skills that were relevant to new conditions of warfare. It had also acquired a new organisational framework. But problems remained:

- Army commanders underestimated the potential of the machine-gun and believed that cavalry charges, with lances or swords, would still win battles.
- The army remained paltry in size. In mid-1914 Germany had 84 divisions, France 66 and Britain just six ready for a European war.

The Royal Navy before 1902

In 1889, Britain had adopted the two-power standard 'ratio' whereby its navy was to be kept up to the combined strength of the next two greatest naval powers. But in 1898, Germany passed a navy law that would double the size of its fleet. This fleet posed a threat to Britain's Empire, trade and security.

Admiral Fisher

In the first decade of the twentieth century Britain embarked on a massive programme of naval reform, presided over by Admiral 'Jackie' Fisher. As second naval lord (1902–3), Fisher pushed through the Selbourne Scheme. All naval officers were to be trained in common. Later they could specialise in engineering, navigation or gunnery. As they reached high rank all would be eligible to command ships and for promotion to admiral. Fisher hoped by this to produce a more meritocratic and less class-bound navy. However, his attempts to open up officer rank to promising young seamen had little success.

In 1904, Fisher became first sea lord, remaining so until 1909. He secured the post because at a time when expenditure was under scrutiny, he claimed that he could see his way 'to very great reduction with increased efficiency'. One way of achieving this was by overhauling the Fleet Reserve, ensuring that ships in reserve were manned with only two-fifths of their normal crew. Money saving was a leading consideration in Fisher's strong advocacy of submarines (first built by Britain in 1902). Submarines were 25 times cheaper to build than battleships. Fisher realised that submarines, armed with torpedoes, were likely to revolutionise naval warfare. While they were a possible threat, they also had the potential to increase Britain's security. Even if Britain's main fleet was defeated or lured away, submarines would deter an invader.

Fisher believed that submarines would free the navy to fulfil its traditional global mission, which would be better achieved through the deployment of a new type of vessel that would combine a battleship's firepower with a cruiser's speed, a hybrid that he called a 'battlecruiser'. Fisher would have preferred to put all his eggs in the battlecruiser basket. However, Selbourne and the Admiralty's Committee on Designs were determined to introduce a new battleship, the *Dreadnought*. The result was that the navy would have battleships and battlecruisers.

The naval race

Brought into commission in 1906, the Dreadnought class was faster and better armed than any battleship afloat. This initially gave Britain a major advantage over Germany. However, the Dreadnought class made the huge number of old battleships that Britain had amassed redundant and gave Germany some hope of catching up. Thus began a new phase in the naval arms race, a phase when the public assumed that Britain's security could be measured by the number of its Dreadnoughts. In 1909, fearing that Germany was accelerating its shipbuilding programme, the Admiralty demanded six new Dreadnoughts. The Liberal government, committed to social reform, was not keen to increase naval expenditure. But the **Navy League**, campaigning with the slogan, 'We want eight and we won't wait', forced the government to build eight new battleships. The naval race continued, pushing the Admiralty's budget up to £48.8 million (twice that of Germany's) by 1914. By August 1914, 40 Dreadnoughts and battlecruisers had been built or were under order. Sixty-four per cent of Britain's defence budget was devoted to the navy, only 36 per cent to the army. This spending ensured that the navy had far more battleships than Germany on the eve of the First World War (see page 150).

 **KEY TERM**

Navy League A patriotic organisation set up to promote the interests of the navy. By 1914 it had 100,000 members.

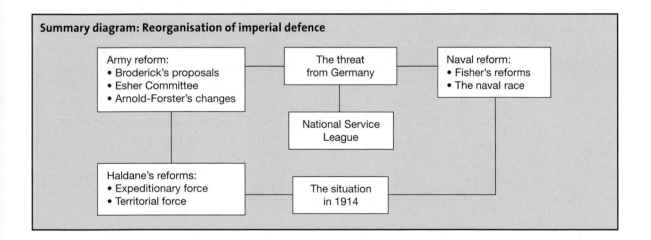

Summary diagram: Reorganisation of imperial defence

Army reform:
• Broderick's proposals
• Esher Committee
• Arnold-Forster's changes

The threat from Germany

Naval reform:
• Fisher's reforms
• The naval race

National Service League

Haldane's reforms:
• Expeditionary force
• Territorial force

The situation in 1914

Chapter summary

In 1899 Britain went to war with the Transvaal and the Orange Free State. The relatively few Boers proved difficult adversaries. In the first three months of the war Ladysmith, Kimberley and Mafeking were besieged and Buller's efforts to relieve the towns ended in disaster in December 1899. The appointment of Lord Roberts and the increase in British troops in southern Africa led to a reversal of fortune. Between February and September 1900 British forces relieved Ladysmith, Kimberley and Mafeking, defeated the main Boer armies and captured the main Boer towns. But Boer commandos continued to wage guerrilla war. Kitchener used blockhouses, a scorched-earth policy and concentration camps to counter the Boer threat. While most Britons supported the war, there were many opponents. The war's end in 1902 led to demands for national efficiency and military reform. Haldane's reforms, which established the Territorial Army, were the most important. The army increasingly prepared for war with Germany, as did the Royal Navy, which was threatened by German naval expansion.

Refresher questions

Use these questions to remind yourself of the key material covered in this chapter.

1 To what extent was the British Army prepared for war in 1899?

2 Why were the Boers initially successful?

3 Why was Britain successful militarily from February to September 1900?

4 How successful was Kitchener in dealing with Boer resistance in 1901–2?

5 Were concentration camps 'methods of barbarism'?

6 What were the main political results of the war?

7 Why did some Britons oppose the war?

8 What impact did the war have on social development?

9 How effective were army reforms in the years 1902–14?

10 What were the main naval developments in the years 1902–14?

Question practice

ESSAY QUESTIONS

1 To what extent was the British Army successful during the Boer War in the years 1899–1902?

2 To what extent was Britain's treatment of the Boers after 1900 'brutal and inhuman'?

3 How far do you agree that the Second Boer War (1899–1902) demonstrated that the British Army was fit for purpose?

4 How far was Britain prepared for war with Germany in 1914?

SOURCE ANALYSIS QUESTION

1 Assess the value of Source 1 for revealing the reasons for the establishment of concentration camps in southern Africa and the attitude of those in command and control. Explain your answer, using the source, the information given about its origin and your own knowledge about the historical context.

SOURCE I

From General Kitchener's orders, issued on 21 December 1900 in Pretoria, quoted in A. Mallinson, *Light Dragoons: The Making of a Regiment*, Pen & Sword Books, 2012.

The General Commander-in-Chief is desirous that all possible means shall be taken to stop the present guerrilla warfare. Of the various measures suggested for the accomplishment of this object, one which has been strongly recommended, and has lately been successfully tried on a small scale, is the removal of all men, women and children, and natives from the Districts which the enemy's bands persistently occupy. This course has been pointed out by surrendered burghers, who are anxious to finish the war, as the most effective method of limiting the endurance of the guerrillas, as men and women left on farms, if disloyal, willingly supply burghers, if loyal, dare not refuse to do so. Moreover, seeing the unprotected state of women now living in the Districts, this course is desirable to assure their not being insulted or molested by natives.

… The women and children brought in should be camped near the railway for supply purposes … The Ordnance will supply the necessary tents and the District Commissioner will look after the food on the scale now in use.

It should be clearly explained to burghers in the field, that, if they voluntarily surrender, they will be allowed to live with their families in the camps until it is safe for them to return to their homes.

CHAPTER 5

The First World War 1914–18

Although the First World War was fought all over the globe and involved many non-European nations, it was essentially a European conflict. It began, and most of the fighting took place, in Europe. Virtually everyone in 1914 expected a short war. Instead, it became a war of attrition on a scale without precedent. This chapter will focus on Britain's role in the conflict, examining the following issues:

★ The situation in 1914

★ The war: 1914–15

★ The war: 1916–17

★ The end of the war

Key dates

1914	Aug.	Britain declared war on Germany	1916	Dec.	Lloyd George became prime minister
	Oct.–Nov.	First Battle of Ypres	1917	April	USA entered the war
1915	April	Allied landings at Gallipoli		July–Nov.	Third Battle of Ypres
1916	Feb.–Aug.	Battle of Verdun	1918	March–July	Ludendorff Spring Offensive
	May	Battle of Jutland		July–Nov.	Hundred Days Offensive
	July–Nov.	Battle of the Somme		Nov.	Armistice agreed

 ## The situation in 1914

▶ *To what extent was Britain prepared for war in 1914?*

By 1914 Europe was divided into two blocs – the Central Powers (Germany and Austria-Hungary) and the Triple Entente (France, Russia and Britain). German policy-makers over the previous two decades were largely to blame for this state of affairs, first driving France and Russia together and then, by constructing a large fleet, making an enemy of Britain. The alliance system did not make war inevitable, however. Nor is there any conclusive evidence that any nation wanted war in 1914. Moreover, if conflict came, British involvement was far from certain. Although British and French military leaders had made some joint plans, Britain was not strictly allied to France or Russia.

The Sarajevo assassination

On 28 June 1914, Archduke Franz Ferdinand, heir to the Austro-Hungarian throne, was murdered in Sarajevo by Gavrilo Princip, one of a number of **Bosnian terrorists** in the town. Suspecting that the terrorists had received encouragement from Serbia, Austro-Hungarian leaders agreed that severe reprisals should be taken against Serbia, even if this meant risking war with Russia, Serbia's protector. On 5–6 July, Germany promised Austria-Hungary full support. Hoping to achieve a diplomatic victory, German leaders were prepared to risk, but did not expect, war. On 23 July, Austria-Hungary presented an ultimatum to Serbia. The Serbs rejected the key demand, to let Austro-Hungarian officials into Serbia to enquire into Franz Ferdinand's death.

War

On 28 July, Austria-Hungary declared war on Serbia. On 30 July, Russia, with French support, agreed to full mobilisation. Unbeknown to Russia and France, this decision made war inevitable. Germany had only one plan to deal with a major war, the **Schlieffen** Plan. As a solution to the problem of fighting a two-front war, Schlieffen had planned an assault on France, via Belgium, with only a holding action in the east. By the time the cumbersome Russian Army was ready to move, the Germans hoped to have defeated France so that troops could be transferred eastwards. If Russia was allowed time to mobilise, the success of the Schlieffen Plan was endangered. Thus, Germany demanded that Russia cease all military activities within twelve hours.

In the absence of a reply, Germany declared war on Russia on 1 August. France was asked for a promise of neutrality. When no such promise was received, Germany declared war on France on 3 August. Meanwhile, on 2 August, Germany demanded free passage for its troops through Belgium. When this was refused, German troops invaded Belgium.

Britain declares war

Herbert Asquith's Liberal government was initially divided on whether it should assist France. But Germany's violation of Belgium's neutrality, guaranteed by Britain in 1839, decided the issue. For centuries, it had been a prime objective of British policy to ensure that no strong power controlled the Low Countries. Virtually all the cabinet agreed that Britain should support Belgium. Britain thus demanded the withdrawal of German troops from Belgium. Receiving no reply, Britain declared war on Germany on 4 August.

Although there had been some opposition to war prior to 4 August, once it was declared, all the major political parties, including the Irish Nationalists, supported it. King George V declared war in the name of the entire British Empire. The governments of the self-governing dominions – Australia, New Zealand, South Africa and Canada – were not consulted. Nor were 250 million

> **KEY TERM**
>
> **Bosnian terrorists** Serbs who wanted Bosnia, part of Austria-Hungary, to become part of Serbia and were prepared to use violence to achieve their aim.

> **KEY FIGURE**
>
> **Alfred von Schlieffen (1833–1913)**
> Chief of the German General Staff 1891–1908.

Table 5.1 The balance of power in 1914

	Great Britain	France	Russia	Germany	Austria-Hungary
Population	46,407,037	39,601,509	167,000,000	65,000,000	49,882,231
Soldiers available on mobilisation	711,000[1]	3,500,000	4,423,000[2]	8,500,000[3]	3,000,000
Merchant fleet (net steam tonnage)	11,538,000	1,098,000	486,914	3,096,000	559,784
Battleships (built and being built)	64	28	16	40	16
Cruisers	121	34	14	57	12
Submarines	64	73	29	23	6
Annual value of foreign trade (£)	1,223,152,000	424,000,000	190,247,000	1,030,380,000	198,712,000
Annual steel production (tons)	6,903,000	4,333,000	4,416,000	17,024,000	2,642,000

[1] Including the Empire.   [2] Immediate mobilisation.   [3] Emergency maximum.

Indians and 50 million Africans. The white populations of the Empire rallied eagerly to Britain's defence.

The British Army's readiness for war

On 4 August 1914, the regular army consisted of 247,432 officers and men. Most of its officers came from the landed classes and military families. Most of its recruits were from the urban poor. The part-time territorial force, with 268,777 men, attracted a broader spectrum of society. Its primary role was regarded as home defence. Although Britain was now committed to fighting in Europe, the implication of that commitment had not been thoroughly explored. Crucially, all British plans were predicated on the war being short. Little thought had gone into how to raise a mass army or increase munitions' output in the event of a long war.

Lord Kitchener's role

On 5 August 1914, Kitchener became secretary of state for war. The public greeted his appointment with enthusiasm and he quickly became a symbol of national unity, standing above political interests. In government circles, his shortcomings as a cabinet minister, administrator and strategist soon became apparent. Nevertheless, he made one vital contribution to Britain's war effort. Virtually alone among British military and political leaders, he forecast a three- or four-year long war, and realised that Britain would have to put huge armies into the field. He set about planning accordingly.

Given the government's view that conscription would be nationally divisive, Kitchener had no option but to raise men by voluntary means. He aimed to construct a series of New Armies, each duplicating the six infantry divisions of the British Expeditionary Force (BEF). This was to be done through the regular recruiting channels rather than through the territorial system. Like many soldiers, Kitchener did not rate the territorials. Nor, as yet, did they have a statutory obligation to fight overseas. Kitchener was unsure about the ultimate size of the army needed. On 25 August he thought it might expand to 30 divisions. By mid-September his estimate had increased to 50 divisions.

Recruitment

SOURCE A

Why did Source A have such a massive impact on the British public in 1914–15?

A 1914 recruitment poster featuring Kitchener.

Recruitment exceeded all expectations. Some 761,000 recruits joined the army in August and September 1914 while the average number of volunteers ran at 125,000 a month until June 1915. Uncomplicated patriotism impelled most men to enlist. Public school codes of duty, self-sacrifice and discipline, which had permeated every level of society through the education system, youth movements and Sunday schools, underpinned the response. But there were a variety of other motives for the mass enlistment:

- The lure of travel and excitement and the opportunity to quit arduous or boring jobs were powerful inducements.
- Pressure from social superiors, employers and peers was important.
- Women put pressure on menfolk. Getting 'shirkers' to enlist was the objective of the Women of England's Active Service League, whose members vowed 'never to be seen in public with any man who, being in every way fit and free for service, has refused to respond to his country's call'.
- The raising of pals battalions (see below) harnessed local loyalties to national patriotism in a manner that proved irresistible to thousands of men.

The huge numbers of volunteers resulted in overcrowding at depots and training centres. There were also severe shortages of weapons, uniforms, equipment, even rations. As a result, the War Office introduced a scheme of deferred enlistment, whereby volunteers could stay at home until the army was able to handle them.

Pals regiments

On 19 August, General Rawlinson, director of recruiting, proposed raising a battalion of London employees who were willing to enlist if 'they were assured that they would serve with their friends'. The War Office approved his proposal and by 27 August the 10th Battalion of the Royal Fusiliers – the 'Stockbrokers' Battalion' – numbered 1600 men. But it was in the northern industrial towns that the idea of pals regiments was particularly strong. Mayors and corporations, MPs, committees of industrialists and leading citizens encouraged men who lived in a particular city or who shared a common social and occupational background to enlist with their friends and workmates on the understanding that they would be allowed to fight together. By 1 October, 50 pals battalions were complete or in the course of formation.

The composition of the army

Rapid expansion threw together volunteers from all occupations and classes, changing the army's social composition almost beyond recognition. Lawyers and teachers drilled alongside miners and labourers. However, the overall patterns of enlistment were complex and uneven:

- Lancashire, Yorkshire and Scotland together furnished over one-third of the 250 battalions in the first three new armies, whereas Devon, Dorset, Cornwall and Somerset produced only eleven battalions between them.

- In 1914–15 finance, commerce, the professions and entertainment all contributed over 40 per cent of their pre-war workforce, while corresponding returns from manufacturing, transport and agriculture were under 30 per cent.

The shortage of officers

In 1914 only 12,738 regular and 9563 territorial officers were available. Merely to cater for the infantry battalions raised during 1914–15, Kitchener had to find at least 30,000 more officers, and that was before taking into account the demands of other branches of the army or the need to replace officer casualties. To ease the problem:

- Courses at Sandhurst and Woolwich were shortened and the age limit for candidates was raised to 25.
- BEF battalions were ordered to leave three officers at depots to provide officers for new units.
- Retired officers were brought back into service.
- Temporary commissions were granted to suitable men. The Officers' Training Corps (OTC) (page 135) was a major source of applications. By March 1915, 20,577 current or former OTC members had been commissioned.

High command

The BEF was commanded by Sir John French. Aged 62, he had seen active service in Egypt and South Africa. Unfortunately, French, his staff at **GHQ** and his divisional and corps commanders had little practice or training at their respective levels of command. Nor had the Staff College prepared senior commanders very well for modern war. The Russo-Japanese War (1904–5) had provided clear indications of the impact of firepower. But, because the aggressive Japanese had defeated the defensive-minded Russians with costly bayonet attacks, the wrong lessons were drawn. The British Army had developed no particular doctrine prior to 1914 except to go on the offensive under almost all circumstances. Senior staff expected to overcome the enemy's firepower through mobility, discipline and moral force.

Munition problems

The army was woefully deficient in modern technology. In 1914:

- each battalion had only two machine-guns
- the entire army had only 80 motor vehicles
- all guns and supplies were drawn by horses
- the army lacked field telephones and wireless equipment.

Worse still, in August 1914, barely 6000 rifles and 30,000 rounds of shells a month were being produced and the stock of munitions was grossly inadequate. Rather than spreading munition production, the War Office concentrated orders in the hands of government ordnance factories and long-established contractors,

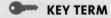

KEY TERM

GHQ General Head Quarters, comprising military staff officers who advised the commander-in-chief on policy and administration and helped him to carry out his plans.

insisting that only experienced firms knew how to produce munitions of satisfactory quality. This limited the industry's ability to respond to the new demands. So did the fact that indiscriminate recruiting had led to the enlistment of many skilled engineers who were not easily replaced.

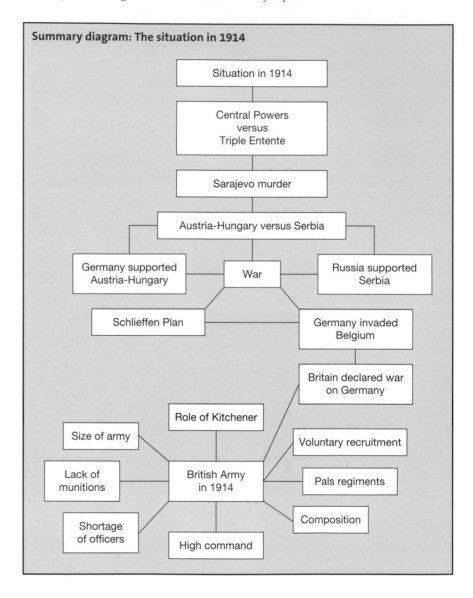

Summary diagram: The situation in 1914

The war: 1914–15

▶ *Why was the war not over by Christmas 1914?*

In accordance with the Schlieffen Plan, 1.5 million German troops marched through Belgium, aiming to capture Paris and crush France. Meanwhile, 300,000 French troops advancing in Lorraine were mown down by German machine-guns and artillery.

Mons and Le Cateau

The 120,000-strong BEF was sent to Maubeuge on the left of the French Army, according to pre-war plans. This decision placed it smack in the path of the advancing German armies. On 23 August, 75,000 troops of the BEF II Corps under General Smith-Dorrian faced 300,000 men of the German 1st Army at Mons. British troops checked the enemy advance but were then forced to retreat. On 26 August, Smith-Dorrian held up the Germans at Le Cateau but lost 8000 men in the process. The BEF continued its retreat. By the start of September, Sir John French contemplated withdrawing the BEF to below the River Seine (or even leaving France altogether) to refit. Kitchener rushed to Paris and ordered French to keep his place in the Allied line.

The Battle of the Marne

On 28 August, German General von Kluck changed his line of advance. Instead of sweeping around Paris from the west, he moved east. This enabled the French commander, General Joffre, to attack the exposed German right flank on 5 September. The fighting, which lasted over the next week, is known as the Battle of the Marne. Sir John French joined the attack, promising Joffre that 'we will do all that men can do'. In fact the BEF did very little, simply marching into a gap between the German 1st and 2nd Armies. In some disarray, the Germans retreated to the River Aisne. Here they dug in, stumbling on the discovery that trenches, barbed wire and machine-guns could stop attackers.

The First Battle of Ypres

Both sides now tried to outflank each other by 'racing to the sea'. The BEF, which moved north to Flanders, encountered German forces at Ypres. Dogged resistance from the outmanned and outgunned BEF ensured that the Allies retained control of crucial Channel ports. But by December, 30,000 British soldiers had been killed and far more wounded or captured.

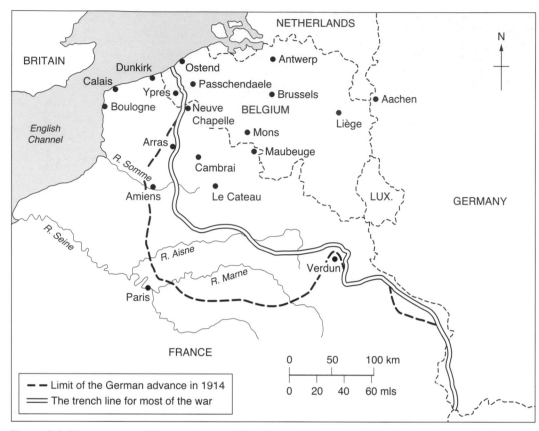

Figure 5.1 The war on the Western Front in 1914–15.

The Eastern Front 1914

The Russians, mobilising faster than Schlieffen had foreseen, attacked the Germans in East Prussia, threatening Berlin. However, German generals Hindenburg and Ludendorff defeated the Russians at Tannenburg in late August and at the Masurian Lakes in early September. The Russians were more successful against the Austrians, winning the Battle of Lemburg in September and driving deep into Galicia before being halted by German intervention.

Stalemate

By December the expectation of a short war had proved false. On the Western Front a line of trenches ran for over 475 miles (760 km) from the Channel to Switzerland. It was a thin line by later standards but solid enough to prevent a war of movement. British forces held about 35 miles (56 km) of this line, including the Ypres **salient**. While the BEF had fought well, French and his GHQ had maintained only tenuous control at critical points. Exuberant one moment, depressed the next, French often operated more by intuition than by rational calculation.

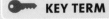 **KEY TERM**

Salient A bulge pushing into enemy lines which could thus be attacked from several sides.

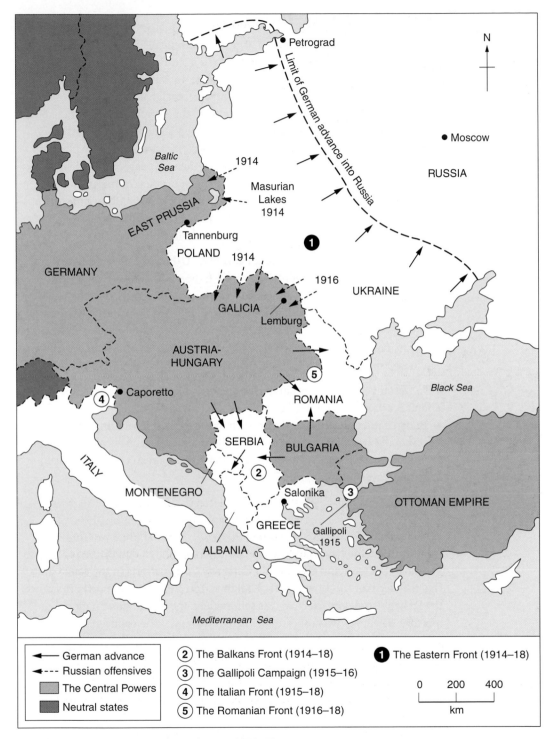

Figure 5.2 The war on the Eastern Front in 1914–18.

The naval war 1914–15

In 1914 the elderly Lord Fisher (see page 136) was recalled as first sea lord. Command of the Grand Fleet was transferred from Prince Louis of Battenberg, whose German origins made him unacceptable, to Admiral Sir John Jellicoe. The Grand Fleet, with twenty Dreadnoughts and 26 pre-Dreadnought battleships, was stationed at Scapa Flow in the Orkneys. To the disappointment of the British public, the German High Seas Fleet, with thirteen Dreadnought equivalents and twelve pre-Dreadnoughts, remained in port. However, German inaction gave Britain command of the seas, permitting the safe passage of British troops and supplies to France and the equally safe transportation of troops from India, Canada, Australia and New Zealand to Europe, Asia Minor and Africa. Moreover, Britain was able to enforce a blockade of Germany. While Germany was deprived of goods, supplies poured into Britain from all over the world.

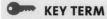

KEY TERM

U-boats German submarines.

The main danger to the Royal Navy came from **U-boats**. On 22 September, three British cruisers were sunk by a single U-boat. Given that Scapa Flow was not secure from U-boat attack, Jellicoe moved his fleet, first to the west of Scotland and then to Ireland, not returning to Scapa Flow until its U-boat defences were completed in mid-1915. Thereafter, Jellicoe, conscious that he was 'the only man on either side who could lose the war in an afternoon', remained cautiously in harbour:

- In December 1914 a German naval squadron bombarded Hartlepool, Whitby and Scarborough, killing 122 people.
- British battlecruisers, based at Rosyth in the Firth of Forth, under the command of Sir David Beatty, caught German battlecruisers at Dogger Bank in January 1915 (see the map on page 164), but as a result of poor British gunnery the outnumbered German ships escaped.

The war in 1915

With the failure of the Schlieffen Plan, Germany had to fight a war on two fronts. In 1915 the new German commander Falkenhayn determined to hold ground in the west and concentrate Germany's main efforts in the east. Given that the Germans occupied most of Belgium and large parts of northern France, the French's strategic objective was self-evident: the liberation of national territory. Kitchener was concerned. The German lines, he believed, had become a fortress 'which cannot be taken by assault'. But what should Britain do instead?

The British Army in 1915

- In January 1915 the BEF was 250,000 strong. It was still composed mainly of regular troops, a fifth of whom were from the Indian Army.
- In March 1915 the first territorial division reached the Western Front.
- Britons continued to volunteer in huge numbers. The lowering of the height standard to 5 feet 3 inches (160 cm) in November 1914 helped recruitment.

- Shortage of munitions remained a serious problem.
- Kitchener's new armies would not be ready for battle until late 1915 at the earliest.

Easterners versus Westerners

In October 1914 the Ottoman Empire joined the Central Powers. The widening of the war presented Britain with new challenges but also new opportunities. In a series of War Council meetings in January 1915, ministers debated British strategic options. 'Easterners', like Lloyd George, favoured pulling out troops from France and Belgium and launching operations in Syria (against Turkey) and in Salonika (against Austria-Hungary). First Lord of the Admiralty Winston Churchill shared some of Lloyd George's views. Anxious that Britain should not be sucked into a continental bloodbath, he wanted to exploit Britain's naval dominance. He claimed that British ships could force their way through the Dardanelles, menacing Constantinople and knocking Turkey out of the war.

'Westerners' opposed an eastern strategy, convinced that the war could only be won if Germany was defeated. Far-flung campaigns against Austria-Hungary and Turkey would not achieve that aim. Moreover, if France was defeated the war would be lost. The War Council compromised. It resolved to persevere on the Western Front. However, it also supported Churchill's proposal for a naval expedition to seize the Dardanelles.

Gallipoli

As the naval force prepared to attack the Dardanelles, Kitchener decided it needed military support. Sir Ian Hamilton, commander of the new force, received one inaccurate map, no staff and virtually no information about the Turkish Army and its fortifications.

On 18 March, an Allied fleet entered the Dardanelles to bombard Turkish forts. When three ships were sunk by mines, Admiral de Robeck called off the attack. On 22 March, Hamilton agreed to occupy the Gallipoli Peninsula. Discovering that the military transports sent out to him were in total confusion, he took his army to Egypt, to prepare it for a landing in three weeks' time. This enabled the Turks to increase their forces at Gallipoli from two divisions to six, one more than Hamilton commanded.

On 25 April, British, Australian and New Zealand troops (Anzacs) attacked at Gallipoli. Seldom has an expedition of such difficulty been so ill prepared. Allied forces lacked artillery, ammunition and proper landing craft. They also lacked the element of surprise. Thus, most beaches were raked with Turkish fire, the initial naval bombardment being insufficient to overwhelm the enemy defences. Once ashore, opportunities were thrown away because of ineffective leadership. Drifting up and down the coast on a warship, Hamilton left matters to his subordinates and was barely in command. Eventually, his men were pinned to the shore.

Figure 5.3
The Gallipoli
landings in 1915.

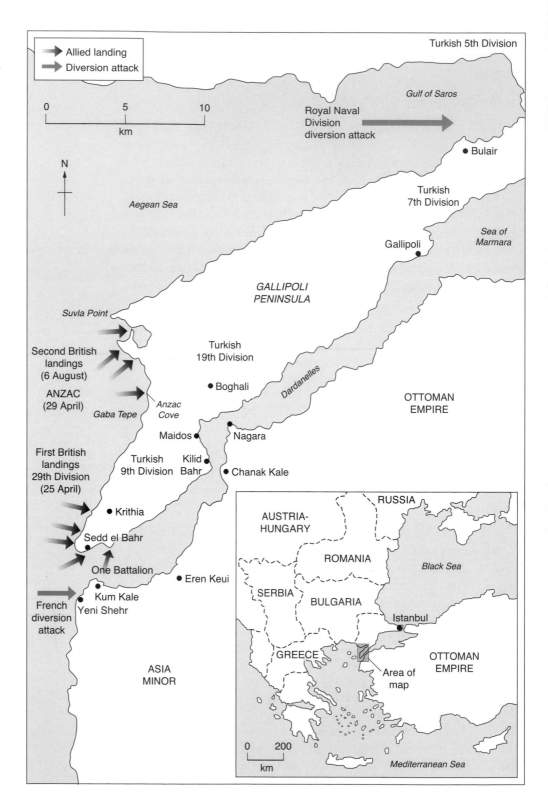

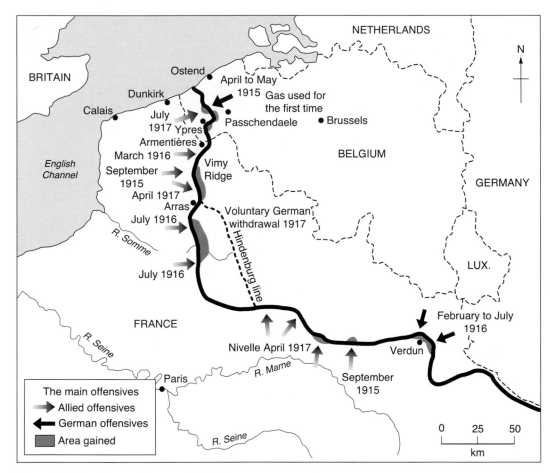

Figure 5.4 The Western Front in 1915–17.

The Western Front: March to May 1915

In early 1915 British and French leaders agreed that in the spring both countries would co-ordinate their attacks around the Ypres salient. Under pressure from Joffre, the BEF engaged in an unsuccessful offensive at Neuve Chapelle on 10–13 March, sustaining 13,000 casualties, double those of the enemy.

On 22 April, the Germans launched an offensive (the Second Battle of Ypres) using chlorine gas for the first time. The British held firm but suffered 60,000 casualties. While the British were indignant at the use of gas, they quickly followed suit. A British gas unit was created which soon developed the far more deadly phosgene.

In early May, British forces attacked at Aubers Ridge. The opening artillery bombardment did not cut the enemy's barbed wire and British troops were mown down. The attack was aborted. This pattern was repeated at Festubert in mid-May. The BEF had suffered 165,000 casualties to little purpose.

Sir John French cloaked his failure by complaining about a shell shortage. There was some truth in the charge. Despite Lloyd George's promptings, Kitchener had refused to extend the list of authorised firms and had deluged these firms with orders that they could not fulfil. Northcliffe (see page 123), the greatest of the press lords, launched an outcry against the 'shell scandal', hoping to drive Kitchener and possibly Asquith from office.

National government

In May 1915 Asquith's government, blamed for Gallipoli and the shell shortage and embarrassed by Fisher's resignation in protest at 'the further depletion of our Home resources for the Dardanelles', faced a crisis. On 17 May Conservative leader Andrew Bonar Law met Lloyd George. Agreeing on the necessity of coalition, they presented Asquith with what amounted to an ultimatum. Asquith acquiesced. Thus, a national government was formed on 25 May, almost half the Liberal ministers stepping down to make way for Conservatives:

- Kitchener survived. Despite his many failings, he remained popular.
- Lloyd George became head of a newly created Ministry of Munitions.
- Churchill, blamed for Gallipoli, was replaced at the Admiralty by Balfour.
- Arthur Henderson joined the cabinet, nominally as president of the Board of Education, but in reality as the voice of the Labour Party.

Lloyd George as minister of munitions

Lloyd George's appointment was crucial. It was from this point that the real transformation of industry began. New munitions factories multiplied, employing growing numbers of women and unskilled men (see pages 197–8). Thanks to Lloyd George's drive, shell deliveries rose from 5.3 million between July and December 1915 to 35.4 million in the second half of 1916. Machine-gun output increased from 287 to 33,507 between 1914 and 1916. The manufacture of heavy artillery similarly soared. Lloyd George also deserves credit for overriding Kitchener on two important issues:

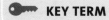 **KEY TERM**

Mortar A short-barrelled gun that lobs shells at the enemy.

- When the War Office rejected Wilfred Stokes' new light **mortar**, Lloyd George persuaded a wealthy Indian prince to finance its production. It proved to be an effective weapon.
- While Kitchener was unimpressed with the tank (see page 168), first demonstrated in 1916, Lloyd George supported its production.

> ## The Vickers machine-gun
>
> The Vickers machine-gun entered service with the British Army in 1912 and soon developed a reputation for reliability. A six- to eight-man team usually operated the machine-gun: one man fired, another fed it bullets, and the rest helped to carry the weapon, its ammunition and spare parts. Able to fire 500 rounds a minute, the weapon came in three parts: a mounting tripod, the gun itself, and a can of water that fed into the 'water jacket' that surrounded the barrel and stopped it overheating.
>
> When the Lewis gun was adopted as a light machine-gun and issued to infantry units in 1916, the Vickers gun was redefined as a heavy machine-gun and withdrawn from the infantry for use by specialist machine-gun companies.

Gallipoli: the second landings

In mid-June, while accepting the primacy of the Western Front, the new cabinet resolved to mount a second landing at Gallipoli. Five divisions were sent to reinforce Hamilton. On 6–7 August troops landed at Suvla Bay, this time taking the Turks by surprise. But little was made of it. General Stopford remained on board ship and slept throughout the afternoon. Most of his men bathed on the beach, instead of capturing the surrounding hills. This gave the Turks time strengthen their defences. The whole expedition should probably have been abandoned at this point but the government feared this would lead to the collapse of British prestige throughout the east.

In October Hamilton was replaced by Sir Charles Monro, who immediately recommended Gallipoli's evacuation. Eventually, in December, the government decided to abort the venture, which had cost nearly 300,000 casualties.

Salonika

In August Bulgaria entered the war on the side of the Central Powers, deepening Serbia's plight. Greece, seemingly about to join the Allies, asked Britain and France to send troops to the Balkans. But by the time the force arrived, the pro-Allied Greek government had been overthrown by the pro-German King Constantine. Despite the withdrawal of Greek support, Allied troops landed at Salonika. The landings came too late to save Serbia. Nevertheless, the 600,000-strong Anglo-French army remained in the malaria-ridden swamps of Macedonia, failing to break through the mountainous terrain.

The Western Front: September to October 1915

By August 1915 there were 28 British divisions on the Western Front; some 900,000 men. The few survivors from 1914 had been supplemented by the arrival of territorial units, troops from the dominions and the first of Kitchener's new armies. Given the inexperience of most of the men, the British government would have preferred to remain on the defensive until all the new armies took the field in 1916. But Kitchener and the French were keen to launch an offensive to help Russia. Consequently, British troops, led by Haig (see page 161), attacked at Loos on 25 September. Thousands of men were mown down by enemy machine-guns. Units that managed to break through failed to make further advances, partly because French mishandled the disposition of his reserve troops. The operation spluttered on until mid-October, by which time Britain had suffered 50,000 casualties, the Germans 20,000.

SOURCE B

According to Source B, why did the British attack fail?

From an official German account describing the fighting at Loos in September 1915, quoted in Richard Holmes, *Tommy: The British Soldier on the Western Front 1914–1918*, Harper Perennial, 2005, p. 37.

Never had machine-guns had such straightforward work to do, nor done it so effectively; with barrels burning hot and swimming in oil, they traversed to and fro along the enemy's ranks unceasingly; one machine-gun alone fired 12,500 rounds that afternoon. The effect was devastating. The enemy could be seen literally falling in hundreds, but they continued their march in good order and without interruption. The extended lines of men began to get confused by this terrific punishment, but they went doggedly on, some even reaching the wire entanglement in front of the reserve line, which their artillery had scarcely touched. Confronted by this impenetrable obstacle, the survivors turned and began to retreat.

The naval war in 1915

In February 1915, the Germans announced the start of unrestricted submarine warfare, whereby any ship in British waters was liable to be torpedoed. Given that merchant seamen were conventionally thought of as non-combatants, Britain denounced the practice as barbarous. Fortunately, Germany's 37 U-boats were not sufficient to starve Britain into surrender. Moreover, the U-boat campaign had serious consequences for Germany. Inevitably, it resulted in the sinking of neutral ships. The USA – Britain's greatest trading partner – protested. In May, the liner *Lusitania* was sunk, with the loss of over 1000 lives, including 128 Americans. This led US President Woodrow Wilson to issue an ultimatum to Germany. Rather than risk war with the USA, Germany agreed to abandon unrestricted submarine warfare. However, it continued building U-boats with the aim of conducting a more concerted campaign in the future.

Air war

Orville and Wilbur Wright had managed to get an aeroplane briefly airborne in 1903. By 1914 aircraft development had taken huge strides and all the major powers realised aircraft's military potential. Nevertheless, the aircraft available to the armies and navies in 1914 were rudimentary. The British FE-2a, for example, could manage no more than 55 mph (88 km/hour).

Reconnaissance

The main use of aircraft was for reconnaissance. Over 90 per cent of aerial sorties flown throughout the war were reconnaissance missions. The role of Allied airmen in detecting German troop movements that led to the Battle of the Marne (see page 147) demonstrated the aeroplane's value. When trench warfare began in 1914, aircraft were used to spot enemy artillery, while aerial photographic reconnaissance enabled accurate maps of enemy trenches to be created. Reconnaissance aircraft became increasingly sophisticated:

- Reconnaissance reports were increasingly delivered by radio rather than in person.
- Bulky hand-held cameras gave way to smaller cameras fitted within the fuselage.
- New types of planes could fly higher and faster.

Fighters

As the value of air reconnaissance became apparent, both sides began to develop fighter aircraft whose main role was to shoot down enemy aircraft and protect friendly reconnaissance aircraft. The first fighters were two-seater planes, fitted with a single machine-gun operated by the observer from the rear of the cockpit. The chief problem was that the machine-gun was easiest to aim when firing forward. However, most aircraft had a wooden propeller at the front of the fuselage and there was no means of firing through its arc without shooting the wood to pieces.

In 1915 the French fitted steel plates to their propellers, which deflected bullets away without causing damage. However, in mid-1915 the Germans produced a device that prevented a machine-gun from firing when a propeller blade passed immediately in front of its barrel. This gave the Germans a crucial advantage in the second half of 1915, and their Fokker planes shot down more than 1000 Allied aircraft. However, by the spring of 1916, the Allies were producing comparable fighters.

Zeppelin bombing

At the start of the twentieth century Germany had embraced the airship for both military and civilian use, launching a programme presided over by Count Ferdinand von Zeppelin. On 19–20 January 1915 two Zeppelins bombed Great Yarmouth and King's Lynn, killing five people. London was bombed by Zeppelins on 31 May 1915. There were a further nineteen missions in 1915, 22 in 1916, seven in 1917 and four in 1918. Most raids were conducted in darkness. In all, 556 British civilians were killed and 1350 injured by the 5750 bombs dropped from Zeppelins. Although relatively trivial, the raids caused some dislocation. Lighting restrictions were imposed and factories stopped work when raiders were sighted. However, Zeppelins cost far more to build than the damage they inflicted. Moreover, as British defences improved, Zeppelins became vulnerable to anti-aircraft guns and fighter aircraft, as well as adverse weather.

Sir William Robertson

In November 1915, Sir William Robertson, an avowed 'westerner', became chief of the Imperial General Staff (CIGS). Henceforth the CIGS, not the war secretary, would determine strategy, advise the government and issue orders to commanders in the field. Kitchener's functions, in his own words, were 'curtailed to the feeding and clothing of the army'.

Haig replaces French

In the wake of Loos, recriminations broke out between French and Haig about responsibility for the misuse of the reserves. Haig, highly regarded by the royal family, told King George V that French was 'a source of great weakness to the army, and no one had confidence in him any more'. In December, French was prevailed on to resign. Haig took his place. Strategy thus passed into the hands of the Robertson–Haig partnership, where it remained for the next two years.

Haig remains a controversial character (see page 161). His critics claim that he was a typical product of the pre-war army, a cavalryman, a stickler for military etiquette, and lacking in imagination. However, Haig had advanced in the army by virtue of hard work and by taking his profession seriously. He was a more stable character than French; resolute and unruffled by defeat. He thought that his role was to set strategy and then let his army and corps commanders get on with the job with minimal interference. Stern and unapproachable, few people dared confront or even approach him for open discussion on critical matters.

Summary diagram: The war: 1914–15

	Air war	Naval war	Western Front	Eastern Front
1914	Reconnaissance fighters	No major battles	Mons and Le Cateau Marne First Ypres Stalemate	Tannenburg Masurian Lakes Lemburg
1915	Zeppelin raids	• Unrestricted submarine warfare • *Lusitania* • US threat • Germany backed down	British Army in 1915 • Neuve Chapelle • Second Ypres • Aubers Ridge • Festubert • Loos – Robertson and Haig Shell shortage National government Lloyd George minister of munitions	• Gallipoli • Salonitia • Gallipoli failure German success on Eastern Front

The war: 1916–17

▶ *To what extent did warfare favour the defender in 1916–17?*

By June 1916, as Kitchener's new armies poured into France, there were 57 British divisions on the Western Front, compared with 95 French divisions and 117 German divisions. Britain now had a continental-sized army on the continent. It was needed because, in 1916, the German high command refocused its attention on the west.

British recruitment problems

In mid-1915, despite an intensive recruiting campaign, the number of men enlisting in the army began to decline. Conservatives and Lloyd George called for conscription, insisting that all citizens had a duty to serve the nation in its hour of peril. But Asquith held back:

- Trade unions opposed conscription. Its introduction might thus imperil the industrial truce (see page 197) essential to Britain's war effort.
- Many Liberals opposed conscription on the grounds that it would undermine traditional liberties as well as harm the country's manufacturing capabilities.

Conscription

On 29 December, faced with the threat of Lloyd George's resignation if compulsion was not adopted, Asquith persuaded the cabinet to accept conscription for unmarried men and widowers aged 18–41. A Military Service Bill, which exempted the unfit, conscientious objectors, sole supporters of dependants and men engaged on essential war work from conscription, passed by 403 votes to 105, the minority consisting of 60 Irish Nationalist, eleven Labour and 34 Liberal MPs. It became law in January 1916. In May a second Military Service Act extended liability for military service to all men, single or married, aged 18–41.

Conscription did not provide more men for the army. Instead of unearthing 650,000 'slackers', it produced 748,587 new claims for exemption, most of them valid, on top of 1.5 million already 'starred' by the Ministry of Munitions. In the first six months of conscription, the average monthly enlistment was around 40,000, less than the rate under the voluntary system. The competing needs of the military and of the war industries remained a contentious issue until November 1918.

The need for British action in 1916

It was apparent that Britain's new armies would have to shoulder a major role:

- Russia had suffered huge losses of life and territory in 1915.
- In February 1916 Germany launched a massive assault on Verdun, a symbolically important French fortress. Gambling on French determination to defend the place, Falkenhayn planned to bleed the French army 'white'. French troops clung on to Verdun, just as Falkenhayn had hoped. However, as more German troops were sucked into the fighting, they too suffered heavy casualties.

Figure 5.5 A British soldier's kit as used in France in 1916.

Helmet: the steel helmet was introduced in 1915. It was soon apparent that sunlight glistening off the helmet aided German marksmen. Thus most soldiers created makeshift covers from hessian sacking.

Bayonet: a 17 inch sword blade

Rifle: the mark III Short Magazine Lee Enfield Rifle, introduced in 1903, had a magazine of 10 rounds. Its bullet could penetrate 18 in. of oak at 200 yards.

Uniform: khaki green tunic, worn over long johns, vest and heavy flannel shirt. The woollen uniform soaked up the damp.

Equipment: soldiers carried two ammunition packets (each holding 75 rounds), an entrenching tool, a water bottle, a small haversack, a large pack and a mess tin. Inside the pack and haversack, men carried great coat, cutlery, sewing kit, washing and shaving equipment, and food rations.

Gas mask: the Small Box Respirator (1916), held in a canvas bag strapped to the chest, was the best gas mask of the war. Its filter box, made of charcoal, gauze and neutralising chemicals, was attached to the rubberised canvas mask by a flexible tube.

Boots: black leather boots with hard hob-nailed soles and steel toecaps. Woollen puttees were worn above the boot.

Douglas Haig

1861	Born in Edinburgh
1880–3	Attended Oxford University
1883–4	Attended the Royal Military College at Sandhurst
1898	Saw active service in the Sudan
1899	Served in the Boer War; mentioned in despatches four times
1906	Appointed director of military training
1915	Became commander-in-chief of the BEF
1916	Directed the Battle of the Somme
1917	Became field marshal; directed the Passchendaele campaign
1918	Led the Hundred Days Offensive
1919	Became the First Earl Haig
1921	Helped to create and presided over the Royal British Legion
1928	Died

Many, then and now, have criticised Haig's leadership. Churchill accused him of blocking enemy machine-gun fire with 'the breasts of brave men'. More recently, Haig's critics have included Gerard De Groot, Paul Fussell and Alan Clark (whose book *The Donkeys* led to the popularisation of the phrase 'lions led by donkeys' used to describe British generalship). Haig is blamed for being unimaginative, for his rigid command style, and for being self-obsessed, devious and disloyal.

Haig had and still has his defenders, however. He was praised by US General Pershing as 'the man who won the war'. Historian John Terraine portrayed him as one of Britain's greatest ever commanders, claiming that he pursued the only possible strategy given the military situation in 1916–18. His attrition tactics wore down the Germans and finally delivered the knockout blow in 1918. Historian Gary Sheffield has called the Hundred Days Offensive (page 179) 'by far the greatest military victory in British history'.

In an effort to take pressure off the beleaguered French, Haig and Robertson accepted Joffre's plan for a combined Anglo-French operation at the River Somme. Robertson believed that an offensive would wear down the German Army more than the Allies. Haig thought there was a chance of achieving a decisive breakthrough. Following a massive artillery bombardment, he envisaged his infantry clearing up the wreckage and his cavalry charging into open country. Hundreds of thousands of horses were kept in France throughout the war for this opportunity.

The Battle of the Somme

The Somme battle commenced in late June with a week-long bombardment; 2200 British guns fired 1.7 million shells. Unfortunately, the artillery did not have the expertise, enough heavy guns or the right shells to do the job it had been given. The bombardment failed to cut German barbed wire and left deep dugouts largely untouched. Many shells detonated in no-man's-land, making the ground even more difficult to cross. Up to a third of shells, hastily produced by the Ministry of Munitions, did not explode.

The first day of the Somme

On 1 July, the day began with an Allied artillery barrage of 600,000 shells, fired by 1500 guns. Then, at 7.30a.m., fourteen British and three French divisions advanced. General Rawlinson, who led the 4th Army, which undertook the offensive, allowed his divisional commanders freedom to decide how they would cross no-man's-land. Most accepted his suggestion that the men attack in slow, methodical waves, walking at intervals of two or three paces. Rawlinson believed that if men were close together this would give them added confidence.

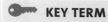

KEY TERM

Mills bomb A type of hand grenade.

The troops were loaded with shovels, sandbags, **Mills bombs** and 200 rounds of ammunition in anticipation of consolidating control of captured trenches and dealing with possible German counterattack. This proved to be wildly optimistic. The artillery barrage was too far ahead of the advancing troops, lifting past the front-line enemy trenches some minutes before the British infantry could reach them. The race for the parapets was won by Germans leaving the security of their dugouts and manning their machine-guns. British troops thus advanced into a hail of fire. Half of the first wave of attackers became casualties within 30 minutes. During the course of the day Britain suffered 57,470 casualties including 19,000 deaths, the greatest loss of life in one day in the British Army's history. German losses were about a tenth of this.

The Battle of the Somme continues

Piecemeal attacks on the Somme continued throughout the summer and, as the Germans counterattacked, the body count no longer told so heavily in their favour. In September, the British used 36 tanks for the first time in the war; virtually all of them broke down. Haig continued to pound away until 19 November when the Somme offensive was finally called off. Britain incurred 420,000 casualties, France 194,000 and the Germans 465,000. After more than four months of fighting, the Allies had advanced no further than seven miles (11 km).

What had the Somme offensive achieved?

- It had some attritional effect. The Germans, with fewer men, could less afford the losses their forces sustained.
- It may have helped to relieve pressure on Verdun.

Was Haig to blame?

It is easy to blame Haig for the debacle of the Somme. But critics, then and later, were unwilling to recognise the dilemma he faced. Something had to be done to help the French. Lloyd George observed that the French thought 'that they are making all the sacrifices and we are endeavouring to preserve our trade and carry on as usual'.

Haig had to attack. And the technology of war continued to operate against attacking forces. Machine-guns, positioned in trenches protected by barbed wire, gave defenders a massive advantage. Heavy artillery bombardment was needed if the attackers were to have any chance of a breakthrough, but such a bombardment warned the enemy of a coming attack. Nor had any army found a foolproof way of co-ordinating artillery and infantry. If the infantry, under cover of an artillery barrage, made initial progress, this merely took it beyond the support of its own gunners, who feared to go on firing because they might hit their own troops. Moreover, if attackers broke through the first defence line, there was a second line. If they broke through the second line, defending generals could move in reserves and plug gaps faster than the attacking side could advance.

There were also problems of battlefield command. If troops advanced in close order they were mown down. If they advanced in open order, officers lost control of them. As historian John Keegan recognised, 'communications consistently lagged behind weaponry'. According to Keegan, 'Generals were like men without eyes, without ears and without voices, unable to watch the operations they set in progress, unable to hear reports of their development and unable to speak to those whom they had originally given orders once action was joined.'

Lloyd George's influence

In June 1916, Kitchener drowned when the ship on which he was travelling to Russia, HMS *Hampshire*, hit a mine. Lloyd George now became secretary of state for war. He had little power over events on the Somme. He grumbled that he was merely a butcher boy, rounding up men for the abattoir. In September, he visited the front and expressed views critical of GHQ. Haig, belying his pose as a bluff, apolitical soldier, was adept at keeping in touch with sympathetic pressmen like Northcliffe and prompted them to warn against government interference in military matters.

The Eastern Front 1916

In June, the Russian commander Brusilov launched an offensive against Austria-Hungary. Over one-third of the Austrian Army was captured or killed. Romania now joined the war on the Allied side, hoping to gain Transylvania. But German forces hit back, halting the Brusilov offensive and defeating Romania's forces. The fall of Bucharest in December marked the end of Romania's war effort.

Mesopotamia

In Mesopotamia British military leaders repeated the mistakes of Gallipoli, underestimating the Turks. General Townshend's army, advancing on Baghdad, failed to break through Turkish defences and was besieged in Kut. A relief force lost 23,000 men in an effort to save the 12,500 men in Kut. In April 1916, Townshend was forced to surrender.

The naval situation in 1916

Germany had difficulty making use of its High Seas Fleet on which it had lavished so much money. In material terms, Britain retained the whiphand. In April 1916 it had almost twice as many modern battleships and battlecruisers

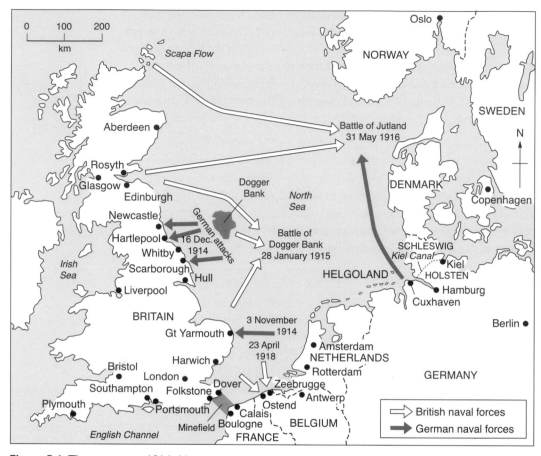

Figure 5.6 The war at sea, 1914–16.

as Germany. Unbeknown to the Germans, Britain had the additional advantage of having captured the German naval codebooks. Intercepted German radio signals were decoded and analysed in a newly created department in Room 40 of the Admiralty Old Building in London.

The Battle of Jutland

Soon after midnight on 31 May the German High Seas Fleet left port. Commanded by Admiral Scheer, it hoped to lure a detachment of the British Grand Fleet into battle. Given that Room 40 had radio intelligence of Scheer's plans, Britain had an opportunity to catch the Germans in their own trap. Jellicoe left Scapa Flow with the Grand Fleet while Beatty's 5th Battle Squadron sailed from Rosyth. The German Fleet seemed to be steaming towards annihilation. But a breakdown of communications at the Admiralty, where staff officers mistrusted the intelligence from Room 40, let Scheer off the hook. Thinking that the High Seas Fleet was still in harbour, Jellicoe sailed south slowly to conserve fuel. Consequently, his ships were too far from the enemy at the very moment that Beatty's force was perilously close.

Early in the afternoon, Beatty spotted enemy battlecruisers. The German ships lured Beatty towards the High Seas Fleet. Beatty followed, his squadron soon coming under heavy fire. Two British battlecruisers were blown up. The appearance of the main body of the German Fleet forced Beatty to flee northwards towards Jellicoe's ships. Soon after 6.00p.m. the only sea battle between two great modern fleets ever fought in European waters took place. Jellicoe commanded 28 battleships, nine battlecruisers, 34 cruisers and 80 destroyers. Scheer commanded sixteen battleships, six pre-Dreadnoughts, five battlecruisers, eleven cruisers and 63 destroyers. Realising the danger, Scheer turned away. Jellicoe, fearing mines and U-boats, did not pursue. Scheer thus escaped back to port.

The Battle of Jutland lasted less than an hour. The Royal Navy lost three battlecruisers, four cruisers and eight destroyers with 6000 dead. The Germans lost one battleship, one battlecruiser, four cruisers and five destroyers with 2500 dead. It seemed that the High Seas Fleet had won a victory. But appearances were deceptive. The High Seas Fleet had fled. It left harbour again only three times during the course of war and then to no purpose. Scheer's 'outing' has been described by Keegan as 'an assault on the gaoler, followed by a return to gaol'. But if Jutland was a British victory, it was also a disappointment to most Britons. Politicians lost confidence in the Admiralty. In November, First Sea Lord Admiral Jackson was replaced by Jellicoe. Beatty replaced Jellicoe as commander of the Grand Fleet.

The December 1916 crisis

By late 1916 Britons were losing confidence in Asquith. Everywhere the war seemed to be going badly. There were tensions among leading Liberals. While Lloyd George and Edwin Montagu, minister of munitions, favoured the conscription of industrial workers, Runciman and McKenna opposed further extension of state controls. Conservative MPs, critical of both Asquith and Bonar Law, demanded that the war was conducted more energetically. On 25 November Bonar Law met Lloyd George and Sir **Edward Carson**, who chaired the influential Unionist War Committee. They agreed a scheme for streamlining the machinery of government by creating a small inner war council, under Lloyd George's chairmanship, which would run the war. Asquith turned down this proposal, insisting that he himself must preside over the council.

On 3 December Bonar Law and his chief Conservative colleagues signed a letter to Asquith calling on him to resign. Meanwhile they offered their own resignations. Alarmed, Asquith now wrote to Lloyd George accepting his war council proposal. The crisis seemed to be over. But the next day *The Times* carried an article describing the war council in terms disparaging to Asquith. Suspecting that the article was Lloyd George's work (it was actually inspired by Carson), Asquith determined to do battle with his secretary of state for war.

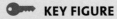 **KEY FIGURE**

Edward Carson (1854–1935)

The leader of the Ulster Unionists 1910–21.

Confident that most Liberals would support him, he withdrew his agreement to the war council.

The end of Asquith

On 5 December Lloyd George resigned. Asquith also resigned, defying Bonar Law or Lloyd George to form a government. On 7 December, assured of Conservative and Labour support, and (according to his ally Christopher Addison) the support of 136 Liberal MPs (the reality was more like 40–50), Lloyd George became prime minister. Virtually all the prominent Liberals refused to serve under him.

Lloyd George

Lloyd George's accession to power, in A.J.P. Taylor's view, was more than a change of government, 'It was a revolution, British-style.' Newspapers and backbench MPs, defying party leaders and whips, had combined to ensure that Lloyd George became prime minister; the first man of humble origin to reach that position. Thereafter, in Taylor's view, he was the nearest thing Britain has known to a Napoleon, a supreme ruler maintaining himself by individual achievement. Almeric Fitzroy, a leading civil servant, wrote in 1918, 'The effects of the change in direction two years ago may be compared to the substitution of dynamite for a damp squib.'

Lloyd George's war cabinet

Lloyd George ran the war through a new war cabinet. Initially it had five members (later six and for a few months seven) chosen, in theory, for their ability, not because of the offices they held. Only the chancellor of the exchequer, Bonar Law, had departmental duties. Henderson spoke for Labour. Lord Curzon and Milner – experienced bureaucrats – were popular with Conservatives and the army. Where the old cabinet rarely met more than once a week and kept no records of its proceedings, the war cabinet met practically every day (300 times in 1917) and Sir Maurice Hankey organised an efficient secretariat, preparing agenda, keeping minutes and ensuring that particular departments carried out decisions made. This ended some of the muddles that had characterised Asquith's regime.

Fearing the collapse of national morale, Lloyd George was anxious to reduce the deaths of soldiers whom he thought Haig and Robertson were squandering. He hoped that the war cabinet's creation would help him to establish mastery over the service departments. This did not happen. The service ministers, no longer in the war cabinet, became more independent than before. Carson, at the Admiralty, fiercely championed his professional advisers, while Lord Derby, secretary of state for war, supported Robertson. The latter, who regarded the war cabinet as 'the enemy' and Lloyd George as 'a real bad 'un', provided the government with little military information.

The U-boat threat

In Germany, Generals Hindenburg and Ludendorff replaced Falkenhayn, effectively becoming military dictators. Fearing defeat, Germany's new leaders renewed unrestricted submarine warfare on 1 February 1917. Aware that this might well bring the USA into the war, Hindenburg and Ludendorff gambled on U-boats starving Britain into surrender before significant US military aid could reach Europe. The hope was realistic. Germany now had over 100 U-boats. In April they sank over a quarter of all ships leaving British ports. British wheat stocks dwindled to six weeks' supply.

The USA enters the war

The reintroduction of unrestricted submarine warfare led to US President Woodrow Wilson severing diplomatic links with Germany, but he was still anxious to avoid war. However, in March, a telegram from German Foreign Secretary Zimmerman to the German ambassador in Mexico, promising that Mexico would receive Texas, New Mexico and Arizona if it declared war on the USA, was intercepted by British intelligence, passed on to Wilson and published in the USA. This caused a wave of anti-German sentiment in the USA. The March Revolution in Russia (see below) removed a further obstacle to US entry into the war; a war which now did seem like a struggle between autocracy and democracy. On 6 April, the USA declared war on Germany. This gave the Allies a tremendous boost. However, it would take many months before the USA was able to mobilise its forces. In the meantime, Britain had to deal with the U-boat threat.

The convoy system

Britain laid mines to try and keep U-boats in their bases but struggled to find a more effective method of defence. While some experts suggested introducing the **convoy** system, which was already operating successfully on selected routes (for example, troopships to France), the Admiralty was sceptical, arguing that:

- merchant captains could not keep station
- convoys would offer a larger target to U-boats
- 2500 ships entered and left British ports each week, too many to convoy.

In April, Lloyd George forced the Admiralty to produce a convoy scheme. It was one of his most decisive achievements. By December 1917, over half of Britain's overseas trade was being conducted under convoy – at a loss rate of under one per cent of tonnage. The official naval history stated, 'the chief objections against the system before it was tried had one and all proved to be unfounded'. Destroyers and new classes of patrol craft, as well as airships and seaplane patrols, which sometimes accompanied convoys, contained the U-boat menace. Aircraft, if not able to destroy U-boats, could alert naval escorts to their presence.

The British Army in 1917

- Conscripted men were recruited for general service and posted to units as required, not raised as distinct formations. This tended to remove or blur many – although not all – of the differences between the regular, territorial and new armies.
- By 1917 the engineers, tank corps and flying corps were growing in importance.
- Given the growth of the army and the heavy casualties, there was a need for more officers; 229,000 had been commissioned by 1918. While many were ex-public schoolboys, there was a noticeable increase in lower-middle-class officers. The change in social tone was particularly marked in the army's technological branches, for example, the tank corps.

British tanks

The first tanks, tracked armoured vehicles fitted with armaments, were developed in Britain. The tank's complex development was partly the responsibility of the Royal Navy, largely because First Lord of the Admiralty Churchill backed the project. The first tanks went into action on 15 September 1916 during the Battle of the Somme. Initially successful in forcing their way through the German trenches, most soon broke down. But they had done sufficiently well for more to be ordered. By 1917 there were several types of tank, with different armaments and features. As the capabilities and limitations of tanks became better understood, they underwent various modifications and improvements, enabling them to cross the mud and shell-craters of no-man's-land. Tanks had some successes and as many failures. Owing to their mechanical unreliability, they were never able to make a decisive breakthrough.

Gambling on Nivelle

Lloyd George thought victory was most likely to be achieved if the Allies acted as one. In January 1917 he attended the first general conference of the Allies in Rome. Italy had joined the war on the Allied side in 1915 and Lloyd George wanted a combined offensive on the Italian front, but Italy refused the doubtful honour. The best hope thus seemed to lie with French General Nivelle, who had replaced Joffre as French commander-in-chief. Nivelle claimed he knew how to win the war with fewer casualties. Oddly, Lloyd George had faith in the French general, while having none in his own generals. In February, to Haig and Robertson's horror, he placed Nivelle in supreme command over British forces for the coming offensive. Meanwhile, the Germans withdrew to the **Hindenburg line**.

 **KEY TERM**

Hindenburg line A heavily fortified German defence system, prepared over the winter of 1916–17 (see the map on page 153).

The Battle of Arras

A preliminary and diversionary offensive – the Battle of Arras (9–14 April 1917) – started well, with British forces advancing three and a half miles (5.6 km) on the first day and Canadian forces capturing Vimy Ridge. Allied troops approached the narrow front through tunnels, and an element of surprise was achieved by shortening the length of the opening bombardment. The artillery now had the equipment and the expertise to fight the sort of battle to which it had aspired on the Somme:

- The new 106 fuse caused shells to explode on the slightest contact and to expend their blast horizontally, thereby cutting barbed wire.
- The Battle of Arras was fought as series of limited attacks, leap-frogging over each other, with pauses to consolidate.

Arras showed that **combined arms tactics** and careful preparation could break the enemy line, but the greatest problems remained unsolved. Cavalry troopers were unable to cross the broken ground and infantry could not easily advance beyond the range of artillery support. New defensive positions were improvised faster than attackers could plod forward. Nevertheless, Arras achieved its purpose. The Germans doubled their strength in the sector, diverting men from the River Aisne where Nivelle intended to attack.

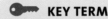

KEY TERM

Combined arms tactics
Fighting the enemy by blending together the different branches of the army, for example, artillery, infantry and tanks.

Nivelle's failure

Nivelle's offensive in mid-April was a disaster: 29,000 Frenchmen died for no gain. After the attack, a large part of the French Army mutinied. Order was restored by Petain, the hero of Verdun, who promised no more bloody offensives. By supporting Nivelle, Lloyd George had undermined his authority with regard to strategic matters.

The war against the Turks

After the humiliation at Kut, Britain strengthened its army in Mesopotamia. With new leadership and improved transport systems, a British expedition took Kut and then Baghdad. Meanwhile, in 1917, Australian General Allenby captured Beersheba, Gaza and then, in December, Jerusalem. In the Hejaz desert, Colonel T.E. Lawrence became a national hero, fomenting an Arab revolt against Turkish rule and capturing Aqaba in July 1917. Other exploits by Lawrence followed, but his military role was not critical to the Middle East campaign.

Haig's 'show'

By mid-1917, the BEF had replaced the French Army as the main force on the Western Front. Haig, confident that 'the German was now nearly at his last resources', was eager to take up an idea which he had long cherished: a great offensive in Flanders. Here he believed he could win the war. British forces

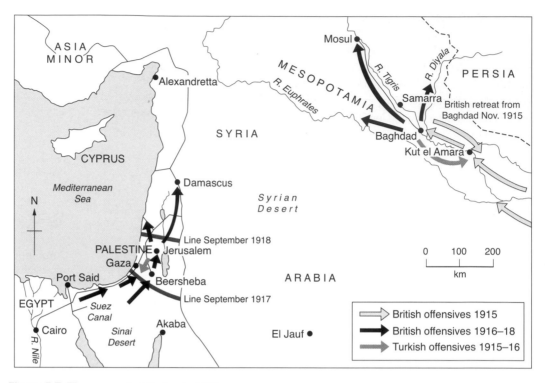

Figure 5.7 The war against Turkey in 1917.

would break out of the Ypres salient and roll up the entire German front. By June an almost unstoppable momentum had built up behind Haig's project. Even the Admiralty supported a Flanders offensive, hoping it would result in the capture of U-boat bases in Belgium. Robertson was also supportive. While doubting whether Haig's 'show' would result in a major breakthrough, he thought there was military advantage to be gained if the Germans could be driven from the heights overlooking the Ypres salient. The fact that the Germans were likely to stand and fight was also a powerful recommendation to Robertson, who still favoured an attritional strategy.

Lloyd George, fearing another bloodbath, remained sceptical. He had little confidence in Haig's ability. However:

- British success at Messines Ridge on 7 June, following the detonation of a million pounds (450,000 kg) of high explosives under German trenches, was a cause for confidence.
- The situation in Russia was dire (see below).
- Fearing that a pro-peace government might come to power in France, Lloyd George accepted that British action somewhere was essential.

The new War Policy Committee (essentially the war cabinet, minus Henderson and with the addition of Jan Smuts, the South African minister of defence) approved the Flanders offensive. The committee agreed with Robertson that the aim should be 'wearing down and exhausting the enemy's resistance' rather than breaking the German line.

Passchendaele

On 31 July, Haig launched the Third Battle of Ypres, popularly known as Passchendaele. The battle began with a massive artillery barrage: 2299 guns, one every five yards (4.6 m), employing four times as many shells as were fired before the Somme. British counterbattery work eliminated around half the German guns. But the fortnight-long bombardment destroyed the Flanders' drainage system, turning the countryside into a quagmire. The attack that followed the bombardment was geared to a **creeping barrage**. Unfortunately, the Germans were ready:

- They had built concrete pillboxes and bunkers.
- They had divided their troops into two separate formations: a trench garrison and counterattack troops in the rearward battle zone.

The German defence-in-depth strategy ensured that Haig's forces gained no more than two miles (3 km). Tactically, the British attack showed more imagination than at the Battle of the Somme. Initial losses were thus smaller: 35,000 casualties before 3 August. Then it rained for a fortnight. A series of costly pushes followed later in August.

Haig persevered through a dry September and a wet October, perhaps misled by John Charteris, his intelligence chief, who insisted that the Germans were 'used up'. A series of battles – Menin Road Ridge (20–27 September), Polgon Wood (26 September to 3 October) and Broodseinde (4 October) – proved costly. Lloyd George was appalled by events. He contemplated making a personal intervention to stop the carnage but was persuaded not to do so on the grounds that Haig had the support of the Conservatives and the press.

The Canadian capture of the village of Passchendaele on 6 November marked the end of the campaign. Haig's forces had advanced no more than 10,000 yards (9 km), failing to reach all the objectives that had been set for the first day. The advance had simply made the Ypres salient more precarious.

Passchendaele: conclusion

The Third Battle of Ypres, more a succession of distinct battles than a single operation, suffered from strategic incoherence, with Haig and – initially – General Gough harbouring ambitions of a breakthrough, while General Plumer and General Rawlinson set greater store by **'bite and hold'**. Haig must bear the ultimate responsibility for this confusion. He had also chosen a battlefield where German defences were strong and where the waterlogged terrain made it impossible to use tanks effectively.

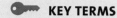 **KEY TERMS**

Creeping barrage
An artillery bombardment, where the shells are meant to keep falling just ahead of the attacking troops.

'Bite and hold' A term used to describe the tactic of capturing part of the enemy trench line and then defending it when the Germans counterattacked.

SOURCE C

Examine Source C.
What problems does this
source suggest British
troops faced at
Passchendaele?

A stretcher party carrying a wounded soldier during the battle of Passchendaele in 1917.

Unreliable casualty statistics makes it hard to know whether the battle was a success in attritional terms. Most authorities agree that some 70,000 British troops were killed and over 170,000 wounded. The Germans probably suffered some 220,000 casualties. 'No doubt the morale of the German army was shaken by Passchendaele', wrote A.J.P. Taylor. 'It is unlikely that the morale of the British army was much improved.'

Cambrai

In November Haig authorised another attack, this time at Cambrai. Some lessons had been learned. A short but accurate artillery bombardment concentrated on eliminating German guns. The attack, when it came on 20 November, took the enemy by surprise. Smokescreens and fake smokescreens aided the infantry assault. So did 324 tanks, which crushed the enemy barbed wire. British troops advanced over three miles (5 km) with the loss of only 5000 men. Bells to celebrate a victory were rung in London for the only time during the war. The rejoicing was premature. There were insufficient infantry reserves to consolidate the opening and German counterattacks quickly recovered lost ground. When the fighting ended on 7 December, Britain had lost two-thirds of its tanks and had suffered 45,000 casualties.

Cambrai gave the lie to Haig's claim that the BEF had broken the spirit of the German Army during the Third Battle of Ypres. For the first time, newspapers started to voice criticisms of Haig. Lloyd George considered making a clean sweep of the military high command but drew back because of Conservative opposition. Instead, he looked towards Allied co-operation as a way of reducing Haig's and Robertson's influence. In November, at Lloyd George's prompting, a Supreme War Council, composed of the Allied prime ministers and their military advisers, was set up at Versailles. The Council was supposed to provide a co-ordinated direction for the war. To some extent it did. But essentially it could only discuss and advise. Robertson, for the most part, refused to work with it.

The aerial war

Under the pressure of war, aircraft development was accelerated and new methods of waging war from the air were introduced.

German bombing

Although there had been German aircraft raids on England since 1914, true strategic bombing did not begin until early 1917. German High Command aimed to crush Britain's will to fight by disrupting war industry, communications and supply. The first raid on London occurred during daylight on 27 May 1917. Seven more raids followed. On 13 June, 162 people were killed in London in a raid by fourteen **Gothas**. While the raids caused alarm, Germany lacked sufficient planes to cause serious disruption to Britain's war effort. As British anti-aircraft defences improved, German bombers suffered heavy losses. In August, the Gothas turned to night operations, which were safer but less accurate. There were a further nineteen raids, the final one coming on 19–20 May 1918. British civilian casualties totalled around 850 dead and 2000 injured.

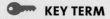 **KEY TERM**

Gotha The main German bomber.

Ground attack

Close co-operation between ground and air units became an important part of offensive operations during 1917–18. Given that few planes were built specifically as ground-attack aircraft, both sides generally used bombers and fighters for close-support missions. Such missions had a limited impact:

- Aerial bombing tended to be inaccurate.
- Pilots and their unprotected aircraft were highly vulnerable to machine-gun and rifle fire as they swooped down to strafe enemy positions.

The importance of reconnaissance

Reconnaissance remained aircraft's most vital work. Indirect artillery fire – shooting at targets not visible from gun batteries – became possible because aeroplanes flew over enemy positions and identified targets. Gunners, aided by accurate maps produced by aerial photographs, were also guided by airmen who used radio to direct artillery fire.

The role of fighter aircraft

The main task of fighters was still to shoot down reconnaissance planes. As the war progressed, the methods of employing air power grew more sophisticated. Baron von Richthofen's 'Flying Circus', a large grouping of fighter aircraft, was a famous example of the tendency towards greater centralisation of air assets. More importantly, the fighter planes of the second half of the war were far superior to their predecessors. Fitted with more powerful engines, they had a better rate of climb, greater speed, and were more manoeuvrable.

The air war was a technological struggle as much as anything else. Better fighters appeared on both sides at regular intervals. Consequently, air superiority switched back and forth as new planes outclassed older opponents. This was demonstrated in the Battle of Arras (see page 169). While the British enjoyed a three to one advantage in aircraft, their BE-2s and RE-8s were no match for the German Albatros D-types. During April 1917, the Royal Flying Corps (RFC) lost 151 aircraft and 316 crew compared to German losses of 66 planes and 119 crew. However, the D-types were soon outclassed by British planes. Between May and September 1917, five Sopwith triplanes downed 87 German aircraft without loss. However, their heyday was soon over as Germany produced better performing fighters.

By late 1917, the British were producing the Sopwith F-1 Camel. The first British aircraft to be built with two synchronised machine-guns, it was agile and had a good rate of climb. It became Britain's leading fighter for the remainder of the war, shooting down some 1300 enemy aircraft.

Aces

Fighter pilots developed the tactics of air combat. Victory usually went to the pilot who exploited the sun and clouds to sneak up behind his opponent and open fire at close range. Pilots who achieved more than five 'kills' were recognised as 'aces'. As well as being expert pilots and skilled marksmen, the great aces invariably had better aircraft than their opponents.

The most successful 'ace' was von Richthofen, the Red Baron. He had 80 'kills' to his credit between August 1916 and his death (probably by ground fire) in April 1918. Edward Mannock, the most successful British pilot, with 73 'kills', was also killed by ground fire.

The activities of the 'aces' captured the public's imagination and became the focus of intense propaganda campaigns to boost morale. While aerial combat was seen as gallant and chivalrous, in reality it was bloody and dangerous. The casualty rate among British pilots was almost 50 per cent.

The RAF

While many Britons demanded bombing attacks on German towns in reprisal for the attacks on Britain, aerial experts opposed the idea, convinced that planes were best used in co-operation with the army. Smuts, given the task of judging air power, claimed, in October 1917, that, given enough planes, Germany could be bombed into submission. Lloyd George and Churchill, whose minds were always open to innovation, liked the idea. An independent air ministry was set up under Rothermere, the younger brother of Northcliffe, the press magnate. In April 1918 the Royal Air Force (RAF) was formed. It was the world's first air service that was independent of either an army or a navy. Major-General Hugh Trenchard, head of the RFC, was made chief of staff to the RAF.

> ### Balloons
> Tethered balloons had a key battlefield role. Equipped with telephones and binoculars, observers could see very long distances into enemy-held territory from their baskets, generating valuable information. As such, they tended to be a priority target for attacking aircraft and were therefore heavily defended.

The Eastern Front 1917

From an Allied perspective, developments on the Eastern Front were disastrous:

- In March, Tsar Nicholas II's government was overthrown.
- Hope that the new provisional government would give fresh impetus to the Russian war effort quickly died.
- In November, the Bolsheviks, led by Lenin, seized power in Russia.
- In December, Lenin signed an armistice with Germany. The Eastern Front had ceased to exist.

Italy

In October 1917, German and Austrian forces trounced the Italians at Caporetto, forcing the Italians into a 50-mile (80-km) retreat. Against Robertson's wishes, tens of thousands of British troops were sent to Italy to bolster Italian resistance.

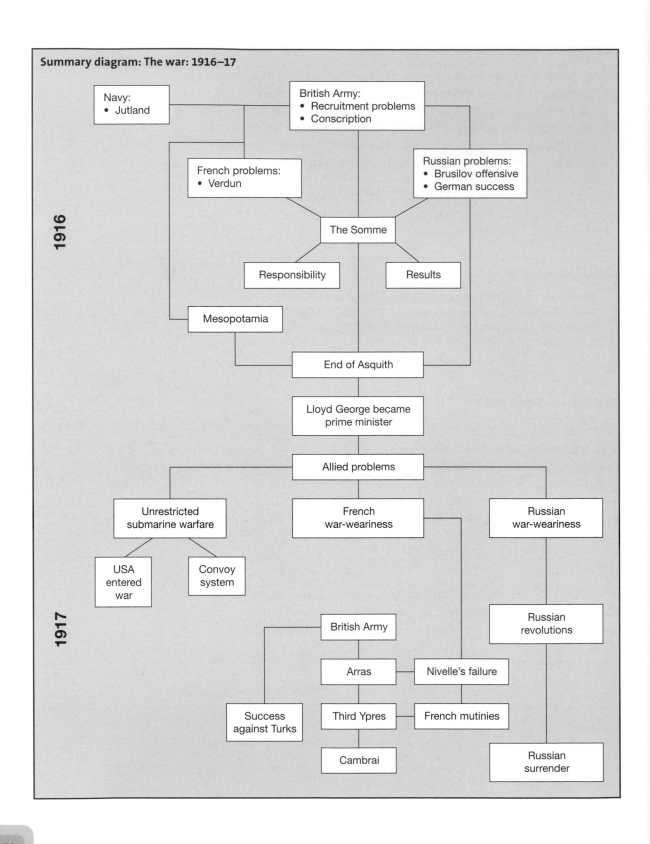

Summary diagram: The war: 1916–17

1916

- Navy:
  - Jutland
- British Army:
  - Recruitment problems
  - Conscription
- French problems:
  - Verdun
- Russian problems:
  - Brusilov offensive
  - German success
- The Somme
  - Responsibility
  - Results
- Mesopotamia
- End of Asquith
- Lloyd George became prime minister

1917

- Allied problems
  - Unrestricted submarine warfare
    - USA entered war
    - Convoy system
  - French war-weariness
  - Russian war-weariness
    - Russian revolutions
    - Russian surrender
- British Army
  - Arras — Nivelle's failure
  - Third Ypres — French mutinies
  - Cambrai
- Success against Turks

The end of the war

▶ *How far is it correct to say that the British Army won the war in 1918?*

With Russia out of the war, Germany was able to transfer large numbers of men to the west. However, Germany faced serious problems. Its allies – Austria-Hungary, Turkey and Bulgaria – were a source of serious concern. There was also the prospect of having to fight huge numbers of US troops. The outcome of the war was thus delicately balanced.

The British Army in 1918

With a 'wastage' level of some 76,000 men a month on the Western Front in 1917, double the rate of enlistments, the army faced a manpower crisis. Moreover, the army was low on the government's December 1917 list of priorities. This put the navy and air force first, followed by the merchant navy, shipbuilding and coalmining, then the manufacture of tanks and aeroplanes, followed by food and timber production. Instead of the 600,000 men that Haig demanded, he was promised only 100,000. Given the manpower shortage, Britain planned to stay largely on the defensive in 1918, awaiting the arrival of US troops.

The end of Robertson

In February 1918, the Supreme War Council, with Lloyd George's support, resolved to create a general reserve of British and French divisions under the control of its own military advisers. If this scheme operated, grand strategy would be determined in Versailles, not by CIGS in London. Robertson resisted. On 16 February, Lloyd George offered Robertson the option of either going to Versailles as Britain's military representative or staying on as CIGS with much reduced powers. Robertson refused both offers. Although Robertson had the support of the king, Lloyd George and Bonar Law were determined to get rid of him. He was replaced by Sir Henry Wilson.

Haig survived. Smuts, after touring the Western Front, reported that there was no one better.

The Ludendorff Spring Offensive

Ludendorff, with 192 German divisions in the west facing 178 Allied divisions, determined to strike before the Americans arrived in overwhelming numbers. His attack, code named Operation Michael, began on 21 March, on the Somme at the join between the British and French armies. It was successful for several reasons:

- The attack was expected in Flanders and took the British by surprise.
- Gough's 5th Army, which bore the brunt of the German attack, was below strength.

- The Germans adopted a new style of attack. There was no warning bombardment beforehand. Specially trained soldiers called stormtroopers broke through weak spots in the Allied line. Instead of consolidating, they pressed forward, leaving pockets of resistance to be dealt with later.
- A heavy fog helped the German attack.

The British line was blown wide open. General Gough lost one-third of his force. While some units fought bravely, others surrendered *en masse*. In a single day the Germans captured over 98 square miles (250 km²), to a depth of four and half miles (7 km), virtually the same area that had been captured by the BEF during the entire Somme offensive. Over the next week, British troops fell back over 40 miles (64 km). The German advance threatened the vital railway junction at Amiens.

Allied co-operation

The crisis drove the Allies into co-operating more effectively. On 3 April, French Marshal Foch was appointed Allied commander-in-chief, with the task of co-ordinating the operations of the Allied armies. Foch shaped the military situation to some extent by his control of the reserves. However, without a staff and with ambiguous powers, his appointment had a limited impact. In Britain, Lloyd George replaced Derby with Milner as secretary of state for war.

German problems

Fortunately for the Allies, the German offensive began to lose momentum. By switching his attack on 28 March to Arras, which was successfully defended by the British 3rd Army, Ludendorff blurred the focus of operations. His advance was also slowed down by:

- heavy German losses, especially of elite troops
- the ill-discipline of some troops who gorged themselves on captured supplies
- the fact that the Germans were far ahead of their supply lines.

On 4–5 April a last German attempt to capture Amiens failed.

Operation George

On 9 April, Ludendorff launched Operation George, an attack in Flanders. Again the initial German assault was successful, threatening the Channel ports. On 11 April, Haig issued his 'Backs to the Wall' order, declaring that troops must fight to the end. The BEF held out. On 25 April, Operation George was aborted. Meanwhile the Allied armies grew stronger:

- The BEF was strengthened by 500,000 troops mustered from Britain, Palestine and Italy.
- US troops were arriving in France at the rate of 250,000 a month.

In April 1918, the British government rushed through a new Military Service Act, which raised the age of compulsory military service to 50 and reduced the minimum age to seventeen and a half.

German failure

In late May, the Germans attacked the French, advancing to within 40 miles (64 km) of Paris. US troops and five British divisions, brought south to recuperate, helped to staunch the German advance. On 15 July, Ludendorff launched his last offensive against the French. It failed.

The Hundred Days Offensive

By late July the Germans had shot their bolt. Foch was keen to attack. But all he could do was make suggestions. His role was more that of a cheerleader than a commander. Haig continued to behave as though he enjoyed virtual autonomy, probably deferring less to Foch than he had once done to Joffre. But well supplied with traditional arms and ammunition and with new weapons, including Mark V tanks, mustard gas shells and rifle grenades, he was ready to attack.

Haig now showed considerable skills in generalship. His most impressive victory was at Amiens on 8 August (dubbed by Ludendorff as 'the black day of the German Army'). The BEF attack, spearheaded by Australian and Canadian troops, gained eight miles (13 km), captured 400 guns and inflicted 27,000

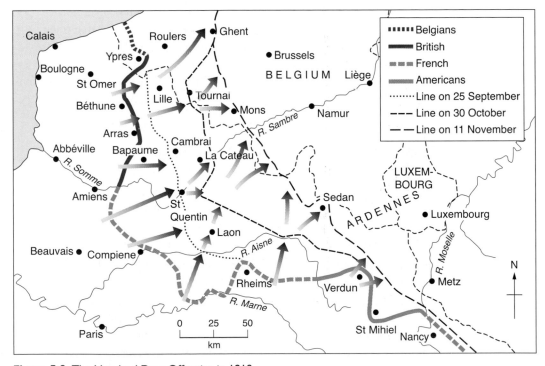

Figure 5.8 The Hundred Days Offensive in 1918.

enemy casualties. The British incurred 8000 casualties. British firepower – 2000 guns, 450 tanks and 1900 planes – overwhelmed the Germans. Learning from previous experience, Haig stopped the attack after a couple of days. Instead of creating an unwieldy salient, he started a second attack at another point where the Germans had depleted their reserves in order to stem the first advance. A succession of short jabs forced the enemy to withdraw back towards the Hindenburg Line.

The importance of aircraft

Aircraft made an important contribution to Haig's success. By 1918, the Allies were producing over 11,000 planes a month while the Germans manufactured below 2000. Control of the skies allowed the Allies to reconnoitre battlefields with impunity. Aircraft could also provide tactical support for infantry and launch raids on enemy supply lines, communication centres and reserves.

By the summer of 1918 British bombers, using French airfields, regularly struck at targets located in the industrial heartland of western Germany. In total, Britain dropped 665 tons of bombs on Germany, losing 450 planes in the process. By late 1918 Trenchard was planning to launch raids deep into Germany, hoping to bomb the country into submission. However, the Allies did not have enough planes to do major damage to Germany's infrastructure or to German morale.

Palestine

The Palestine theatre demonstrated what could happen when an air force dominated the skies. In the summer of 1918, British and Australian airmen fought and won a battle for air superiority over their Turkish and German counterparts. This was important during and after the Battle of Megiddo on 19 September. As Turkish troops retreated, British planes bombed and machine-gunned them with devastating effect, ensuring the battle was a decisive victory.

The importance of artillery

By mid-1918 the Allies had overwhelming superior artillery; a crucial advantage. Further advances in mapping, aerial photography, surveying, calibration and communications helped to produce accurate fire. Artillery, using a variety of specialised shells, became the decisive weapon on the battlefield.

Allied advance

Allied armies continued to push home their advantage. On 29 September British troops crossed the Canal du Nord, a seemingly impregnable part of the Hindenburg Line. The attack followed a 56-hour artillery bombardment, using 1637 guns on a 10,000-yard (9100-m) front. Almost a million shells were fired in a 24-hour period. French and American troops also pressed forward. German front-line troops continued to fight, but in the rear there were problems of desertion and disobedience.

On 29 September, Ludendorff insisted that Germany must seek an armistice. Believing they would get better terms from the USA than from Britain or France, German leaders appealed to Wilson to open peace negotiations.

The military situation in autumn 1918

The Hundred Days Offensive rolled on. Nevertheless, the German line was never broken for more than a few hours. The BEF incurred 264,383 casualties between 21 August and 11 November. This was a daily loss of 3645 men, higher than the daily loss sustained on the Somme or during the Third Battle of Ypres. One-third of all officers and men of the tank corps became casualties during the final 96 days of the war. By late October, given deteriorating weather, the offensive seemed set to slow down. German troops still controlled most of Belgium and large parts of France. American troops would not be ready to fight in large numbers until 1919. However, Germany faced even greater problems.

The defeat of Germany's allies

Germany's allies collapsed in the autumn of 1918:

- On 15 September, Allied forces in Salonika (see page 155) at last broke out, forcing Bulgaria to surrender a fortnight later.
- After defeating the Turks at Megiddo, Allenby went on to capture Damascus. On 30 October, the Ottoman government signed an armistice with Britain.
- On 23–24 October, the Italians defeated the Austrians at Vittorio Veneto. On 3 November, Austria-Hungary concluded an armistice with Italy.

Armistice

Amid mounting chaos, a new German government dismissed Hindenburg and Ludendorff on 26 October. Admiral Scheer now planned to break the Allied blockade by a 'do or die' assault on Britain's Grand Fleet. He was defied by mutinous sailors who joined striking workers. The domestic situation in Germany forced Kaiser Wilhelm II to abdicate on 9 November and flee to the Netherlands. Germany now accepted the armistice terms and agreed that the war would end at 11.00a.m. on 11 November 1918.

The armistice terms were designed to remove Germany's ability to fight:

- German troops had to withdraw beyond the River Rhine.
- Germany had to hand over large quantities of war *matériel*.
- The blockade of Germany would continue until peace terms had been drawn up and accepted.

Desperately short of manpower, British leaders were happy to accept the armistice. Work ceased in factories, shops and offices as crowds spilled out into the streets to celebrate.

 **KEY TERM**

Matériel Military equipment.

Military losses

Ten million men died in the war; 30 million were wounded. Britain lost 750,000 men. International comparisons suggest that, demographically Britain, escaped relatively lightly. Of British males in the age range 15–49, some 6.3 per cent were killed. Serbia lost 22.7 per cent, France 13.3 per cent, Germany 12.5 per cent, Austria-Hungary 9 per cent and Turkey 14.8 per cent. Unlike earlier wars, most of the deaths were due to battle, not disease. Deaths from battle outnumbered deaths from disease in a ratio of one to fifteen. British soldiers benefited from the use of antiseptics and from a mass inoculation programme against various diseases. Although **trench foot** and **venereal disease** immobilised large numbers, various sanitary precautions limited the damage. Improved anaesthetic and X-ray techniques and the impressive work of the Medical Service Corps all contributed to a high recovery rate from wounds. Blood transfusion developments, especially the ability to preserve and therefore store blood, also did much to save lives in 1917–18.

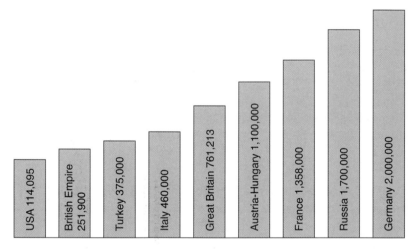

Figure 5.9 Military losses over 1914–18.

The military experience

During the war, 5.7 million men served in the British Army, over a fifth of the male population. Roughly half were volunteers, the other half conscripts. There was no 'universality of experience':

- Not all men served on the Western Front.
- The experience of officers was different from that of privates, the experience of the artillery different from that of the cavalry or infantry.
- The experience of those who served in 1914 was different from that of those who served in 1918.
- Many soldiers never **went over the top**. Over a third of a million men in the BEF in 1918 were involved in supply and support work.

Nevertheless, over half of all combatant troops were infantry and most infantrymen fought on the Western Front.

Whatever romantic expectations soldiers may have had about war quickly dissipated. Tedium and discomfort, punctuated by moments of sheer terror, formed the lot of most infantrymen. For many **Tommies**, the principal fight was waged against the weather, rats and lice:

- Inclement weather caused frostbite and trench foot.
- Rats carried disease and spoiled food.
- The blood-sucking louse was even more irksome. Ninety-five per cent of soldiers coming out of the line were infested.

At the front, the men's main concerns were food, clean water and cigarettes. About two-fifths of an infantryman's time was spent in the front line but participation in major battles was infrequent. For long periods, soldiers were on leave or recuperating in the rear. When they did go over the top, many experienced panic but others felt exhilaration and – if they got the opportunity – killed the enemy with relish, avenging the deaths of former pals. Surviving letters, diaries and memoirs show a vast array of attitudes on this, as on other attitudes. It is a gross oversimplification to see the soldiers as mere sacrificial victims. Expressions of enthusiastic patriotism frequently crop up in correspondence. Some men enjoyed the adventure and camaraderie of war. Among non-commissioned officers and privates the predominant stance seems to have been one of stoicism, tinged with black humour.

Discipline in the BEF never broke down. Most men performed their duty more or less uncomplainingly. Nor, except when the 5th Army's positions were overrun in the spring of 1918, did British soldiers surrender in droves. Most seem to have been determined not to let down their 'mates'. Censors in early 1918 made a careful examination of the letters troops sent home. They found a great deal of grumbling about food but no sign of serious disaffection. The relationship between officers and men was generally harmonious. While soldiers sometimes voiced complaints about incompetent and bullying officers, most seem to have borne no general grudge against the officer class as a whole, reserving their hatred for the officers carrying out staff work. The staff were also unpopular with junior officers: this was a functional, not a class dispute.

British military authorities operated a strict disciplinary regime. During the war 300,000 soldiers were court-martialled, mostly for trivial offences, especially drunkenness. There were 3080 men sentenced to death but only 346 were executed. Those who faced the firing squad had, mostly, been found guilty of desertion while on active service. Half of those executed had committed a serious offence for at least a second time. It is likely that some of the executed men were suffering from shell-shock (see page 210).

KEY TERM

Tommies The nickname for British soldiers in the First World War.

The naval experience

While 84 per cent of all servicemen were troops, over 500,000 men served in the Royal Navy. The navy lost one in sixteen of its officers and men, 43,244 in all. While naval engagements were few and far between, stress was constant for the blockade enforcers – as it was for merchant seamen – who spent long spells at sea in conditions of acute discomfort. Boredom was a problem for those at Scapa Flow.

The airmen's experience

Initially airmen seemed to be participating in an older kind of war, one marked by individual heroism and gallantry. But fatalities among British air crews were exceptionally high: 14,166 men died, 8000 of these in training accidents.

The female experience

Fighting remained an almost entirely male activity. It was with reluctance that the service ministries sanctioned the use of female personnel. Nevertheless, in 1917 volunteer bodies were consolidated into the Women's Auxiliary Army Corp (WAAC) followed by the Women's Royal Naval Service (WRNS) and later the Women's Royal Air Force (WRAF); in total over 100,000 women. Serving as typists, drivers, telephonists, clerks and cooks, they released more men for combatant duty. A further 40,000 women worked as nurses or female orderlies in Britain and France.

The purpose of the war

The dominant image of the First World War has usually been one of futile carnage, an image heavily dependent on:

- a few poets, such as Wilfred Owen
- a number of anti-war novels, especially G.E. Remarque's *All Quiet On The Western Front* (1928)
- the view of the political left, which sought to condemn the conflict as a capitalist struggle.

But most contemporaries did not view the war this way. The war inspired a huge literary outpouring, particularly of poetry. There have been 2225 poets, whose works were published between 1914–18, identified. Very few expressed sentiments similar to those of Owen. Instead, most celebrated heroism and sacrifice. Most combatants believed the war had a purpose, saving Britain from German domination. The Victory medal, issued to all those who had served, put it simply: 'For Civilisation'.

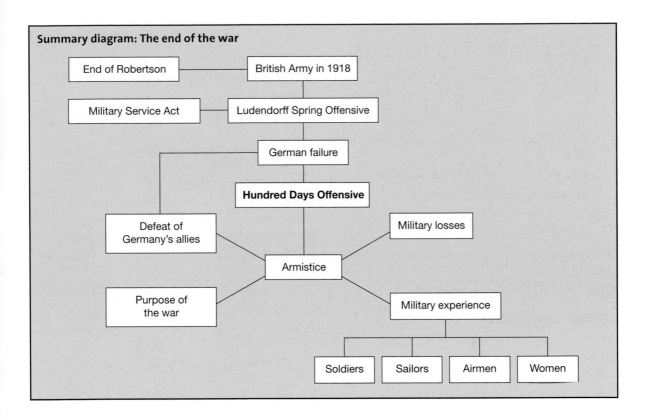

Summary diagram: The end of the war

- End of Robertson — British Army in 1918
- Military Service Act — Ludendorff Spring Offensive
- German failure
- **Hundred Days Offensive**
- Defeat of Germany's allies
- Military losses
- Armistice
- Purpose of the war
- Military experience
  - Soldiers
  - Sailors
  - Airmen
  - Women

Chapter summary

In 1914 Kitchener set about raising a large army. The BEF fought effectively in 1914–15 on the Western Front but the Gallipoli campaign failed to knock Turkey out of the war. The Royal Navy ensured that the German fleet rarely left port. U-boats posed more of a problem but, fearing war with the USA, Germany abandoned its unrestricted U-boat campaign in 1915. Lloyd George, as minister of munitions, greatly increased Britain's output of war materials. Conscription was introduced in 1916.

While failing to defeat the German fleet at the Battle of Jutland in 1916, the navy retained control of the sea. The BEF, now led by Haig, suffered terrible losses on the Somme. In December 1916 Lloyd George replaced Asquith as prime minister. Germany's reintroduction of unrestricted submarine war in 1917 brought the USA into the war. Haig's hope of defeating the Germans at Passchendaele failed. In 1918, having defeated Russia, German troops launched a major offensive, threatening to capture Paris and the Channel ports. But the allies clung on and in July went on the attack. Haig's Hundred Days Offensive was important in forcing Germany to accept peace in November 1918.

Refresher questions

Use these questions to remind yourself of the key material covered in the chapter.

1 How well prepared was the British Army in 1914?

2 Why did so many men volunteer to fight in 1914–15?

3 How well did the BEF fight in France in 1914–15?

4 Why did the Gallipoli campaign fail?

5 To what extent was Haig responsible for the Somme failure?

6 Was the Battle of Jutland a British victory or a British defeat?

7 Why did Lloyd George replace Asquith as prime minister?

8 Was Haig unlucky at Passchendaele?

9 Why did the Ludendorff Spring Offensive initially succeed but ultimately fail?

10 Why was the Hundred Days Offensive so successful?

11 Did British soldiers share a common experience?

 Question practice

ESSAY QUESTIONS

1 To what extent were British soldiers badly led on the Western Front in the years 1914–18?

2 To what extent was the British Army transformed in the years 1914–18?

3 To what extent did aerial warfare affect the outcome of the First World War?

4 How far do you agree that the Royal Navy was successful in the years 1914–18?

SOURCE ANALYSIS QUESTION

1 Assess the value of Source 1 for revealing the nature of the First World War and the attitude of officers to the conflict. Explain your answer, using the source, the information given about its origin and your own knowledge about the historical context.

SOURCE 1

From an account by Lieutenant Edwin Campion Vaughan of 8/Royal Warwicks advancing on a German pillbox (nicknamed Springfield) on 27 August 1917 in the battle known as Passchendaele. Quoted in Richard Holmes, *Tommy: The British Soldier on the Western Front 1914–1918*, Harper Perennial, 2005, pp. 61–2.

Up the road we staggered, shells bursting around us. A man stopped dead in front of me, and exasperated I cursed him and butted him with my knee. Very gently he said 'I'm blind, sir', and turned to show me his eyes and nose torn away by a piece of shell. 'Oh, God! I'm sorry, sonny', I said … Around us were numerous dead, and in the shell-holes where they had crawled for safety were wounded men. Many others, too weak to move, were lying where they had fallen and cheered us faintly as we passed: 'Go on boys! Give 'em hell!' Several wounded men of the 8th Worcesters and 9th Warwicks jumped out of their shell-holes and joined us. A tank had churned its way slowly round and opened fire; a moment later I looked and nothing remained of it but a heap of crumpled iron: it had been hit by a large shell. It was now almost dark and there was no firing from the enemy; ploughing across the final stretch of mud, I saw grenades bursting around the pillbox and a party of British rushed in from the other side. As we all closed in, the Boche [German] garrison ran out with their hands up … We sent the 16 prisoners back but they had only gone a hundred yards when a German machine-gun mowed them down.

CHAPTER 6

The impact of the First World War on Britain

The First World War broke the empires of Germany, Russia, Austria-Hungary and Turkey, triggered the Russian Revolution and paved the way for the Second World War. It thus shaped the twentieth-century world. It also helped to shape Britain's political, economic and social future. This chapter will consider the war's impact on Britain by examining the following themes:

★ The political impact

★ The impact of the media and propaganda

★ The economic impact

★ The social impact

The key debate on *page 211* of this chapter asks the question: To what extent did the British Army contribute to Allied victory?

Key dates

1914		Defence of the Realm Act
1915	May	Lloyd George became minister of munitions
	July	Munitions of War Act
	Sept.	McKenna war budget

1916		Lloyd George became prime minister
1917	May	Strikes
1918	July	Representation of the People Act

1 The political impact

▶ *What were the main political results of the war?*

In August 1914 Parliament enacted the Defence of the Realm Act (DORA). This gave the government sweeping power to rule by decree. Its provisions were progressively extended to cover press censorship, requisitioning, direction of the munitions industry, control of the sale of alcohol and food regulations. Piecemeal, the state acquired the right to intervene in most aspects of daily life. Many Liberals had an ideological aversion to government intervention. As the war wore on, they had constantly to choose between betraying their principles and damaging the war effort.

David Lloyd George

1863	Born in Manchester
1864	Moved to Llanystumdwy in Wales
1890	Elected as a Liberal MP
1899–1902	Gained fame by his opposition to the Boer War
1905	Became president of the Board of Trade
1908	Became chancellor of the exchequer: responsible for introducing old-age pensions
1915	Became minister of munitions
1916	Became secretary of state for war in June and prime minister in December
1918	Won the December general election
1922	Resigned as prime minister
1945	Died

Lloyd George had many critics at the time and has had many since. The economist J.M. Keynes portrayed him as being without principles and 'rooted in nothing'. He is often depicted as being devious, unscrupulous and delighting in improvisation, so much so that for him the means justified themselves almost irrespective of the ends. He cared nothing for conventional rules, neither those economic rules of free enterprise to which his Liberal colleagues attached so much importance nor rules of personal behaviour. He left office flagrantly richer than he entered it and, as prime minister, lived openly with his mistress. His reputation as a womaniser led to his being nicknamed 'the Goat'.

Lloyd George also had and still has his supporters. Some regard him as the most inspired and creative British statesman of the twentieth century. Historian A.J.P. Taylor thought him, 'The greatest ruler of Britain since Oliver Cromwell.' It is certainly possible that, without Lloyd George, Britain might have lost the war.

Asquith's failings

Asquith, a competent peacetime prime minister, was a far less successful war leader. He is sometimes attacked for doing too little. However, far from being a doctrinaire liberal, he was prime minister when most of Britain's traditional liberal 'freedoms' were suspended. Perhaps his main failings were:

- his reluctance to interfere in military matters, even when it was clear that many army leaders were incompetent
- not ensuring a sense of urgency in many departments of government.

In May 1915, Asquith tried to counter growing criticism by bringing leading Conservatives – Bonar Law, Lansdowne, Balfour, Carson and Curzon – together with the Labour leader, Henderson, into the cabinet. His most important move, however, was the appointment of Lloyd George as minister of munitions (see page 154). Lloyd George's vigour and ability to get things done contrasted sharply with Asquith's apparent lethargy.

Lloyd George as prime minister

In December 1916, Lloyd George replaced Asquith as prime minister (see page 166). According to historian K.O. Morgan, 'Lloyd George's war premiership was almost without parallel in British history. No previous Prime Minister had ever exercised power in so sweeping and dominating a manner.'

SOURCE A

From Lloyd George's *War Memoirs*, Oldhams Press, 1938, p. 602.

There are certain indispensable qualities essential to the Chief Minister of the Crown in a great war … Such a minister must have courage, composure and judgement. All this Mr. Asquith possessed in a superlative degree … But a war minister must also have vision, imagination and initiative – he must show untiring assiduity, must exercise constant oversight and supervision of every sphere of war activity, must possess driving force to energise this activity, must be in continuous consultation with experts, official and unofficial, as to the best means of utilising the resources of the country in conjunction with the Allies for the achievement of victory. If to this can be added a flair for conducting a great fight, then you have an ideal War Minister.

> According to Source A, what qualities did Lloyd George imply that he had as prime minister?

Few Conservatives, on whom he was dependent, trusted him, but most recognised his talent.

From the start, Lloyd George was a more dynamic leader than Asquith:

- He set up a small war cabinet, which took all the main decisions (see page 166).
- He often relied more on unofficial advisers than on cabinet members.
- He appointed men from outside Parliament to head important ministries.
- More government controls than ever were introduced (see pages 201–4). Most of the organisations he created were replicated at the start of the Second World War. As press magnate Lord Beaverbrook observed, 'There were no signposts to guide Lloyd George.'

Lloyd George's advent to power – heralded by new departments of state, new men and new methods of control – gave a boost to the nation's morale. Nevertheless, his leadership was far from perfect:

- He was a poor administrator and delegator.
- It is easy to exaggerate the changes brought about by the new regime.
- Not all his new ministries operated effectively.

Most of Lloyd George's acts sprang from no particular doctrine; they were the response to the challenge of events. He has also been blamed for the decline of the Liberal Party, but in his defence, his paramount aim was to win the war, not to preserve the Liberal Party.

Liberal decline

Arguably, the Liberal Party was in trouble before 1914:

- It was divided. The radical wing favoured state action to bring about social reform. The traditional wing wanted to keep government intervention to a minimum.

- The growing trade union movement preferred to fund Labour rather than the Liberals.
- The Liberals failed to deal effectively with serious problems before 1914 – including the potential civil war in Ireland, the suffragette campaign and industrial unrest – leaving Britain, according to historian George Dangerfield, on the verge of anarchy.

However, none of this proves that the Liberal Party was in terminal decline in 1914:

- Its policies attracted support from workers.
- The Labour Party was seriously divided prior to 1914.
- Dangerfield's claims are not generally accepted.

Nevertheless, the First World War seriously harmed the Liberal Party. Its prestige was damaged by its (perceived) fumbling conduct of the first years of the war. Then came the split between Lloyd George and Asquith. Asquith, who continued to be Liberal leader, was unable to forgive Lloyd George for his 'betrayal'. The seriousness of Liberal divisions was demonstrated during the Maurice debate in May 1918, a Parliamentary debate about whether Lloyd George had lied to Parliament about British Expeditionary Force (BEF) numbers. Ninety-eight Liberal MPs voted against him, 71 voted for him and 85 abstained.

The rise of Labour

During the war the Labour Party extended its influence. The war gave some of its members cabinet experience and at local level working-class representatives were co-opted on to a variety of public bodies. Although deeply divided over the war, common grievances and shared ideals held the Labour movement together. Trade union expansion (see page 200) swelled Labour's coffers, making an extension of its organisation at constituency level possible. Labour did well in a series of by-elections in 1917–18. The extension of the franchise (see below) seemed certain to further help Labour's cause.

The Representation of the People Act 1918

In 1914 Britain had the most restrictive franchise of any European state except Hungary. Many working-class men and all women did not have the vote. The Representation of the People Act, passed in July 1918, improved matters:

- The right to vote was given to all males at the age of 21.
- Women householders were given the right to vote at the age of 30. MPs feared that if women had electoral equality, female voters would outnumber male voters.

The act added more voters to the voting register than all previous parliamentary reform acts put together. The war thus smoothed the way for democracy, 'one of the few things to be said in its favour', according to A.J.P. Taylor.

The December 1918 election

On 14 December 1918, the first general election since 1910 took place. The new voters – six million women and two million extra men – faced a complicated situation. Lloyd George was determined to continue the wartime coalition. This meant that in many constituencies there were two Liberal candidates, a Lloyd George coalition Liberal and an Asquith Liberal. The coalition won easily, largely because of Lloyd George's popularity as the man who had led Britain to victory and his promises to create a 'fit country for heroes to live in'. His coalition won 478 seats, made up of 335 Conservatives, 133 coalition Liberals and ten coalition Labour and other supporters. The opposition consisted of 63 Labour MPs, 28 Asquith Liberals and 48 Conservatives who refused to support the coalition. Seventy-three Sinn Féin MPs did not take their seats at Westminster (see page 192).

The election result was a disaster for Asquith's Liberals. Labour, which secured over a fifth of the vote, became the main opposition party. But the overwhelming victor was the Conservative Party. Between 1918 and 1939, there were only three years (1924 and 1929–31) when the Conservatives were not in government.

Ireland and the First World War

In 1914 Ireland seemed on the verge of civil war. There were two private armies: the Ulster Volunteers, formed to resist the Third Irish Home Rule Bill, and the Nationalist Volunteers, formed to defend it. In August 1914 Home Rule was postponed until the end of the war. Most Irish people accepted this and Irish Nationalist leader John Redmond placed his men at the disposal of the government. The Ulster Volunteers were, of course, even more willing to become part of the British Army. Not all Irish nationalists were happy about Redmond's action, however, and southern Irish enthusiasm for the war soon dissipated. Less than eleven per cent of eligible Irish males enlisted up to December 1915. The British government, anxious not to arouse unrest, ensured that the Military Service Acts of 1916 (page 159) did not apply to Ireland.

The Easter Rising 1916

Extreme Irish nationalists saw Britain's preoccupation with the war as a chance to win independence. On Easter Monday 1916 nationalists proclaimed an Irish republic and seized key points in Dublin, hoping that the rest of the country would rise in sympathy. No such uprising took place. After five days of sporadic fighting, which resulted in the loss of 100 British soldiers and 450 Irish rebels, the rebels surrendered. The execution of sixteen rebel leaders caused an outburst of anti-British feeling. More Irish now demanded not just Home Rule but complete independence.

The rise of Sinn Féin

After 1916 many southern Irish turned away from the Irish Nationalists, supporting instead the more extreme Sinn Féin Party, which won four by-elections in 1917. The emergence of republican nationalism reduced the flow of southern Irish volunteers to the British Army to a trickle: only 14,000 in 1917. Many Britons fumed at the privileges accorded to Irish 'slackers'. But no effort was made to enforce conscription in Ireland because it would have tied down more British soldiers than it would have raised. By 1918, much of Ireland had effectively seceded from the UK. The war, which had initially seemed to promise a more amicable relationship between Ireland and the rest of Britain, instead drove the two apart. Southern Ireland was finally granted independence in 1921.

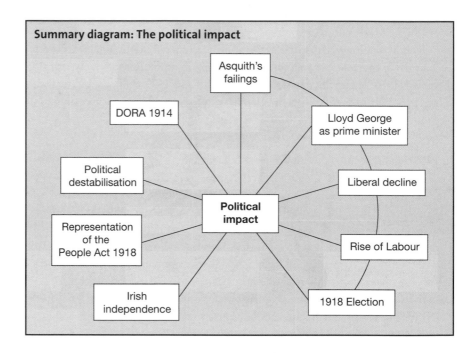

Summary diagram: The political impact

2 The impact of the media and propaganda

▶ *To what extent did the government control the press?*

From the start of the war, the government was concerned about military secrecy, using DORA to censor all cables and foreign correspondence. As well as regulating the flow of information, it was involved in a range of attempts to shape opinion and maintain the commitment of the British public to the war.

Newspaper censorship

In 1914 the government was concerned that newspapers might divulge information which might be of use to the enemy. Therefore:

- Any paper publishing unauthorised news, or speculating about future strategy, ran the risk of prosecution.
- No war correspondent followed the army to France in 1914. In 1915, six correspondents were invited to General Head Quarters (GHQ) 'for a limited period'. They remained in this privileged position for the rest of the war.
- A press bureau was established. This distributed statements from GHQ and from government departments, provided advice about the publication of other news, and could recommend prosecutions if it thought that DORA regulations had been infringed.

In practice, the press largely censored itself. Northcliffe, for example, did not allow his papers – the *Daily Mail* and *The Times* – to criticise the Gallipoli campaign, however much he fumed in private. Northcliffe's papers, like the press generally, took a patriotic line. Thus, the **D-Notice system**, which was introduced to warn newspapers off 'sensitive' topics, was rarely employed. While a few papers were prosecuted for breaches of security, none was prosecuted for expressing unwelcome opinions. Despite the limitations on their freedom, newspapers provided a vital service.

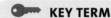

KEY TERM

D-Notice system
Instructions sent by the government to newspapers, ordering them not to publish certain information. D is short for defence.

Propaganda

It has been claimed that gullible Britons were manipulated into supporting the war by government propaganda. It is certainly true that the Parliamentary Recruiting Committee (PRC), which drew together MPs from all parties, worked tirelessly to get across its message, sending out 50 million posters and other publications as well as hosting countless rallies. This must have had some effect. But given that the first dramatic surge in recruiting took place before the PRC was established, it is likely that it was preaching to the converted.

The government's first direct initiative on the propaganda front was taken in September 1914 when it established a bureau at Wellington House in London. But Wellington House directed its propaganda almost entirely at opinion in neutral countries, especially the USA, and not at Britons.

In February 1917, a Department of Information was set up. It became a full ministry, under Lord Beaverbrook, proprietor of the *Daily Express*, a year later. The department/ministry made use of a wide variety of populist devices, including pamphlets, posters and films. Over 700 films were made for propaganda purposes. However, it too was concerned more with international than home opinion.

Worried by what it saw as flagging commitment at home, the government established a National War Aims Committee in 1917. This body issued propaganda literature, printed a stream of posters (on such issues as the need for food economy) and organised speakers to address public meetings.

The effectiveness of government propaganda

It is a moot point how effective official propaganda was in generating support for the war. In some respects it may have been a self-defeating activity. Many saw it as being somehow un-British. Arguably, German behaviour constituted the most effective propaganda of all. The invasion of Belgium, the savage treatment of some of its people and the naval bombardment of towns on the east coast of England created intense anger in 1914. Thereafter, whenever it seemed enthusiasm for the war was flagging, the German army, navy or government did something sufficiently barbarous – such as the sinking of the *Lusitania* or the Zeppelin raids on civilian targets – to confirm Britons in the belief that they were engaged in a righteous cause.

SOURCE B

? What is the purpose of the poster in Source B?

A home front poster from about 1915.

Non-government propaganda

Much of the wartime propaganda was generated by private individuals, firms and agencies rather than by the government:

- Journalists, academics and writers churned out anti-German material.
- A variety of groups and associations campaigned for British victory.
- British film-makers produced some 250 pro-British war films between 1915 and 1918. Few of these were directly inspired by government departments.

It is hard to gauge the effectiveness of propaganda. However, there seems little doubt that most Britons, from 1914 to 1918, were solidly patriotic and committed to victory.

Opposition to the war

There were a number of organisations that opposed the war and campaigned for peace. However, pacifists – a word used for the first time – were small in number and far from united.

Socialist opposition

In 1914, the British Socialist Party was the only political party to call for an immediate end to hostilities. But by 1917 the party had only 6435 members. Socialist 'Stop-the-War' candidates performed poorly in by-elections. While the Labour Party supported the war effort, some of its members opposed the war, mainly because they thought it was being fought in pursuit of capitalist interests.

Other anti-war groups

- Most Quakers opposed the war, often providing support to peace organisations.
- The Union of Democratic Control supported the securing of peace by negotiation.
- The No-Conscription Fellowship was pledged to resist all war service. Drawing support from socialists, the Quakers and radical intelligentsia, it never had more than 5500 members.

Conscientious objectors

Britain and the USA were the only combatant nations that recognised the existence of conscientious objectors during the war. Lloyd George had little sympathy for objectors; 'I will make their path as hard as I can', he declared. Those who objected to military service (amounting to only 0.33 per cent of the men in the armed services) were allowed to state their case before tribunals. Over 80 per cent were given some form of exemption. Ninety per cent of those whose claims for exemption were rejected, accepted an alternative form of national service, often undertaking ambulance work on the Western Front. There were 1300 'absolutists' who refused all compulsory service. These men were drafted into military units and sentenced to imprisonment by court martial when they refused to obey an officer's order. They received harsh treatment; ten died as a result of the experience.

The threat of class war

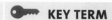
'Troublemakers' within the industrial working class were more a government concern than pacifists. The industrial truce established in 1914 (see below) worked reasonably effectively. However, there were signs in 1917–18 that the truce was breaking down. Left-wing activism, led by militant **shop stewards**, was growing stronger and it seemed that working men's economic grievances might become political. Events in Russia, where workers overthrew the tsar and went on to create a Bolshevik government, revived faith in the notion of an international brotherhood of the working class.

Yet industrial unrest did not translate into serious political action. Glasgow experienced more strikes than most British cities. But even here militant shop stewards suspended industrial action during the 1918 Ludendorff Spring Offensive (see pages 177–8). Industrial disputes died down and productivity soared as people, sacrificing their Easter holidays, worked flat out to replace lost material.

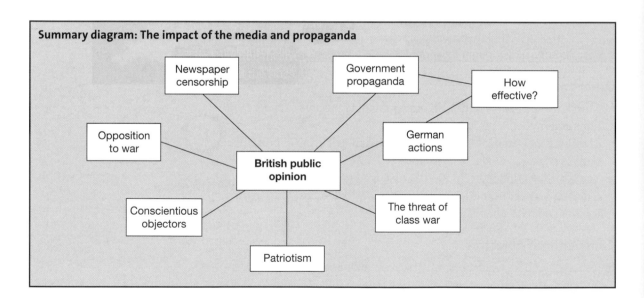

Summary diagram: The impact of the media and propaganda

3 The economic impact

> ▶ *What were the main economic effects of the war?*

The war demonstrated the strength and flexibility of Britain's economy. In spite of millions of men being mobilised for the armed forces, industrial output hardly fell and factories produced huge quantities of war materials.

The immediate economic effects

In August 1914 the Liberal government, although still imbued with the philosophy of **laissez-faire**, took some economic actions:

- Merchant ships were requisitioned for the transport of armed forces.
- Railways were taken over by the government.

On 24 August, trade unions declared an industrial truce for the duration of the war. Despite the government's slogan, 'Business as Usual', the war brought a substantial degree of economic dislocation. While some industries boomed, others saw an increase in unemployment. However, the surge of men into the army and the demand for military supplies led to an improvement in job prospects in late 1914.

The Treasury Agreement

The most urgent problem in munitions factories was 'dilution'. Unskilled workers and women had to be brought in if output was to expand. However, skilled workers refused to 'dilute' or relax their traditional standards. The government, fearing industrial strife, was reluctant to use its compulsory powers under DORA. In March 1915 Lloyd George persuaded engineering union leaders to accept 'dilution' in return for three promises:

- Traditional practices would be restored at the end of the war.
- Profits in the munitions industry would be restricted.
- Unions were to share in the direction of industry through local joint committees.

The Treasury Agreement established Lloyd George's claim to be the man who could enlist 'the people' for the war effort.

Munitions production

Lloyd George became the first minister of munitions in May 1915. His task was to increase the production of munitions (see page 154). The Munitions of War Act, passed in July 1915, gave the Munitions' Ministry the power to declare any essential plant a 'controlled establishment' where 'dilution' of jobs could be introduced and where restrictive practices were suspended, strikes banned, fines could be levied for absenteeism, and workers could only move jobs if they

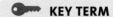

KEY TERM

Laissez-faire The principle that governments should not interfere in social and economic matters.

received 'leaving certificates' from their employers. While trade unions were unhappy with the regulations, Lloyd George won them over by guaranteeing reasonable minimum wages and by favouring firms that used union labour.

Lloyd George contracted out work so that firms could, with appropriate guidance, adapt their plant to munitions production. There were soon 20,000 'controlled establishments' and a host of new state-owned munitions enterprises.

The Ministry of Munitions was, as Lloyd George recognised, 'from first to last a businessmen's organisation'. Staffed by businessmen, it handled other businessmen – who ran the munitions effort at a local level – gently. Manufacturers were glad to accept the system of 'costing' which gave them the costs of production plus 'a reasonable profit'. Usually the costs were those of the least efficient firm. Thus, many businesses were well rewarded.

In a desperate haste to boost production, Lloyd George took some dangerous shortcuts. It needed his successors, Edwin Montagu, Christopher Addison and Winston Churchill, to impose method on the ministry's operations. But under Lloyd George's inspiration, the Ministry of Munitions ensured the massive production of weaponry that eventually helped to win the war. By 1918 the ministry employed a headquarters staff of 25,000 and had over 3 million workers under its direction.

Women's economic role

In 1914 suffragette groups suspended their campaign for women's right to vote, demanding instead that they be allowed to serve the country by undertaking work that would release men for military duty. Trade union opposition initially made this difficult. Unions feared that female labour would reduce wages for men. But as the labour shortage intensified and the principle of dilution was accepted, women began to find work. The number of females employed in munitions production, where women had long been engaged in shell-filling, rose from 82,859 in July 1914 to 947,000 by November 1918. There were 200,000 women in government departments and 500,000 took over clerical work in private offices, while the number of females in the transport sector rose from 18,200 to 117,200.

It would be wrong to overstate the extent of the changes in women's roles:

- The total number of women doing waged work did not increase dramatically. In 1914, 5.9 million women were employed, and in 1918, 7.3 million, an increase of 22.5 per cent. Many of those taking up work in munitions transferred from other employment, a quarter coming from domestic service. Munitions work offered better remuneration.
- By 1918 five-sixths of women were still doing what was considered to be 'women's work'. While the number of domestic servants declined by 400,000, most working women were still employed as domestic servants.

SOURCE C

A poster produced in Britain in 1918.

> What does the poster in Source C show about the British economy in 1918?

- The increase in women's employment was not built on secure foundations. By 1917 one woman in every three in employment had replaced a male worker. Under industrial agreements, these jobs would revert to men once the war was over. Work in munitions would also cease when the war ended.
- Women still earned substantially less than men doing the same work.

Industrial unrest 1915–16

The Treasury Agreement and the Munitions of War Act did not end industrial action. Many workers believed that trade union leaders had caved in too easily to patriotic blackmail. Local shop stewards took up their grievances, leading resistance to:

- the infringements of customary trade union rights
- employers' high profits which were not shared with workers
- the employment of female workers.

There was unrest in Clydeside throughout 1915. In 1916, militant shop stewards feared that conscription would be extended to industrial life or even used as an instrument of industrial discipline, with men who went on strike being conscripted into the army. These fears seemed to be confirmed when skilled engineers who thought that they had been guaranteed exemption from military service found themselves called up. Strikes in Sheffield and Barrow followed. The government capitulated, accepting the Trade Cards Agreement which allowed the main engineering union to decide which of its members could be exempted from military service.

The May strikes 1917

In early 1917 there was a wave of strikes. Workers were angry at the government's decision to extend 'dilution' to private work and at its repudiation of Asquith's Trade Cards Agreement. By the end of May, trouble had led to the loss of 1.5 million working days. The government was conciliatory:

- It fixed the price of certain essential foodstuffs.
- It offered skilled men in the industrial workforce a 12.5 per cent war bonus, which was later extended to semi-skilled and unskilled workers.
- Leaving certificates (see page 198) came to an end in August 1917.

In July 1917 Lloyd George made a significant gesture towards removing workers' discontentment by turning the Reconstruction Committee into a ministry, holding out to workers the prospect of extensive social reforms as a reward for wartime co-operation. The government measures ensured that the protests petered out.

The war and the unions

The war had a positive effect on the trade union movement:

- The number of workers affiliated to the Trades Union Congress (TUC) grew from 4.1 million in 1914 to 7.8 million by 1918.
- Trade unions were seen as necessary partners in the war effort.
- The creation of the Ministry of Labour and promises of social reform were concessions to the power of organised workers.
- Unions enhanced their reputation with their responsible attitude. The number of working days lost in strikes during the war averaged a quarter of those lost before the war.

War socialism

In 1916 there were demands for greater government control of the economy. For those Liberals who put their faith in free enterprise, the implications were alarming. Lloyd George had no such qualms. After coming to power, he created twelve new ministries: Blockade, Reconstruction, Information, Munitions, Shipping, Food Control, National Service, Labour, Pensions, Air, Health and Transport. The new ministries were headed by new men, mostly businessmen with no political background. They enlisted the co-operation of producers and owners, who largely ran what some called **war socialism**.

Perhaps Lloyd George has been given too much praise for his role in expanding the wartime government:

- Several of the new state agencies were in the pipeline prior to his becoming prime minister.
- The new ministries, running side by side with old departments, sometimes created more confusion than they resolved.

The allocation of manpower

In August 1917, General Auckland Geddes, formerly director of recruiting, became minister of national service. At long last, the properly co-ordinated use of mobilised manpower began, a fact underlined by the transfer of control of recruiting from the War Office to the new ministry in November 1917. From this point on, the army's manpower demands were accorded a lower priority than those of shipbuilding, tank and aircraft production. However, not until mid-1918 did Geddes receive powers to allocate labour and to monitor its distribution. Only at the end of the war, therefore, did the government have a coherent manpower policy.

Merchant shipping

Requisitioning for naval and military purposes took nearly a quarter of British merchant shipping out of ordinary service in 1915. Given the demands on men and materials from the Admiralty and the Ministry of Munitions, merchant shipbuilding sank to a third of its pre-war figure. The lack of merchant ships became even more serious with unrestricted German submarine warfare in 1917.

The Ministry of Shipping, led by Glaswegian ship-owner Joseph Maclay:

- extended requisitioning to cover all ocean-going mercantile ships; the owners thus became virtually agents of the state, working at a limited rate of profit and on fixed freight charges
- reorganised the ports, cutting delays in unloading and reloading cargo

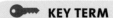 **KEY TERM**

War socialism
The government's wartime control of many aspects of British economic and social life.

- began a vast merchant shipbuilding programme which required many skilled workers to be brought back from the front. After March 1917 the gross tonnage of ships launched each month doubled. By June 1917, new ships overtook the tonnage lost in U-boat attacks.

The government supplemented these efforts by taking responsibility for Britain's imports. In 1918 it managed to reduce the volume of imports by 5 million tons, thanks largely to Lord Milner (see page 178). His Priority Committee:

- adjudicated between claims on materials being made by the armed services and by key civilian industries
- graded imported goods according to their national importance.

The British government was thus more in control over the general economic situation, particularly Britain's requirements from abroad.

The food situation

Shipping and food were related problems. In 1914, 60 per cent of food consumed in Britain was imported. In 1914–15 there were no real shortages but food prices rose. By mid-1916, they were on average 59 per cent above the level of July 1914, a fact resented by many working-class families. In late 1916 supplies of food began to dwindle and long queues formed outside shops.

In December 1916, Lloyd George set up a food agency, with Lord Lee as its director. This began the process whereby food production became subject to national planning:

- Landowners were directed to use their land more efficiently. If not, they could be dispossessed and their land worked by others.
- In July 1917 skilled agricultural labourers were exempted from conscription.
- The Corn Production Act, passed in August 1917, was designed to make Britain more self-sufficient in agricultural products. Under state direction 3 million acres (1.2 million hectares) of pasture and parkland were converted to cereal production.

By 1918, despite a shortage of fertilisers, the wheat crop was 65 per cent higher than the pre-war average, while allotments became a useful source of vegetables.

Rationing

In early 1918 there was a sudden panic about food distribution, even though the situation was much better than it had been in 1917. The U-boat menace was no longer so serious and the 1917 wheat harvest was the best of the century. To allay alarm, the new Food Control Ministry introduced rationing. Individuals who registered with a particular shop received coupons for particular foodstuffs. The system, geared to human needs rather than capacity to pay, was designed to help the poor. While there was no rationing of wheat, the price of bread was kept stable by government subsidy.

By the end of the war, 85 per cent of all food consumed by the civilian population was being bought and sold through government agencies that fixed prices and profit margins for each stage of distribution. This eliminated shortages and discontent. In 1917–18 the calorific content of the average diet dropped by three per cent, a limited fall compared with the experience of most Europeans.

Control of alcohol

Given the view that drunkenness was a major cause of absenteeism and as such an impediment to the war effort, a government campaign against excessive drinking was launched. King George V was persuaded to take the King's Pledge of total abstention of alcohol for the duration of war. Few followed his example, certainly not Lloyd George or Asquith.

In 1915, the government set up the Central Liquor Control Board, which:

- reduced pub opening hours, usually from noon to 2.30p.m. and from 6.30p.m. to 9.30p.m.
- banned the sale of alcohol to those aged under eighteen
- took steps to weaken beer
- took responsibility for drinking habits in the area around the great munitions centre at Gretna, acquiring 119 licensed premises and purchasing breweries.

These measures, while probably having little effect on industrial production, were beneficial in other ways:

- Beer consumption had halved by 1918.
- Consumption of spirits, mainly as a result of heavy increases in duty, declined from 35 million gallons (159 million litres) in 1915 to 15 million gallons (68 million litres) in 1918.
- England and Wales averaged 3388 convictions a week for drunkenness in 1914. In 1918 there were just 449.
- The nation's health improved.

Other government initiatives

- The government fixed the prices of many commodities, not just food, in an attempt to prevent speculation and profiteering and to stabilise the cost of living.
- Coalmines were **nationalised** for the duration of the war.
- The Ministry of Munitions pioneered a range of reforms, aimed at improving working conditions and thereby increasing workers' productivity.
- Cocoa magnate Seebohm Rowntree (see page 130), who headed the Health of Munitions Workers' Committee, demonstrated that the reduction of excessive factory hours actually increased output, mainly by reducing absenteeism and accidents.
- Model housing was provided for workers in areas like Gretna.

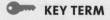 **KEY TERM**

Nationalised Taken over and run by the government.

- Workers canteens proliferated.
- The ministry subsidised the creation of crèches in factories.

Socialism or free enterprise?

While there was far more state control in 1917–18, it was not quite socialism. Most industry was left in private ownership. Those who had run things before 1914 generally continued to do so. For example, Maclay, having requisitioned all merchant ships, then employed the owners as managers. The county committees which directed agriculture were composed of local landowners.

Scientific and technical advances

For two decades before 1914 efforts had been made to improve scientific research at British universities and make its results more widely available to industry. This became even more vital after 1914. In 1916, the government created the Department of Scientific and Industrial Research. Scientists and engineers were recruited in large numbers by the service departments and the Ministry of Munitions, where they assumed responsibility for a host of projects.

The war gave an enormous boost to the automobile and aeronautical industries and to wireless telegraphy, while technological advances created what were in effect a range of new industries geared to the production of such commodities as scientific instruments and ball bearings.

Trade

Given that British industry was geared to producing war materials, Britain lost lucrative markets, especially in Latin America and the Far East, to the USA and Japan. However, it gained other markets at Germany's expense.

Financing the war

Initially, Chancellor of the Exchequer Lloyd George hoped to pay for the war by borrowing. Reginald McKenna, who took charge of the Treasury in May 1915, initially continued Lloyd George's policy. But the government bond, issued in June 1915, brought in only half of the £1000 million that McKenna had hoped to raise. To meet the war's spiralling costs, he introduced a war budget in September 1915:

- Income tax went up from 1s. 2d. to 3s. 6d. in the pound (from 6 to 17.5 per cent) and the exemption limit was lowered, meaning that people on lower incomes had to pay.
- Supertax rates went up.
- An Excess Profits Duty (EPD) of 50 per cent was imposed on any increase in pre-war profits on all war-related industries.
- McKenna imposed duties at 33.33 per cent on some 'luxury' articles, for example cars and watches.

Nevertheless, McKenna still faced a huge deficit. This meant that he and his successors had to further increase taxes. In 1916 the standard rate of income tax went up again, this time to 5s. in the pound and ultimately to 6s. in 1918. The sugar duty was increased and new duties were placed on a range of products. EPD rose to 60 per cent and then 80 per cent in 1917. This tax provided a quarter of the total tax revenue in the war period. Direct taxes were the easiest to increase. Reliance on them was also a matter of social policy. It appeased the working classes by 'soaking the rich' and it did not push up the cost of living as the increase of indirect taxation did.

By 1916 only twenty per cent of national expenditure was being met from taxation. New and higher taxes raised it to 30 per cent in 1917–18. Thus, most war expenditure was met from public borrowing. Treasury officials were not greatly disturbed by this. McKenna laid down the doctrine that there need be no limit on government borrowing so long as taxation was enough to cover the payment of interest on the national debt. This rose during the war from £625 million to £7809 million. Servicing it took nearly half the yield from taxation in the 1920s, against fourteen per cent before the war.

International finance

Government financial policies, which resulted in the printing of a great deal of extra money, coupled with the fact that there were fewer goods available, inevitably led to inflation. By 1919 the pound bought only a third of what it had done in 1914. Britain was able to pay for the rising costs of imports because exports, though much reduced in volume, brought in as much sterling as before the war, thanks to the rise in their prices. Britain's **balance of payments** remained favourable until 1918: positive balances of £200 million in 1915 and £101 million in 1916, an equal balance in 1917 and a negative balance of £107 million in 1918. Britain was wealthy enough to provide loans to its allies. Russia received £585 million, France £434 million, Italy £412 million – a total, including money given to lesser countries and the dominions, of £1825 million.

Britain's main financial problem was with the USA. The war increased Britain's need for supplies from the USA without increasing British exports to the USA. There was therefore a dollar shortage. This was met partly by raising loans on the American market, partly by sales of American securities held by British citizens. While some politicians feared that Britain was becoming dependent on US credit and might end up bankrupting itself, most agreed with Bonar Law that bankruptcy was preferable to defeat. The USA's entry into the war in 1917 meant that Britain no longer had any difficulty raising loans in the USA. By November 1918, Britain had amassed debts to the USA of about £1000 million.

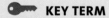 **KEY TERM**

Balance of payments
The difference between a nation's total receipts from foreign countries and its total payment to foreign countries. Most of this money comes from trade.

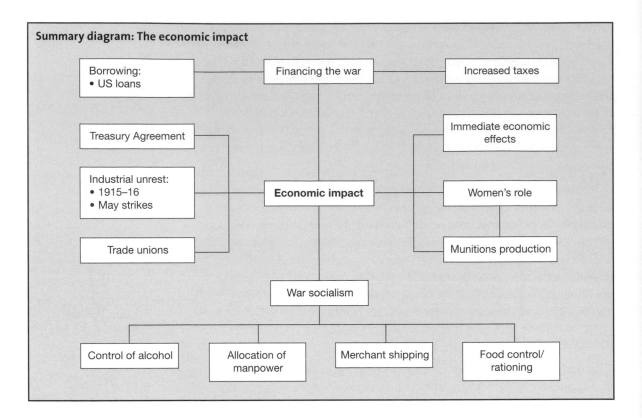

Summary diagram: The economic impact

4 The social impact

▶ *What impact, if any, did the war have on social development?*

Historians continue to debate the effect the war had on social developments. Derek Fraser claims, 'The war quite simply swept away a whole world and created a new one and the Edwardian epoch became a vision of the distant past.' Martin Pugh is more cautious, 'On investigation, many of the trends and innovations attributed to the great war turn out to be not so much the direct product of war as the outcome of long-term developments whose origins lie in the pre-1914 period.'

State involvement in life

By 1918 the state was involved in all aspects of life in a way it had not been in 1914. Civilian life became more regimented and controlled the longer the war went on. During the course of the war, the notion spread that working-class people deserved some rewards for their sacrifices. By 1917 it was taken for granted that the state would play a large role in this process. In response to the May strikes (see page 200), Lloyd George created a Ministry of Reconstruction, headed by Addison. It soon sprouted dozens of committees, which surveyed practically every aspect of British life. Reconstruction, claimed its spokesmen, would not only be a culmination of the earlier quest for national efficiency (see pages 130–1), it would, in Addison's words, 'mould a better world out of the social and economic conditions which have come into being during the war'. Lloyd George and Addison thus raised expectations of a brave new post-war world – expectations that would prove difficult to meet.

Redistribution of wealth

The war encouraged the redistribution of wealth. The high rates of income tax, supertax and death duties introduced during the war were not reduced much afterwards. A rich man paid eight per cent of his income in tax before the war, one-third after it. This helped to fund improvements in welfare.

Women's role in society

Arguably, the war led to a revolution in women's position in society:

- During the war women undertook a variety of jobs previously done by men (see pages 198–9). This may have increased women's self-confidence. It certainly gave some women more economic independence and a legitimate excuse for escaping the confines of domesticity.
- The horizons of many young women opened out after 1914. They were able to smoke, spend money on entertainments and come and go without the protection of chaperones. 'Flappers' wore short dresses, cut their hair and donned lipstick. These developments caused widespread dismay, especially among older women.
- In 1918 women were allowed to vote in parliamentary elections and stand as MPs for the first time.

However, the war's positive effects on women's status may have been exaggerated:

- Women rarely did skilled work during the war and were usually paid much less than men. This did little for gender equality.
- Most women were forced to leave their wartime jobs after 1918.
- The notion that the war revolutionised men's minds about the sort of work women were capable of is probably a deception. Traditional views of a woman's role remained strong.
- If most men continued to think that a woman's place was at home, many women agreed. Indeed, the war may have strengthened the ideology of domesticity. Motherhood was increasingly presented as an honourable state service, akin to soldiering.
- Women would probably have received the vote even if there had been no war. The war simply created the circumstances in which 'Votes for Women' could be granted. Given that the suffragette movement had ended its disruptive campaign in 1914, MPs could give women the vote without being reproached

for giving into violence. The argument that women deserved the vote because of their wartime service was something of a myth. Those who had really helped the national cause – women under 30 who had worked in munitions factories – did not get the vote.

- Few women stood as prospective MPs, just seventeen in 1918. Only Countess Markievicz of Sinn Féin won a seat in 1918, and she refused to take it.
- In the two decades after 1918 there were never more than twenty women MPs, no women directors of large companies, no women judges and virtually no women professors at universities.

Heartache and gender imbalance

The war brought heartache and loneliness for many women. Constant anxiety over the fate of loved ones often culminated in the agony of bereavement. In the longer term women had to endure another of the war's legacies: a worsening of the gender imbalance. Among those aged 20–34, the female surplus rose from 463,000 in 1914 to 773,300 in 1921. Because of the war, one woman in six could look forward to being single.

Life on the home front

Those on active service were often dismayed, when on leave, to discover life at home apparently going on much as usual. While music halls may have lost customers, their place was taken by cinemas; part of the growing Americanisation of popular culture. But many civilians had a drab time. Clothing, shoes and furniture were scarce and often of poor quality. Food and coal sometimes ran short.

Civilian status no longer conferred safety:

- 14,287 merchant seamen and fishermen died as a result of U-boat attacks.
- Civilians in coastal towns faced German naval bombardment.
- Bombing raids, by Zeppelins and planes, killed over 1000 people.
- The workforce employed in the munitions industry ran the risk of injury and death. Some 300 female munitions workers died from **TNT** poisoning or explosions.

KEY TERM

TNT Short for trinitrotoluene, a chemical used as an explosive, which is poisonous.

War and class

People of different social class contributed to the war effort, and were affected by the war, in different ways.

The upper class

Imbued with a strong sense of patriotic duty, public schoolboys rushed to enlist in 1914. All but eight of the 5439 boys who left Winchester School between 1909 and 1915 volunteered. Virtually all received commissions. They paid a price for this. In the armed services, 13.6 per cent of all serving officers were killed compared with 11.7 per cent of other ranks.

Some landed families were hit hard economically, particularly when the death of the head of the household was followed by the death in battle of his heir. The estate was then saddled with two sets of death duties. Finding themselves in straitened circumstances, many landowners sold parts of their estates after 1918, so much so that almost a quarter of Britain's land changed hands as a result of the war.

Businessmen generally did well out of the war. By 1916, average profits in coal, iron, engineering and shipbuilding were a third higher than in 1914. While profits were heavily taxed (see pages 204–5), most businessmen involved in munitions work made money.

The middle class

Middle-class men were more likely to end up in uniform than working-class men. They were more likely to volunteer and more likely to be conscripted. For example, in London only 45 per cent of the former manufacturing workforce served in the armed forces compared with 63 per cent of men in finance and commerce. Many middle-class entrants into the army received commissions. Thus, middle-class status carried with it increased risks of becoming a casualty. Sixteen per cent of London's pre-war banking employees died during the war, compared with only four per cent of its pre-war manufacturing workforce.

As a result of high inflation, middle-class citizens living on fixed incomes were among the war's economic losers. Given that they had to pay higher taxes, many middle-class families saw the value of their earnings decline.

The working class

There were great variations among working-class families and their experiences of the war varied considerably. By February 1916, 28.3 per cent of the industrial workforce was in uniform. However, after 1916, many skilled workers were exempt from conscription while a third of the urban poor were deemed unfit for military combat. To generalise broadly, a working man's chances of surviving the war were least promising if he was unskilled yet possessed good health. But he still stood a better chance than a man with a middle-class occupation.

While many working-class households were hard hit by the rise in prices of food, fuel, alcohol and tobacco, several factors helped to protect living standards:

- The war resulted in the virtual disappearance of unemployment.
- By 1917 real wages had caught up with prices and were running slightly ahead by 1918.
- On average, workers did ten hours of overtime a week. This allowed some workers to accumulate substantial savings.
- The expansion of the female workforce meant that many households drew a double income.

The 'lost generation'

Some 750,000 Britons died in the war. One in three males aged between 19 and 22 in 1914 were killed. After 1918 people talked about the 'lost generation'. Some imagined a cohort of extra-gifted young men who, if they had lived, would somehow have averted the errors made by inter-war governments. **Eugenicists** feared that Britain had lost the cream of its youth while the physically and mentally unfit had survived.

Despite the horrendous fatalities, the 1921 census revealed a 2.4 per cent increase in population since 1914. The reason for this was that the war greatly reduced emigration. Between 1910 and 1914, 300,000 people a year – mainly young men – emigrated to the dominions or the USA. Thus, the net result of the war was to make the loss of men less than it would have been if emigration had continued at its old rate. The lost lives, and the decline in births during the war, were partly compensated by the baby boom of 1920 when the birth rate rose to 25.5 per thousand, just above its pre-war level.

Such statistics offered scant consolation to wives who found themselves widowed and children left fatherless. Something was done to ease material suffering through the payment of war pensions. By 1921, 239,000 allowances were being paid to soldiers' wives and 395,000 to soldiers' children. But for many, the loss of loved ones had a lifelong impact.

While the war was in progress, the process of grieving was eased by the establishment of street shrines which sprang up in all British cities. Civic war memorials and church monuments later played an important part in the rituals of remembrance, as did the war graves in France and Belgium and the national two-minute silence on Armistice Day.

Wounded men

Both during the war and thereafter, Britain had to cope with treating hundreds of thousands of wounded men:

- Some 40,000 men were left blind or partially blind by the war.
- In 1922 some 50,000 men received war pensions on mental health grounds. Most had suffered from a newly designated condition called 'shell-shock', a mental collapse due as much to the stress and horror of trench warfare as to intense artillery bombardment. Today the condition is known as post-traumatic stress disorder. Soldiers exhibited a range of symptoms, the most severe being hysteria, delusion, limb paralysis and loss of speech. Special hospital units were established for shell-shock patients.
- Over 40,000 men lost at least one limb. By 1918 artificial limb quality had improved and generous post-war government grants ensured that development continued.

- The Queen's Hospital at Sidcup, opened in 1917, specialised in facial wounds. Despite advances in surgical procedures, especially the use of skin grafts, there were limits to what could be achieved.

While injuries were initially badges of courage, this heroic status gradually diminished as the war wounded became subsumed into the general disabled population.

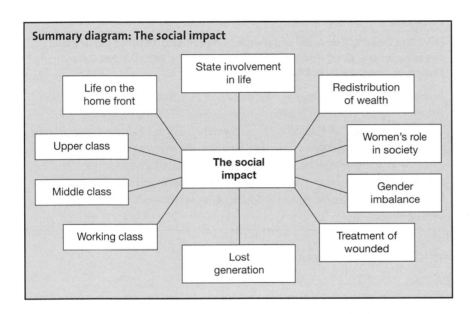

Summary diagram: The social impact

State involvement in life

Life on the home front

Redistribution of wealth

Upper class

Women's role in society

The social impact

Middle class

Gender imbalance

Working class

Treatment of wounded

Lost generation

5 Key debate

▶ *To what extent did the British Army contribute to Allied victory?*

Historians have different views about the British Army in the First World War. Arguably, it was poorly led, performed rather badly, and did not have a decisive effect on the war's outcome.

EXTRACT I

From Kenneth O. Morgan, editor, *The Oxford Popular History of Britain*, Oxford University Press, 1993, p. 583.

For almost four years, the war in France showed little movement. There were occasional British attempts to seize the initiative. Always they ended in huge casualties …. The British offensive at Loos was beaten back in September 1915. More damaging still, in June 1916 a new British advance on the Somme proved a calamitous failure with 60,000 men falling on the first day. British casualties here alone amounted to 420,000. The most terrible of these experiences came at Passchendaele in August–September 1917, when over 300,000 British troops were recorded as dead or wounded … As on other occasions, the class divide that cut off commanding officers from the rank-and-file infantrymen and hindered communication between them was fatal throughout. In effect, the British ceased to be a viable offensive force for the next few months.

But it is also possible to claim that the army fought splendidly and played a crucial role in Allied victory.

EXTRACT 2

From Tim Travers, 'The Army and the Challenge of War 1914–1918', in David Chandler, editor, *The Oxford Illustrated History of the British Army*, Oxford University Press, 1994, p. 240.

In conclusion, and to answer the fundamental question posed earlier: did the British army significantly improve its performance between 1914 and 1918? Yes it did, especially technically, and ultimately it played as large a part as any army in winning the war … In 1914 and 1915, the army still essentially operated in a pre-war mode of thinking and fighting, and changes were those of scale rather than substance. The turning-point came in 1916 despite massive losses during the Somme offensive, as the army began to learn lessons and improve technically.

> ? Which of these two extracts provides the more convincing interpretation?

British Army ineffectiveness?

Arguably:

- The British Army was badly led from start to finish, not just on the Western Front but also at Gallipoli and in the Middle East.
- Haig needlessly sacrificed the lives of hundreds of thousands of soldiers on the Somme and at Passchendaele.
- British forces, over the course of the war, were far smaller than French and Russian forces. France lost twice as many men as Britain. Although it pulled out of the war in 1917, Russia inflicted huge casualties on the enemy, suffering even more losses in the process.
- The British Army was overrun in the Ludendorff Spring Offensive in 1918.
- British military success only came in late 1918 when the German Army was short of men and war materials.
- The prospect of fresh US troops, arriving at the rate of 300,000 a month by August 1918, not the BEF demoralised the Germans.

British Army effectiveness?

Arguably:

- The BEF fought well in 1914–15 on the Western Front.
- A case can be made for Haig. He had little option but to fight a war of attrition. Moreover, the cumulative effects of attrition on Germany were critical. The Somme and Passchendaele thus played their part in fatally

weakening the German Army, which could afford to lose fewer soldiers than the Allies.

- By 1917–18 the BEF had overwhelming superiority in technology and war material. By August 1918, for every shell the Germans fired at the BEF, they received ten or twenty back.
- Haig's Hundred Days Offensive in 1918 won the war.
- By 1918 the BEF bore the brunt of the fighting. On the Western Front in 1918, the BEF captured 188,700 prisoners and 2840 guns. In contrast, the French Army captured 139,000 prisoners and 1880 guns and the Americans captured 43,300 prisoners and 1421 guns.
- By 1918 the British Army was the best in the world:
  - There was co-ordination, helped by wireless telegraphy, of the various military branches: artillery, infantry, tanks, engineers, gas and aircraft.
  - Enormous strides had been made in the use of the creeping barrage and in survey techniques.
  - The BEF was the world's most highly mechanised army.
  - Tactical lessons had been learned. Rather than aiming to capture predetermined objectives, the 1918 offensives took place across a wide front with the centre of attack repeatedly switched from one area to another, preventing German resistance solidifying. The new tactics entailed a departure from earlier centralised battle-plans, masterminded from GHQ. Army commanders, at every level, had to show greater initiative and flexibility as the war became more mobile.

Other British contributions to Allied victory

The BEF was by no means Britain's only contribution to Germany's defeat.

The Royal Navy's role

- It ensured Britain's safety from invasion.
- It transported men and supplies to France.
- It maintained links with the Empire.
- Its blockade gradually throttled the German economy, contributing to the deprivation (of most things but essentially food), which eventually helped to destroy civilian morale.

Britain's economic role

By 1918 the German Army was outgunned by the BEF alone in nearly all areas of munitions. Under Churchill, minister of munitions from June 1917, the volume and variety of weaponry pouring out of factories gave British armies the means to defeat Germany.

Britain's financial role

Britain loaned huge sums of money to its Allies.

Britain's technological role

Churchill viewed the war as an 'engineers' war' in which Allied technology and ingenuity in weapons design was a decisive factor. The Royal Naval Air Service was particularly innovative; its engineers and inventors can claim to have originated tanks and aircraft carriers. Tanks were certainly a useful weapon in 1918, the most striking evidence of Britain's ability to integrate science, technology and tactics with greater success than the Germans. However, technological inventiveness, by itself, could not guarantee victory. The tank is a case in point. While tanks were put to good use in August 1918 at Amiens, subsequently Britain was only able to place 100 or more tanks in the field once more, so prone were the machines to breaking down.

British political leadership

Lloyd George was a magnificent war leader. As minister of munitions, he ensured that Britain began to produce the materials that eventually won the war. As prime minister he kept Britain united and committed to victory.

British morale

British morale, among both soldiers and civilians, remained high. Unlike all the other European armies, British troop morale never crumbled.

The contribution of the British Empire

Dominion troops, as well as mopping up German colonies in their vicinity, fought at Gallipoli and on the Western Front. In 1916 New Zealand adopted conscription, as did Canada in 1918. Although the Australian electorate rejected conscription, 413,000 Australians enlisted; 30 per cent of all eligible males. This was a higher contribution than that made by Canada (27 per cent) but smaller than New Zealand (40 per cent). In total, the dominions provided some 1.3 million men to the Allied cause. Haig thought the dominion troops his finest and, in 1917–18, used them for the BEF's most difficult operations. For this, they paid a high price. Canadians sustained 42,000 casualties in the final four months of the war while Australians and New Zealanders incurred a heavier death rate than Britons.

There were 827,000 Indian troops mobilised during the war. Many fought in the Middle East and in Africa. African troops helped to capture Togoland and took part in fighting in East Africa. By 1918, many Africans, Indians, West Indians and Chinese were participating on the Western Front as members of the labour corps.

The Empire's contribution to the war was not confined to raising troops, however. All parts of the Empire helped the war effort by placing their resources at Britain's disposal. In economic terms, the greatest assistance was rendered by Canada. One-third of the BEF's munitions in 1917–18 were made in Canada.

Chapter summary

The Defence of the Realm Act 1914 gave Parliament sweeping powers. Lloyd George, who replaced Asquith as prime minister in December 1916, was prepared to use the powers at his disposal to win the war. Throughout the war, the government tried to control opinion by censuring newspapers and setting up propaganda agencies. But newspapers generally regulated themselves. While there was some opposition to the war, there were few conscientious objectors and no threat of a class war. The economy produced the war materials which ultimately defeated Germany. The trade unions generally co-operated with the government. By 1918, the government controlled many aspects of economic life, including allocation of manpower, merchant shipping and food distribution. The war was paid for by increasing the national debt. Women's role changed during the war, but many of the changes were reversed after 1918. Britain's contribution to Allied victory was crucially important.

 Refresher questions

Use these questions to remind yourself of the key material covered in this chapter.

1 Why was Lloyd George perceived to be a better war leader than Asquith?

2 What were the main political results of the war?

3 How effective was government propaganda?

4 How strong was opposition to the war?

5 What were the main economic impacts of the war?

6 How significant was women's war work?

7 How successfully did the government deal with trade unions?

8 How successfully did the government tackle food and drink problems?

9 How did Britain pay for the war?

10 What impact did the war have on social development?

11 Which class was hit hardest by the war?

 Question practice

ESSAY QUESTIONS

1 To what extent did Haig's major offensives ensure British success in the First World War from 1914 to 1918?

2 'During the First World War, the British Army's technology improved dramatically.' How far do you agree with this statement?

3 How far were government agencies successful in manipulating public opinion in the years 1914–18?

4 'The creeping barrage, not aerial combat, brought Britain victory on the Western Front.' How far do you agree with this statement?

SOURCE ANALYSIS QUESTION

1 Assess the value of Source 1 for revealing the nature of aerial combat in the First World War and the attitudes of the source to such combat. Explain your answer, using the source, the information given about its origin and your own knowledge about the historical context.

SOURCE 1

This report was published in the *Daily Telegraph* on 3 January 1918. The reporter was based at the War Correspondents' Headquarters in France. Quoted in G. Fuller, editor, *The Telegraph Book of the First World War*, Aurum Press, 2014, pp. 409–11.

Over the snow-bound battle-ground of France, high in the icy sky, beardless boys of Britain have again been proving that they belong to the breed of the unafraid. Christmas week and the New Year have been made glorious by acts of pure courage, outshining the fairest deeds of the lion hearts of the classics …

Take the story of just one youngster of twenty-two as an example … Today to his credit is a list of over thirty enemy planes which he has engaged in mortal combat amongst the outposts of cloudland, and sent hurtling to the ground wrecked and splintered. Three of these were accounted for in one day at the very end of the Old Year. Flying at 17,000ft this boy engaged a two-seater at fairly close range. Both his guns he brought to bear on the enemy, who, attempting to get off went into a right-hand spiral dive. Immediately both right wings broke off, and in two parts the wreckage fell behind our lines. Before ten minutes passed he engaged another similar machine, which after a short burst from the deadly machine-gun, burst into flames, and went down like a misdirected rocket …

I hear that German air officers are complaining of the difficulty they are now experiencing in getting first-class fighting machines. Prisoners say only a small percentage of the newer and improved varieties is to be found in the various flying units.

CHAPTER 7

Conclusion

Between 1790 and 1918 Britain fought a number of major wars, notably the French Revolutionary and Napoleonic Wars, the Crimean War, the Boer War and the First World War. The British experience of warfare in these years resulted in a changing relationship between the state and the people, as various governments at different times attempted to create an effective fighting machine and organise the nation for war. This concluding chapter will consider Britain's changing experience of war from 1790 to 1918 by examining the following issues:

★ Britain's position in the world 1790–1918

★ Changes in organising the military

★ Changing weaponry

★ Changes in the role of the people

★ The situation in 1918

 # Britain's position in the world 1790–1918

▶ *Why was Britain a great world power in the period 1790–1918?*

Throughout the period 1790–1918 Britain was a great world power. Its power rested on its economic strength, its empire, political and social stability, the Royal Navy and the British Army. Despite some criticism, both at the time and from historians since, Britain's armed forces proved themselves very much fit for purpose in the period 1790–1918.

Economic strength

In 1790, despite its defeat in the American War of Independence, Britain was one of Europe's strongest economic and financial powers. Its economic and financial strength was a major factor enabling it to defeat France in the wars between 1793 and 1815. By 1850 Britain had become the world's first urban industrialised economy, accounting for 50 per cent of the world's trade in coal, cotton and iron. Its **gross national product (GNP)** was higher than that of China and Russia combined. The steady expansion of the British economy was achieved with only two per cent of the world's population. (Britain's population grew from 9 million

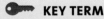 **KEY TERM**

Gross national product (GNP) The total value of all goods and services produced within a country plus the income from investments abroad.

in 1801 to 18 million in 1851 and 36 million by 1901.) Large cities mushroomed. A whole new banking and finance system based in London spread its influence around the world. Britain was both the workshop of the world and the world's banking house by 1870.

By 1900, Britain's economic position was no longer so strong. Germany and the USA had become serious industrial rivals and Britain seemed to be falling behind in a number of new areas (for example, motor car production and electrical goods). Some people thought this was due to inadequate investment in science and technology. However, the British economy was stronger than many pessimists feared. By 1914:

- Britain's merchant fleet carried one half of the world's sea-borne traffic.
- Britain maintained a positive balance of trade balance thanks to its overseas investments.
- London remained the world's financial centre and **sterling** the world's main currency.

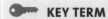

KEY TERM

Sterling The British currency.

Additionally, between 1876 and 1900 some fifteen per cent of all the world's significant inventions were of British origin. British facilities for imparting scientific and technological instruction improved significantly in the five decades after 1870 as the government (and big business) began to fund university research and expansion. The government also funnelled large sums of money into scientific projects designed to improve the armed services: the Admiralty, for example, subsidised the development of wireless technology.

The empire

Economic and naval supremacy enabled Britain to acquire an extensive empire. By 1919 it amounted to a quarter of the world's land surface and population. While the empire is often regarded with a mixture of embarrassment and indifference, in the period covered by this book, it was a source of considerable pride to most Britons. It was perceived as:

- conferring great power status on Britain
- providing Britain with reliable sources of food and raw materials and a captive market for British exports
- providing the Royal Navy with important naval bases from which it was able to dominate the world's sea lanes.

The acquisition of empire was not the result of a co-ordinated policy of conquest. New territories came under British rule largely because of a number of local circumstances. In many cases, they were acquired for defensive or strategic reasons or to safeguard trading interests that were under threat. Some colonies were acquired because enterprising individuals like Cecil Rhodes in southern Africa (see page 106) acted almost independently of the government.

India was the most important and prized part of the British Empire. The largest single element of Britain's army spending in the nineteenth century was devoted to the Indian Army. While the Royal Navy's first task was to defend Britain, its second was to protect the trade route to India. Lord Curzon, a famous viceroy of India, claimed that 'as long as we rule India, we are the greatest power in the world. If we lose it, we shall drop straightaway to a third rate power'. After the Indian Mutiny of 1857–8 (see below), the whole civil and military system of British India was reorganised: the involvement of the East India Company (see page 25) in the operation of British rule was ended. The British government adopted full responsibility for most of the Indian subcontinent, an area larger than all of Europe (excluding Russia), with a population of 300 million people by 1900.

Political and social stability

In many respects, Britain was far from united politically and socially in the period 1790–1918:

- *There was a marked difference between the 'haves' and have-nots'.* The 'haves' were the landed classes and wealthy merchants, bankers and industrialists who wielded huge political, economic and social power. At the other end of the social spectrum were paupers for whom the workhouse was the last resort. By the late nineteenth century most Britons lived and laboured in the mushrooming industrial towns. Many worked long hours for poor wages and often lived in squalor.
- Religion divided Britons as much as class. While Britons were overwhelmingly Christian, Christianity was a source of ideological discord. The deepest divide was between Protestants (the vast majority of Britons) and Catholics (most of whom were of Irish stock). But the divisions between Church and Chapel were also important. Chapel going **nonconformists** were themselves a diverse group. The Wesleyan Methodists were the largest sect but there were also Presbyterians, Baptists, Congregationalists, Quakers and Unitarians.
- There were important national divisions. By 1913 over 75 per cent of Britons were English. Most Scots, Welsh and Protestant Irish were also proud to call themselves British. But the same could not be said of Irish Catholics. Ireland was the least integrated part of the British state. Politically, much of the period was dominated by Irish nationalists' demands for recognition of Ireland's separate identity.
- Women, who on average lived longer than men, were a majority of the population. Emigration (largely by men) tilted the balance still further towards females. Most Britons, whatever their political persuasion, wealth or gender, believed that a woman's place was the home. Indeed, this was where most nineteenth-century women spent a great deal of their time, thanks to frequent childbirth. In the early twentieth century some women – for

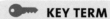 **KEY TERM**

Nonconformists
Protestants who rejected the authority (and some of the practices) of the Church of England.

example, suffragettes – fought for votes for women, but they did not fight for equal rights as such. The prevailing view was that men and women had different but complementary social roles.

Despite these divisions, Britain, unlike many European countries, was not convulsed by revolution in the period 1790–1918. Most Britons were proud of their nation and their government which they perceived as being democratic and better than the authoritarian governments which controlled most of the rest of Europe.

In reality, Britain was far from being a genuine democracy:

- Before the Reform Act of 1832, less than a sixth of the male population had the vote.
- Less than a third of (essentially rich) men had the vote in 1854.
- Only 60 per cent of men had the vote by 1914.
- Not until 1918 were women (over the age of 30) able to vote in general elections.
- The landed gentry dominated the House of Lords, controlled the House of Commons and were a majority in virtually all cabinets pre-1905.

Nevertheless, for most of the period, Parliament did not impinge much on people's lives. Britain's lack of extensive government machinery was seen as a 'good thing' by most – lightly taxed – Britons who espoused *laissez-faire* principles. They contrasted their position favourably with that of most Europeans who (they believed) were harassed by armies of petty officials and subjected to all-pervasive systems of control. Until the start of the twentieth century, Britons were affected more by local than central government. Not until the First World War did the national government impinge heavily on the lives of most Britons (see pages 197–210).

Britain's monarchy probably helped to maintain political calm. Queen Victoria's longevity (she ruled from 1837 to 1901) led to her becoming a symbol of stability. Her Gold and Diamond jubilees in 1887 and 1897 were occasions of national celebration. The British monarchs – George III, George IV, William IV, Victoria, Edward VII and George V – were essentially figureheads with their political power strictly limited, although in practice, particularly at times of crisis, they could exert considerable influence, especially over appointments to the army.

Crucially, in time of war, most Britons rallied to what was perceived to be the national cause.

The Royal Navy

The Royal Navy received far less criticism than the army for most of the period 1790–1918. Regarded as Britain's senior service, it ruled the waves throughout the eighteenth and nineteenth centuries, continuing to do so throughout the First World War. As well as ensuring Britain's security, the navy maintained trade routes with the empire and with other commercial partners. It was an important factor in European politics and proved invaluable in a host of colonial campaigns, providing safe passage for the troops, coastal bombardments and protection for bridgeheads ashore.

The British Army

For most of the period from 1790 to 1918 (with the exception of the First World War), the British Army was relatively small – rarely more than 130,000 strong in peacetime, excluding the troops stationed in India – compared with the armies of the major continental powers. The army's function was essentially two-fold: home defence and maintenance of the empire. It was successful on both these scores. It also had considerable success on the continent in the Napoleonic Wars, particularly under the Duke of Wellington in the Peninsular War and at Waterloo, was well as in the First World War.

The army's colonial success

Virtually every year between 1790 and 1914, the army saw active service overseas in:

- campaigns of conquest
- actions to suppress insurrections
- expeditions to avenge perceived wrongs or to overthrow a dangerous enemy.

The army generally performed well. **Garnet Wolseley**, Britain's most successful late nineteenth-century soldier, claimed that officers and men benefited from 'the varied experience and frequent practice in war'.

In most colonial wars, the army was successful because it was far better armed than its opponents. Despite this huge advantage, some campaigns were first-rate achievements, requiring considerable improvisation given the immense diversity of the foes, terrain, weapons and tactics encountered. The skills of the Royal Engineers, for example, were essential in building roads, bridges and forts was well as providing telegraphic communications and sometimes rail transportation. In general, the army depended on personal qualities of courage and resolution, a highly disciplined organisation, and innovative leadership.

Colonial troops

Given the difficulty of recruiting at home, Britain made use of colonial troops, especially in India. Using locals was cheap. Moreover, in tropical countries, indigenous soldiers had far lower rates of mortality and sickness than Europeans. But some Britons mistrusted colonial troops, doubting their commitment and efficiency. Overreliance on Indian troops almost led to catastrophe in 1857 when a large part of the Indian Army in Bengal mutinied. The Indian Mutiny was suppressed only after fourteen months of hard fighting. Given the need for internal control and possible external threat, 75,000 British

 KEY FIGURE

Garnet Wolseley (1833–1913)

Fought successfully in the Crimean War, in India, Canada and Africa. He later became commander-in-chief of the British Army.

troops were permanently stationed in India from 1858 to 1914 in addition to over 150,000 Indian troops.

Large numbers of Indian and African soldiers fought and died in campaigns in the First World War. Australian, Canadian, New Zealand and South African troops provided the British Army with many of its best soldiers in the First World War.

The army: positives and negatives

Although successful in most colonial campaigns as well as in all the major wars between 1790 and 1918, there were problems with the army:

- In the French Wars (1793–1815), the army had little initial success.
- In the Crimean War, there were leadership, administrative and supply issues.
- In the Boer War, problems initially stemmed from poor leadership.
- In the First World War, the army learned the lessons of fighting a continental war the hard way. This resulted in the deaths of hundreds of thousands of men.

However, in each case, army leaders learned from their mistakes:

- In the French Wars, the army and government finally gave Sir Arthur Wellesley (the Duke of Wellington), who had proved his military ability in India, command of British forces in Portugal and Spain. His success in the Peninsular War and at Waterloo was remarkable. By 1815, the British Army was considered, man for man, the best in the world.
- While the Crimean army suffered over the winter of 1854–5, it did not suffer unduly the following winter.
- The British Army quickly defeated the main Boer armies and then waged a difficult but ultimately successful war against opponents who used guerrilla tactics.
- In 1918, the British Army played a crucial role in winning the First World War.

② Changes in organising the military

▶ *What were the main organisational changes in the British armed forces?*

▶ *What were the main developments in the recruitment of the fighting forces?*

Britain's great power status and the various wars it undertook ensured that there were considerable changes in the nature of its armed forces over the period

1790–1918. Britain was the world's strongest economic power for most of the period and could afford to spend money on its armed forces. The surprising thing is how little money it actually spent. Military and naval leaders had to meet steadily expanding commitments invariably within the constraints of tight budgetary limits and voluntary enlistments. When a major war did occur, therefore, it was hardly surprising that the armed forces were sometimes found wanting. Setbacks and early defeats invariably led to demands for changes in the way that Britain's military forces, but particularly the army, were organised.

The Royal Navy

The navy was generally well organised in 1790 and remained so until 1918. The Admiralty ensured that Britain controlled the seas during the Napoleonic Wars. Nelson's victory at Trafalgar was proof of Britain's naval supremacy. Nevertheless, after 1815 the Royal Navy was greatly reduced in size and most of its ships were decommissioned, enabling the government to cut taxation (see page 60). New developments during the nineteenth century, particularly the change of vessels from sail and wood to steam and steel, forced Britain to keep modernising its navy – a costly business. After centuries of very slow change, warships could now be obsolete on completion.

With the ever-changing technology and the constant threat of new weapons appearing, there were occasional doubts about whether the Royal Navy could defend Britain adequately. This resulted in government reforms, for example, those of Graham in the early 1830s (see page 72) and more money being spent on the navy, especially in the three decades before 1914. Naval expenditure increased by 65 per cent between 1889 and 1897. Nevertheless, the Royal Navy's relative advantage continued to erode. In 1883 Britain had 38 **capital ships** compared to the 40 belonging to the combined fleets of France, Russia, the USA, Japan, Germany and Italy. By 1897, the ratio had slipped to 62:97. After 1900, Britain no longer ruled all the waves. More fears were generated in the first decade of the twentieth century when Germany began to build a large fleet. Britain's response was two-fold:

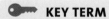 **KEY TERM**

Capital ships Large warships.

- reforms at the Admiralty, usually associated with Admiral Fisher, improved the capability of the navy (see pages 136–7)
- a huge Dreadnought shipbuilding programme ensured that the Royal Navy maintained its supremacy (see page 137).

While it did not always capture the headlines, the Royal Navy's strength underpinned Britain's performance in the French Revolutionary and Napoleonic Wars, the Crimean War, the Boer War and the First World War, ensuring that Britain itself was not unduly threatened by the enemy, and that troops and supplies could be sent to where they were needed.

The army

For much of the period from 1790 to 1918, the army was organised in what appears – and appeared to many contemporaries – a haphazard manner. A host of agencies were involved in its administration. Ultimately, the main bodies responsible for the army were:

- The War Office, responsible for the day-to-day administration of the army and for the cavalry and infantry.
- The Board of Ordnance, responsible for the supply of weapons and ammunition and for helping administer the Royal Artillery and the Royal Engineers.
- The Commissariat, responsible for the supply of rations and transport.

None of these bodies were usually represented in the cabinet. Nor were they responsible for overall strategy, which was in the hands of the secretary of state for war and the colonies. The resulting tangled lines of control often hampered efficiency through and beyond the French Revolutionary and Napoleonic Wars. The army's inefficiency was particularly condemned during the Crimean War, not least for its inability to supply its troops and look after their medical well-being.

Perceived deficiencies in organisation, ordnance and supplies eventually led to a series of reforms in the course of the late nineteenth century, not least those initiated by the McNeill–Tulloch Report (see page 97) and Cardwell's initiative (see pages 98–9). More changes, for example, those associated with Haldane (see pages 134–5), occurred after the setbacks in the Boer War. As a result the army was reasonably prepared for war in 1914, albeit not for the kind of war it ultimately had to fight.

Recruitment

Until 1916, during the First World War, Britain's fighting forces were recruited by voluntary means. The only exception was the Royal Navy which was allowed to use impressment measures (see page 3) in the French Revolutionary and Napoleonic Wars.

Recruitment in the nineteenth century

Harsh discipline, poor conditions and low wages meant than both the navy and army constantly had manpower problems. While a few men may have dreamed of foreign adventure, the bulk of the rank and file of the army and naval crews were unskilled, casual labourers who had joined as a result of economic necessity.

As the nineteenth century wore on, there were changes in the national and social composition of the army. In 1851, Irishmen had constituted 37 per cent of all non-commissioned personnel. By 1913, the Irish element was only nine per cent. Demographic changes meant that both the army and navy drew increasingly on recruits from urban areas rather than from the countryside or small ports. Most army officers preferred men from agricultural backgrounds, assuming that those brought up in the open air were better fitted than town dwellers to be soldiers. The reality may have been different. The experience of soldiers in the American Civil War (1861–5) suggests that those born in towns lived longer than those born in rural areas, probably because they had more resistance to germs. Disease was a far greater killer of soldiers in the nineteenth century than battle.

Most army officers came from the landed classes or from military families. By the late nineteenth century, many public schools specialised in preparing boys for the army. In some regiments, especially the cavalry and guards, most officers were from aristocratic families. Only a few officers managed to advance their careers without money or patronage. The Royal Navy was scarcely more egalitarian. Most of its officers came from families with a naval tradition: they were the sons or nephews of previous naval officers.

The casualty rates in the French and Napoleonic Wars saw some changes in the composition of the officer class, particularly in the army. Men who were not necessarily wealthy but who proved their ability on the battlefield or on the battle-deck were frequently promoted much quicker than would have been the case in peacetime.

The First World War and conscription

Britain initially tried to fight the First World War by relying on voluntary recruitment and for two years did so amazingly successfully. However, in 1916 the Military Service Acts ensured that all men aged 18 to 41 (outside of Ireland) were liable to conscription (see page 159). Ironically, this did not have as much impact as was envisaged. Large numbers of men were exempted from conscription, particularly those working in vital industries. In the first months of conscription, the average monthly enlistment was less than the rate under the voluntary system (see page 159). Nevertheless, the fact that the government could now enforce compulsory service was crucial. The introduction of conscription for the fighting forces and government efforts to control industrial workers and utilise women's labour was testimony to the threat posed by Germany. Britain was fortunate that it could also rely on the loyalty of Canadians, Australians, New Zealanders and South Africans, as well as the Indian Army, all of which contributed considerably to British victory.

The terrible losses sustained in the First World War ensured that the nature of the officer class – but not so much the high command – changed. By 1918 large numbers of officers were men from the lower middle classes, particularly in the army's technological branches, for example, the Royal Engineers and the new tank corps (see page 168).

③ Changing weaponry

▶ *What were the main improvements in weaponry?*

British wealth, scientific and technological resource, and industrial might ensured that the country's armed forces were well armed throughout the period.

The Royal Navy

The Royal Navy led the world in the development of naval weaponry and new warships throughout the period 1790–1918. This was apparent in the French Revolutionary and Napoleonic Wars, for example the introduction of carronades (see page 4) and gunlocks (see page 5). It was equally apparent in the First World War as the navy developed methods to deal with the threat posed by German U-boats (see page 167).

In 1790 the Royal Navy had been dependent on wooden ships of the line. By the mid-nineteenth century, its major ships were ironclad and propelled by steam. Nevertheless, Nelson would probably have felt at home on them. (Interestingly, one of Nelson's successful contemporaries Lord Cochrane hoped to command the Royal Navy in the Crimean War.) But by the First World War the nature of naval warfare had changed totally. Battleships could move at speed, fire at enemy ships that were miles away, and could communicate with each other by wireless (rather than flags). Submarines and aircraft carriers were also changing the nature of naval warfare.

The army

As with the navy, the role of science and technology ensured that the British Army often had better weapons than its adversaries. In the French Revolutionary and Napoleonic Wars, the army was provided with Shrapnel shells, Congreve's rockets and accurate rifles. In 1854–5, the troops had rifled-muskets, much better than the smoothbore muskets of their Russian opponents. Although William Armstrong's new artillery, introduced in 1859–60, had not been an initial success (see page 98), by the final decades of the nineteenth century the army had effective breech-loading and rifled artillery pieces.

The Duke of Wellington (like Nelson) might have felt comfortable in command of the British Army in the Crimean War. (His military secretary Lord Raglan actually led the British expeditionary force sent to Russia in 1854.) Wellington would not have felt so comfortable in the First World War. By 1915–16 the nature of land warfare had changed considerably. New weapons, particularly the machine gun and the development of heavy artillery, led to a change in the nature of warfare. Expectations of a war of movement had ended on the Western Front by 1914 with the coming of trenches (see page 148). The conflict became a war of attrition as both sides, but particularly the Germans, built defensive systems even stronger than those built by Wellington at Torres Vedras in 1810 (see page 53). In an effort to pierce enemy defences, both sides developed new weapons: poison gas, improved types of shells and machine guns, aircraft and tanks. The British Army, supported by an economy geared to war, was at the forefront of military developments, especially the invention of the tank (see page 168). By the summer of 1918 it had the means and the know-how to break through the German defences. The co-ordinated use of tanks, aircraft and particularly heavy artillery was crucial (see page 213).

Technological inventiveness, by itself, however, could not guarantee victory. Good leadership, troop morale and the provision of supplies, equipment and weapons were all equally vital ingredients of success.

4 Changes in the role of the people

▶ *What impact did the major wars have on the British population as a whole?*

The major wars in which Britain engaged in the period 1790–1918 had a varying effect on the population as a whole. The Crimean and Boer Wars engendered a great deal of passion among the public without impacting too greatly on ordinary life. The French Revolutionary and Napoleonic Wars, fought for the best part of 22 years, had a much greater impact on the general population, most of whom were involved in some way in the war effort. The First World War had an even greater impact. By 1918 the government was organising the home front, conscripting men for the armed forces and orchestrating economic and social development in ways designed to assist the war effort.

British patriotism

Most of the major wars fought between 1790 and 1918 were supported by the mass of the population. The British public was strongly patriotic. Men volunteered for the fighting forces in most of the conflicts but particularly in the First World War. Patriotism in the second half of the nineteenth century may well have been generated by the popular press, but it is just as likely that jingoistic newspapers like the *Daily Mail* reflected the public's views. Papers that were seen as unpatriotic were unlikely to sell. Only in the First World War did the government make a deliberate attempt to limit freedom of information and to issue propaganda material in an effort to maintain morale and commitment.

Newspapers did not just toe the government line:

- In the French and Napoleonic Wars, newspapers were often critical of the government and military commanders.
- In the Crimean War, war correspondents like Russell of *The Times* revealed the army's failings.
- In the Boer War, the Liberal press campaigned against the dreadful conditions in the South African concentration camps.
- In the First World War, newspapers were critical of government and military leaders.

Although the bulk of the population supported the wars, there were opponents, mainly from the left of the political spectrum:

- Radicals like William Cobbett were critical of many aspects of the French Revolutionary and Napoleonic Wars and many Whig politicians favoured making peace with the enemy.
- Radicals like Richard Cobden opposed the Crimean War.
- Radical Liberals like David Lloyd George opposed the Boer War.
- Socialists like Keir Hardie opposed the First World War.

The political impact

All the major wars had far-reaching political consequences:

- The French Revolutionary and Napoleonic Wars led to the dominance of the Conservative (Tory) Party.
- Perceived government failure led to Palmerston replacing Aberdeen as prime minister in 1855 and Lloyd George replacing Asquith in 1916.
- The Boer War resulted in serious political division between the political forces of right and left.
- The First World War helped to bring about major parliamentary reform, the decline of the Liberal Party and the rise of Labour. It also saw a massive expansion of government control and intervention, far beyond anything previously experienced or envisaged.

The financial and economic impact

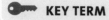 **KEY TERM**

Consols Government-issued securities that people could buy. Unlike war bonds, no date was stipulated for the return of the capital invested.

The wars had to be paid for. This was done by raising taxes and by government borrowing including the issuing of bonds, **consols** and war loans. This inevitably resulted in an increase in the national debt. The French Revolutionary and Napoleonic War had less of an economic impact than might have been expected. Britain enjoyed the benefits of industrialisation which helped provide the means and the money to fight the 22-year long conflict. The Crimean and the Boer Wars had only a limited effect on Britain's finances and economic development. The First World War had a far greater impact. Arguably, it led to the loss of overseas markets and left Britain indebted to the USA. However, it is equally arguable that the war had a limited impact on general economic trends and that Britain was able to pay for it with relative ease. It is certainly the case that Britain's great wealth and manufacturing capacity enabled it to fight and win all four wars.

The social impact

The relatively short Crimean and Boer Wars had only a limited impact on British society. The same could be said of the long French Revolutionary and Napoleonic Wars that had less impact than might have been imagined. The same cannot be said so convincingly with regard to the First World War.

Some historians are convinced that the First World War had huge consequences for Britain's social evolution, especially with regard to state involvement in all aspects of life, general welfare development, the redistribution of wealth and for women's roles. However, other historians claim that the continuities between pre- and post-war First World War Britain were more significant than the changes. Arguably:

- The social measures that were introduced between 1914 and 1918 were a continuation of the expansion in state welfare in late Victorian and Edwardian Britain.
- Most of the First World War's effects were of short-term significance.
- Social change would have occurred if there had been no war.

What can be said with more certainty is that most British civilians in the various conflicts prior to 1914, while assisting and generally supporting the war efforts, were not actually organised for war by the government. This was to change during the course of the First World War. By 1918 the home front was becoming almost as regimented and controlled as the fighting forces themselves. No longer mere 'camp followers', British civilians had become a vital part of the national war effort.

 # The situation in 1918

> ▶ *How strong were British military forces after 1918?*

Although the First World War had resulted in a huge loss of life and resources, Britain emerged the victor. In November 1918, it had:

- an army of 3.5 million men which had learned how to fight a successful war on the Western Front
- a Royal Navy with 58 major battleships and hundreds of other warships
- an RAF with over 20,000 planes.

Britain's strong position in 1918 was enhanced by the weakness of its rivals. Germany was defeated; its army was no longer a major force and its fleet scuttled itself at Scapa Flow in 1919. Russia, a rival for much of the nineteenth century, was in chaos. Moreover, Britain seemed to have little to fear from the other victorious powers:

- France had been hard hit by the conflict.
- Common ties of language, culture and tradition meant that there was already talk of a 'special relationship' between Britain and the USA.

In 1918 Lloyd George's government decided, and the armed forces planned on the assumption that 'the British Empire will not be involved in any large war over the next 10 years'. This Ten-Year Rule, which was used to justify keeping defence spending as low as possible, continued until 1932. In 1913, 30 per cent of Britain's government expenditure had been on defence. By 1933, this had fallen to ten per cent. Given that there was no major threat to world peace in the 1920s, this made some sense. However, savage defence cuts meant that Britain's arms industry virtually disappeared. There was thus no guarantee that the country would have the capability to rearm if a serious threat appeared.

Despite its military success pre-1918, preserving peace seemed to be the greatest of Britain's national interests post-1918. The cost of the First World War in human and financial terms made politicians and the public recoil from the prospect of a new war. The country, it seemed, had everything to lose and little to gain from another major war. That war – the Second World War – came in 1939. It proved that Britain did indeed have everything to lose and little to gain from involvement in a major conflict.

 Question practice

ESSAY QUESTIONS

1 How far do you agree that the Cardwell army reforms brought about most significant change in the organisation of the military in the period 1790–1918?

2 How far do you agree about that Graham's naval reforms of 1832 were the most significant turning point in military organisation in the period 1790–1918?

Edexcel A level History

Edexcel's Paper 3, Option 35.2: The British Experience of Warfare, c.1790–1918 is assessed by an exam comprising three sections:

- Section A is a source analysis assessment. It tests your knowledge of one of the key topics in depth.
- Section B requires you to write one essay from a choice of two, again testing your knowledge of key topics in depth (see page 236 for guidance on this).
- Section C requires you to write one essay from a choice of two. Questions relate to themes in breadth and test your knowledge of change over a period of at least 100 years (see page 240 for guidance on this).

The sections of the exam relate to the sections of the exam paper in the following way:

Sections A and B	Test your knowledge of the key topics in depth	Britain at war overseas: • Britain and the French Wars, 1793–1815 • The Crimean War, 1854–6 • The Second Boer War, 1899–1902 • Trench warfare on the Western Front, 1914–18 • The war in the air, 1914–18
Section C	Tests your knowledge of the themes in breadth	The changing role of government in preparing the nation for war, c.1790–1918: • Changes in organising the military • Changes in the role of the people

Paper 3 is only available at A level, therefore there is no AS Level version of this paper.

Sources guidance

Paper 3 Section A

Section A of Paper 3 comprises a single compulsory question which refers to one source. The Section A question will begin with the following stem: 'Assess the value of the source for revealing …', for example:

> **Assess the value of the source for revealing Mary Seacole's motives for travelling to the Crimea and the condition of British troops in the Crimea in late 1854.**

See the next page for details about the source.

The source

The source will be a primary or contemporary source: it will have been written in the period that you are studying: *c*.1790–1918. The source will be around 350 words long. It will be accompanied by a brief passage that sets out the essential provenance of the source. Here is an example:

SOURCE 1

From Mary Seacole's autobiography, *The Wonderful Adventures of Mrs. Seacole in Many Lands*, published in 1857.

Before I left Jamaica for Navy Bay [a harbour in Panama], war had been declared against Russia, and we were all anxiously expecting news of a descent upon the Crimea. Now, no sooner had I heard of war somewhere, than I longed to witness it. As time wore on, the inclination to join my old friends of the 97th, 48th, and other regiments, battling with worse foes than yellow fever or cholera, took such exclusive possession of my mind, that I threw over the gold speculation altogether, and devoted all my energies to my new scheme.

I arrived in London, in the autumn of 1854, just after the battle of Alma had been fought, and my old friends were fairly before the walls of Sebastopol. As the winter wore on, came hints from various quarters of mismanagement, want, and suffering in the Crimea; and after the battles of Balaclava and Inkermann, and the fearful storm of the 14th of November, the worst anticipations were realized. Then we knew that the hospitals were full to suffocation, that scarcity and exposure were the fate of all in the camp, and that the brave fellows for whom any of us at home would have split our last shilling, and shared our last meal, were dying
thousands of miles away from the active sympathy of their fellow-countrymen.

I had seen much of sorrow and death elsewhere, but that had never daunted me; and if I could feel happy binding up the wounds of quarrelsome Americans and treacherous Spaniards, what delight should I not experience if I could be useful to my own 'sons,' suffering for a cause it was so glorious to fight and bleed for! I made up my mind that if the army wanted nurses, they would be glad of me, and with all the ardour of my nature, which ever carried me where inclination prompted, I decided that I would go to the Crimea; and go I did, as all the world knows.

My first idea was to apply to the War Office for the post of hospital nurse. Among the diseases which I understood were most prevalent in the Crimea were cholera, diarrhoea, and dysentery, all of them more or less known in tropical climates; and with which, I was tolerably familiar. My funds, carefully husbanded, would carry me over the three thousand miles, and land me at Balaclava.

Understanding the question

To answer the question successfully you must understand the question. The question is written precisely in order to make sure that you understand the task. Each part of the question has a specific meaning.

> Assess the value of the source[1] for revealing Mary Seacole's motives for travelling to the Crimea[2] and the condition of British troops in the Crimea in late 1854[3].

1 You must evaluate how useful the source could be to a historian. Evaluating the extent of usefulness involves considering its value and limitations in the light of your own knowledge about the source's historical context. Important information about the context of the source is included in the information given about the source.
2 The question focuses on two specific enquiries that the source might be useful for. The first is Mary Seacole's motives for travelling to the Crimea.
3 The second enquiry is the condition of British troops in the Crimea in late 1854.

In essence, you should use the source, the information about the source and your own knowledge of the historical context to make a judgement about how far the source is useful to a historian engaged in two specific enquiries. Crucially, you must consider both enquiries. An answer which only focuses on one of the enquiries is unlikely to do well.

Source analysis skills

Generally, Section A of Paper 3 tests your ability to evaluate source material. Your job is to analyse the source by reading it in the context of the values and assumptions of the society and the period in which it was written. Examiners will mark your work by focusing on the extent to which you are able to deploy the following skills (in the table below):

Skill	At a basic level …	At a higher level …	At the highest levels …
Interpret and analyse source material	This means you can understand the source, and select, copy, paraphrase and summarise the source to help answer the question	Your interpretation of the source includes the ability to explain, analyse and make inferences based on the source	You will be expected to analyse the source in a sophisticated way. This includes the ability to distinguish between information, opinions and arguments contained in the source
Apply knowledge of historical context in relation to the source	This means the ability to link the source to your knowledge of the context in which the source was written, and using this knowledge to expand or support the information contained in the source	You will be able to use your contextual knowledge to make inferences, and to expand, support or challenge the details mentioned in the source	You will examine the value and limits of the material contained in the source by interpreting the source in the context of the values and assumptions of the society from which it is taken
Evaluate the usefulness and weight of the source material	Evaluation of the source will be based on simplistic criteria about reliability and bias	Evaluation of the source will be based on the nature and purpose of the source	Evaluation of the source will be based on a valid criterion that is justified in the course of the essay. You will also be able to distinguish between the value of different aspects of the source

Make sure your source evaluation is sophisticated. Avoid crude statements about bias, and avoid simplistic assumptions such as: 'a source written immediately after an event is reliable, whereas a source written years later is unreliable'.

Try to see things from the writer's perspective:

- How does the writer understand the world?
- What assumptions does the writer have?
- Who is the writer trying to influence?
- What views may the writer be trying to challenge?

Basic skill: comprehension

The most basic source skill is comprehension: understanding what the source means. There are a variety of techniques that you can use to aid comprehension. For example, using the sources included in this book and in past exam papers, you could:

- read the sources out loud
- look up any words that you don't understand and make a glossary
- make flash cards containing brief biographies of the writers of the sources.

You can demonstrate comprehension by copying from, paraphrasing and summarising the sources. However, keep this to the minimum as comprehension is a low-level skill and you need to apply higher level skills.

Advanced skill: contextualising the sources

First, to analyse the sources correctly, you need to understand them in the context in which they were written. Source 1 reflects Mary Seacole's world view. Your job is to understand the values and assumptions behind the source:

- One way of contextualising the source is to consider the nature, origins and purpose of the source. However, this can lead to a formulaic essay.

- An alternative is to consider two levels of context. First, you should establish the general context. In this case, Source 1 was written shortly after the end of the Crimean War. Second, you can look for specific references to contemporary events, people or debates in the sources. For example, when considering her motives for travelling to the Crimea, the details in the source can be put in context in the following way:
  - '97th, 48th, and other regiments': Seacole knew these soldiers as they had served in Jamaica. She may have wanted to go to the Crimea to work with them again.
  - 'Gold speculation', 'My funds, carefully husbanded': Seacole was a businesswoman and entrepreneur. She had become successful establishing 'hotels' in various parts of the world. Consequently, she saw a business opportunity and had the money to travel across the world to establish a new business venture. The date of publication also indicates that she capitalised on a business opportunity – it was published shortly after the war ended, when interest in the events of the war was high.
  - 'Hints from various quarters of mismanagement': Seacole was aware that the British administration was in disarray and therefore wanted to use her business expertise to help improve conditions in the Crimea.
  - 'My own "sons," suffering': as a Jamaican, Seacole was a subject of the British Empire. She may have been motivated by patriotism.
  - 'I understood were most prevalent in the Crimea were cholera, diarrhoea, and dysentery, all of them more or less known in tropical climates; and with which, I was tolerably familiar': Seacole was an experienced nurse who understood how to treat the kinds of diseases that were most common in the Crimea.

Using context to make judgements: writing the answer

- Start by establishing the general context of the source:
  - What was going on at the time when the source was written, or the time of the events described in the source?
  - What are the key debates that the source might be contributing to?
- Next, look for key words and phrases that establish the specific context. Does the source refer to specific people, events or books that might be important?
- Make sure your contextualisation focuses on the question.
- Use the context when evaluating the usefulness and limitations of the source.

Here is an example:

Source 1 is valuable to a historian investigating Seacole's motives for travelling to the Crimea because it highlights several of her reasons for making the trip. First, there is considerable evidence in the source that Seacole saw the Crimean War as a business opportunity. For example, her decision to throw 'the gold speculation altogether' is a reference to her involvement in a company in South America which was mining gold. Indeed, Seacole had set up a series of 'hotels' across the British Empire that made money by providing food, clothing and medical aid for soldiers.

Therefore, Seacole may well have seen the Crimean War as an opportunity to expand her business. Second, Seacole was also motivated by patriotism. As a Jamaican she was a subject of the British Empire. For this reason she viewed the soldiers as her 'own "sons"'. Additionally, some of the soldiers fighting in the Crimea, including 'the 97th, 48th, and other regiments, were known to her from their stay in Jamaica. She refers to them as 'old friends', and may also have thought of them as regular customers. Finally, Seacole was an experienced nurse. According to the source, she had tended 'quarrelsome Americans and treacherous Spaniards' in previous conflicts and had experience of 'cholera, diarrhoea, and dysentery' and other tropical diseases that were also common in the Crimea. In this sense, the source is extremely useful as it points to a variety of complementary motives for Seacole's journey to the Crimea, specifically that she was an experienced businesswoman who could set up an enterprise, looking after troops that she cared for using the skills that she had acquired in previous conflicts.

This paragraph makes inferences from details in the source to uncover a variety of motives, showing that Source 1 is of considerable use for this enquiry. Significantly, for the answer to reach a high level, it would also have to deal with the other enquiry in the question: the extent of the source's usefulness for revealing the condition of the troops in the Crimea in late 1854.

Essay guidance (1)

Paper 3 Section B

To get a high grade in Section B of Paper 3, your essay must contain four essential qualities:

- focused analysis
- relevant detail
- supported judgement
- organisation, coherence and clarity.

This section focuses on the following aspects of exam technique:

- the nature of the question
- planning an answer to the question
- writing a focused introduction
- deploying relevant detail
- writing analytically
- reaching a supported judgement.

The nature of the question

Section B questions are designed to test the depth of your historical knowledge. They can focus on relatively short periods, or single events. Additionally, they can focus on different historical processes or 'concepts'. These include:

- cause
- consequence
- change/continuity
- similarity/difference
- significance.

These different question focuses require slightly different approaches:

Cause	1 How far was Lord Kitchener's military leadership responsible for British victory in the Second Boer War?
Consequence	2 To what extent, in the years 1854–6, did medical practitioners succeed in addressing the needs of sick and wounded British soldiers in the Crimea?
Continuity and change	3 'British officers were unfit to lead their men in both the Crimean War and the Boer War.' How far do you agree with this statement?
Similarities and differences	4 'Public support for the First World War was more consistent and broadly based than public support for the Second Boer War.' How far do you agree with this statement?
Significance	5 How significant was aerial warfare to the success of the British war effort during the First World War?

Some questions include a 'stated factor'. A common type of stated factor question would ask how far one factor caused something; for example, the first question in the table: 'How far was Lord Kitchener's military leadership responsible for British victory in the Second Boer War?' In this type of question you would be expected to evaluate the importance of 'Lord Kitchener's military leadership' – the 'stated factor' – compared to other factors.

Planning your answer

It is crucial that you understand the focus of the question. Therefore, read the question carefully before you start planning. Check:

- The chronological focus: which years should your essay deal with?
- The topic focus: what aspect of your course does the question deal with?
- The conceptual focus: is this a causes, consequences, change/continuity, similarity/difference or significance question?

For example, for question 5 in the table opposite, you could point these out as follows:

> How significant[1] was aerial warfare[2] to the success of the British war effort during the First World War[3] 1914–18[4]?

1 Conceptual focus: significance, specifically to the success of the British war effort.
2 Topic focus: aerial warfare.
3 Topic focus: First World War.
4 Chronological focus: 1914–18.

Your plan should reflect the task that you have been set. Section B asks you to write an analytical, coherent and well-structured essay from your own knowledge, which reaches a supported conclusion in around 40 minutes:

- To ensure that your essay is coherent and well structured, it should comprise a series of paragraphs, each focusing on a different point.
- Your paragraphs should be logically ordered. For example, you could write your paragraphs in order of importance, so you begin with the most important issues and end with the least important.
- In essays where there is a 'stated factor', it is a good idea to start with the stated factor before moving on to the other points.
- To make sure you keep to time, you should aim to write three or four paragraphs plus an introduction and a conclusion.

The opening paragraph

The opening paragraph should fulfil the following:

- answer the question directly
- set out your essential argument
- outline the factors or issues that you will discuss
- define key terms used in the question (where necessary).

Different questions require you to define different terms, for example:

A level question	Key terms
'Public support for the First World War was more consistent and broadly based than public support for the Second Boer War.' How far do you agree with this statement?	Here it is worth distinguishing between the notions of 'consistent' and 'broadly based'.
How accurate is it to say that it was the use of new fighting techniques and new technology that accounts for the speed of German defeat in 1918?	In this example, it is worth distinguishing between new fighting techniques and new technology.

Here's an example introduction in answer to question 4 in the table on page 236:

> 'Public support for the First World War was more consistent and broadly based than public support for the Second Boer War.' How far do you agree with this statement?

Public support for the First World War was undoubtedly more consistent and broadly based than public support for the Second Boer War[1]. Public support for the Second Boer War was less consistent than public support for the First World War in the sense that it fluctuated more due to the events of the war[2]. Additionally, public support for the First World War was more broadly based than public support for the Boer War because although a minority of the public opposed both wars, the working class tended to support the First World War to a greater extent than they supported the Boer War, meaning that the war had firmer support among all sections of society[3].

1 The essay starts with a clear focus on the question.
2 This sentence simultaneously defines 'consistent' and provides an initial answer to the first part of the question.
3 This sentence simultaneously defines 'broadly based' and provides an initial answer to the second part of the question.

The opening paragraph: advice

- Do not write more than a couple of sentences on general background knowledge. This is unlikely to focus explicitly on the question.
- After defining key terms, refer back to these definitions when justifying your conclusion.
- The introduction should reflect the rest of the essay. Do not make one argument in your introduction and then make a different argument in the essay.

Deploying relevant detail

Paper 3 tests the depth of your historical knowledge. Therefore, you will need to deploy historical detail. In the main body of the essay your paragraphs should begin with a clear point, be full of relevant detail and end with an explanation or evaluation. A detailed answer might include statistics, proper names, dates and technical terms. For example, if you are writing a paragraph about public support for the Second Boer War, you might include the impact of reports in specific newspapers, such as the *Manchester Guardian* or the *Daily Mail,* on specific stories such as Black Week, or the revelations about the concentration camps.

Writing analytically

The quality of your analysis is one of the key factors that determines the mark you achieve. Writing analytically means clearly showing the relationships between the ideas in your essay. Analysis includes two key skills: explanation and evaluation.

Explanation

Explanation means giving reasons. An explanatory sentence has three parts:

- a claim: a statement that something is true or false
- a reason: a statement that justifies the claim
- a relationship: a word or phrase that shows the relationship between the claim and the reason.

Imagine you are answering question 1 in the table on page 236:

> **How far was Lord Kitchener's military leadership responsible for British victory in the Second Boer War?**

Your paragraph on Lord Kitchener's military leadership should start with a clear point, which would be supported by a series of examples. Finally, you would round off the paragraph with some explanation:

Therefore, Lord Kitchener's military leadership was one reason for British victory in the Second Boer War[1] because[2] his tactics ultimately defeated the Boer's guerrilla campaign[3].

1 Claim.
2 Relationship.
3 Reason.

Make sure of the following:

- The reason you give genuinely justifies the claim that you have made.
- Your explanation is focused on the question.

Reaching a supported judgement

Your essay should reach a supported judgement. The obvious place to do this is in the conclusion of your essay. Even so, the judgement should reflect the findings of your essay. The conclusion should present:

- a clear judgement that answers the question
- an evaluation of the evidence that supports the judgement.

Finally, the evaluation should reflect valid criteria.

Evaluation and criteria

Evaluation means weighing up to reach a judgement. Therefore, evaluation requires you to:

- summarise both sides of the issue
- reach a conclusion that reflects the proper weight of both sides.

So, for question 1 in the table on page 236:

How far was Lord Kitchener's military leadership responsible for British victory in the Second Boer War?

The conclusion might look like this:

In conclusion, Lord Kitchener's military leadership was largely responsible for British victory in the Second Boer War because his tactics led to the defeat of the Boer's guerrilla campaign**[1]**. Clearly, Lord Roberts and General Buller also played a part**[2]**. Roberts' campaign reversed the defeats suffered in the first phase of the war and led to a conventional victory over the Transvaal Republic and the Orange Free State. Furthermore, while Buller's initial campaign was unsuccessful, it was not as much of a disaster as the media made it out to be**[3]**. Nonetheless, Lord Roberts' apparent victory in mid-1900 was short lived. While he initiated the scorched earth policy which was part of the final victory against the Boer guerrillas, it was Kitchener's military leadership in the last phase of the campaign that finally defeated the Boer forces. Therefore, Kitchener's leadership was largely responsible for the ultimate victory**[4]**.

1 The conclusion starts with a clear judgement that answers the question.
2 This sentence begins the process of weighing up the different factors involved in victory by acknowledging that other leaders also played a role.
3 The conclusion summarises the role of Lord Roberts and General Buller.
4 The essay ends with a final judgement that is supported by the evidence of the essay.

The judgement is supported in part by evaluating the evidence and in part by linking it to valid criteria. In this case, the criterion is the distinction between the short-lived conventional victory achieved by Lord Roberts in 1900 and the ultimate victory against the guerrillas achieved by Kitchener.

Essay guidance (2)

Paper 3 Section C

Section C is similar in many ways to Section B. Therefore, you need the same essential skills in order to get a high grade:

- focused analysis
- relevant detail
- supported judgement
- organisation, coherence and clarity.

Nonetheless, there are some differences in terms of the style of the question and the approach to the question in Sections B and C. Therefore, this section focuses on the following aspects of exam technique:

- the nature of the question
- planning your answer
- advice for Section C.

The nature of the question

Section C questions focus on the two themes in breadth:

- Changes in organising the military c.1790–1918.
- Changes in the role of the people c.1790–1918.

Questions can address either theme or both themes. There are two questions in Section C, of which you must answer one. Section C questions are designed to test the breadth of your historical knowledge, and your ability to analyse change over time. Therefore, questions will focus on long periods of no less than 100 years.

Section C questions have a variety of forms but they will always focus on either:

- the causes of change: for example, the factors, forces or individuals that led to change

or

- the nature of change: the ways in which things changed.

Significantly, the exam paper may contain two causes of change questions or two nature of change questions: you are not guaranteed one of each. Finally, questions can focus on different aspects of change over time:

- Comparative questions: ask you to assess the extent of change and continuity of an aspect of the period.
- Patterns of change questions: ask you to assess differences in terms of the rate, extent or significance of change at different points in the chronology.
- Turning point questions: ask you to assess which changes were more significant.

Comparative question	'The key factor in promoting military reform in the period 1790–1918 was military defeat.' How far do you agree with this statement?
Patterns of change question	How accurate is it to say that there was a continuous development of British military technology in the period 1790–1918?
Turning point question	How far do you agree that the introduction of conscription in 1916 was the key turning point in the recruitment of the fighting forces in the period 1790–1918?

Planning your answer

It is crucial that you understand the focus of the question to make an effective plan. Therefore, read the question carefully before you start planning. Different questions require a different approach. Here are suggestions about how to tackle some of the common types of question:

'The key factor in promoting military reform in the period 1790–1918 was military defeat.' How far do you agree with this statement?

This is a comparative question which focuses on the causes of change. In this case you should examine the significance of 'military defeat', the stated factor, and compare it to other possible causes of change.

How accurate is it to say that there was a continuous development of British military technology in the period 1790–1918?

This is a pattern of change question which focuses on the nature of change. Here, you should examine the pattern of the development of British military technology in the period 1790–1918. You should consider how far development took place at an even rate, as opposed to developing in fits and starts.

How far do you agree that the introduction of conscription in 1916 was the key turning point in the recruitment of the fighting forces in the period 1790–1918?

This is a turning point question which focuses on the nature of change. Therefore, you should examine the significance of the stated turning point, and compare it to two or three other turning points from the period 1790–1918. Significantly, you should not just focus on conscription, or the year 1916: you must consider other possible turning points. Additionally, when considering how far an event was a turning point you must consider both the changes it caused *and* the ways in which things stayed the same.

Advice for Section C

In many ways a Section C essay should display the same skills as a Section B essay (see page 236). However, Section C essays focus on a much longer period than Section B essays and this has an impact on how you approach them.

The most important difference concerns the chronology. To answer a Section C question properly you must address the whole chronology, in this case the period 1790–1918. In practice, this means choosing examples from across the whole range of the period. Specifically, it is a good idea to have examples from the early part of the period, the middle of the period and the end of the period. For example, if you were answering the question:

How far do you agree that the introduction of conscription in 1916 was the key turning point in the recruitment of the fighting forces in the period 1790–1918?

The question states a possible turning point from 1916 – the end of the period. Therefore, if you are considering other possible turning points you should choose one from the early part of the chronology, and one from the middle to make sure you cover the whole period.

Equally, if you are dealing with the question:

How accurate is it to say that there was a continuous development of British military technology in the period 1790–1918?

you should analyse examples of the development of military technology throughout the whole period. These could include developments such as:

- early: naval developments in the 1790s
- middle: William Armstrong's artillery 1859–60
- late: the Vickers machine-gun 1914–18, development of the tank 1915–18.

In so doing. you would be addressing the full chronological range of the question.

Glossary of terms

1s. (one shilling)   Twelve old pence (12*d.*) or 5 pence in modern money.

Armistice   An agreement to suspend fighting.

Autocratic regimes   Governments where one (unelected) ruler has total power.

Balance of payments   The difference between a nation's total receipts from foreign countries and its total payment to foreign countries. Most of this money comes from trade.

Bandsmen   Most battalions had a small band, useful in attracting recruits at home and maintaining morale on the march and in action.

Bioscope   The first moving film apparatus.

'Bite and hold'   A term used to describe the tactic of capturing part of the enemy trench line and then defending it when the Germans counterattacked.

Boer   The Dutch word for farmer.

Bomb vessels   Small ships that carried mortars – short guns that fired heavy shells.

Bosnian terrorists   Serbs who wanted Bosnia, part of Austria-Hungary, to become part of Serbia and were prepared to use violence to achieve their aim.

Breaches   Gaps or openings.

Broadsides   The firing of all the guns on one side of a ship simultaneously.

Capital ships   Large warships.

Carbine   A short-barrelled, light gun.

Cat-o'-nine-tails   A whip with nine knotted tails.

Ceylon   Present-day Sri Lanka.

Cholera   An infection of the intestine caused by bacteria transmitted in contaminated water. This causes severe vomiting and diarrhoea, which leads to dehydration that can be fatal.

Combination Acts 1799 and 1800   These acts, designed to prevent strikes, made it illegal for workers to gather together in large numbers.

Combined arms tactics   Fighting the enemy by blending together the different branches of the army, for example, artillery, infantry and tanks.

Commando   An armed group of Boers, varying in size from a few dozen men to several hundred.

Comptroller of the Navy   The man who headed the Navy Board, which was responsible for building and maintaining ships.

Consols   Government-issued securities that people could buy. Unlike war bonds, no date was stipulated for the return of the capital invested.

Convoys   Groups of merchant ships sailing in formation and protected by warships.

Coppering   Covering a ship's hull with copper sheeting to protect it from wear and tear.

Creeping barrage   An artillery bombardment, where the shells are meant to keep falling just ahead of the attacking troops.

D-Notice system   Instructions sent by the government to newspapers, ordering them not to publish certain information. D is short for defence.

Division   A formation usually comprising 4000–5000 soldiers.

Dysentery   An infection of the bowel causing painful diarrhoea. This results in dehydration, which can be fatal. Dysentery occurs wherever there is poor sanitation.

Enfield rifle   An improved version of the minié rifle.

Entente   A friendly agreement.

Esprit de corps   Morale.

Eugenics   The idea that there should be 'scientific' breeding. The 'fit' should be encouraged to have large numbers of children while the 'unfit' should be discouraged from reproducing.

Flintlock   A gunlock or gun with a flint from which a spark is struck to ignite gunpowder.

Forecastle   The raised deck at the front of a ship.

French Revolution   The term used to describe the political turbulence in France 1789–94. These years saw the overthrow (and execution) of King Louis XVI and an attempted destruction of the aristocracy.

Gangrene   This can result from infected wounds or frostbite. Lack of blood, usually to an arm or a leg, causes body tissue to decay.

GHQ   General Head Quarters, comprising military staff officers who advised the commander-in-chief on policy and administration and helped him to carry out his plans.

Going over the top   Leaving the trench and attacking the enemy across no-man's-land.

Gotha   The main German bomber.

Government bonds   Securities issued by the government, allowing it to borrow money. Those who bought the bonds were guaranteed to receive their money back in the future.

Grapeshot   Iron shot, contained in a canvas bag, that scattered widely when fired.

Gross national product (GNP)   The total value of all goods and services produced within a country plus the income from investments abroad.

Guerrillas   Irregular forces that harass an enemy. The word was coined by the Spanish during the Peninsular War.

Gunlock   The mechanism in some guns by which the charge is exploded.

Hanover   A small German state.

Hansard   The printed reports of debates in Parliament.

Heliograph   An apparatus for signalling by reflecting the sun's rays.

Hindenburg line   A heavily fortified German defence system, prepared over the winter of 1916–17 (see the map on page 153).

Horse Guards   The administrative headquarters of the British Army in Whitehall.

Imperial Guard   Napoleon's bravest and most loyal soldiers.

Independent Labour Party (ILP)   Formed in 1893, it hoped to unite various socialist groups. In the 1895 election it fielded 28 candidates, all of whom finished bottom of the poll.

Khaki   A dull-brownish cloth used for military uniforms. It provided better camouflage than red tunics.

Laissez-faire   The principle that governments should not interfere in social and economic matters.

Landsmen   Men with no seafaring or riverboat experience.

Lanyard   A short piece of rope.

Leader of the Commons   The prime minister, Salisbury, was a peer and sat in the Lords. Therefore, Balfour led the Conservatives in the Commons.

Linstock   A staff holding a lighted match for firing a cannon.

Luddites   The people who destroyed labour-saving machinery in 1811–12. They took their name from a mythical leader, Ned Ludd.

Magazine   A military storehouse of weapons.

Magazine rifles   Rifles which can fire a succession of shots without reloading.

Marines   Soldiers on board ships.

Matériel   Military equipment.

Merchantmen   Trading ships.

Mills bomb   A type of hand grenade.

Minié rifle   A minié rifle fired the minié ball, an inch-long (2.5 cm) lead bullet that expanded into the groove of the rifle-musket's barrel. The minié rifle was accurate at over 400 yards (366 m); the smoothbore musket had an effective range of less than 100 yards.

Mortar   A short-barrelled gun that lobs shells at the enemy.

Nationalised   Taken over and run by the government.

Navalists   Those who believed that Britain's best line of defence was the Royal Navy.

Navy League   A patriotic organisation set up to promote the interests of the navy. By 1914 it had 100,000 members.

Nepotism   Undue favouritism to one's relations and close friends.

Nonconformists   Protestants who rejected the authority (and some of the practices) of the Church of England.

Nore   The area at the mouth of the River Thames.

Ordenanza   A kind of Portuguese home guard, supposed to turn out in time of invasion.

Ordnance Board   The government agency responsible for arms, armaments and munitions.

Patronage   The process of bestowing jobs and offices.

Peelites   Supporters of Sir Robert Peel who split with the Conservative (Tory) Party in 1846 over the Repeal of the Corn Laws.

Pell-mell An aggressive, confused head-to-head brawl.

Petty officers Seamen who were not commissioned officers but who had some authority.

Piedmont A kingdom in northern Italy.

Poet Laureate A title bestowed by the monarch on a poet whose duties include writing poems to celebrate important occasions.

Pontoon A flat boat that can be used as a bridge.

Portuguese East Africa Present-day Mozambique.

Privateers Private vessels commissioned to seize and plunder an enemy's ships in wartime.

Prize money Captured enemy ships were sold. The money made was then allotted to the men. Officers took the lion's share but ordinary crewmen did receive something.

Quarterdeck Part of the deck behind the main mast, used by officers.

Radical(s) Supporters of profound economic and social change.

Requisitioned Forcefully acquired – without paying.

Salient A bulge pushing into enemy lines which could thus be attacked from several sides.

Sappers Soldiers skilled in digging trenches.

Scorched-earth policy This involves destroying all crops and animals in the path of the enemy, making it hard for them to find food.

Scurvy A disease caused by deficiency of vitamin C. The symptoms are weakness and aching joints and muscles, progressing to bleeding of the gums and other organs.

Seditious Meetings Act 1796 This banned lectures or meetings of more than 50 people unless permitted by local magistrates.

Sepoys Indian soldiers who were trained and employed by the East India Company.

Shop stewards Trade unionists who represent factory or other groups of workers.

Sinecures Well-paid jobs without much work.

Slowmatch A slow-burning rope used for firing a gun.

Social Darwinism Social Darwinists believed that only the fittest nations and social systems could thrive and prosper.

Social Democratic Federation (SDF) The SDF advocated violent revolution to overthrow the capitalist system.

Staff work Preparatory planning and administrative work undertaken by the commanding officer's personal team.

Sterling The British currency.

Stern The back of a ship.

The Straits The Bosphorus and the Dardanelles, which link the Black Sea to the Mediterranean.

Subsidies Sums of money given to Britain's allies.

Suzerainty Overlordship; ultimate power.

TNT Short for trinitrotoluene, a chemical used as an explosive, which is poisonous.

Tommies The nickname for British soldiers in the First World War.

Treasonable Practices Act 1796 This expanded the definitions of treason to include attempts to coerce Parliament or attacks on the constitution.

Trench foot Prolonged exposure to water led to soldiers' feet swelling, blistering and rotting.

TUC The Trades Union Congress.

Typhoid A disease contracted by drinking infected water.

Typhus A dangerous fever transmitted by lice, fleas, mites or ticks.

U-boats German submarines.

Uitlanders White foreigners living in the Transvaal and the Orange Free State.

Veldt Open grass-country.

Venereal disease The term for a number of diseases transmitted by sexual intercourse contracted while on leave in France and/or Belgium. Called sexually transmitted diseases nowadays.

Volunteers Men with some basic military training who could be called on to fight if Britain was invaded.

War of the Third Coalition In 1805 Britain was allied with Austria and Russia against France. Prussia joined the coalition in 1806.

War socialism The government's wartime control of many aspects of British economic and social life.

Yeomanry Volunteer cavalry who served in Britain.

Further reading

General texts

D. Chandler and I. Beckett, editors, *The Oxford Illustrated History of the British Army* (Oxford University Press, 1994)
An excellent collection of essays; probably the definitive one-volume history of the British Army

J.R. Hill, *The Oxford Illustrated History of the Royal Navy* (Oxford University Press, 1996)
An enjoyable, compact account

A. Mallinson, *The Making of the British Army* (Bantam, 2011)
A clear, concise book from a former soldier and a best-selling historical novelist

B. Wilson, *Empires of the Deep: The Rise and Fall of the British Navy* (Weidenfeld & Nicolson, 2013)
A gripping tale of Britain's naval exploits

Chapter 1

R. and L. Adkins, *The War for all the Oceans: From Nelson at the Nile to Napoleon at Waterloo* (Penguin, 2008)
A superb account of naval warfare in the Napoleonic War

A. Lambert, *War at Sea in the Age of Sail* (Orion, 2000)
A very good introduction to naval conflict between 1650 and 1850. It is also well illustrated

N.A.M. Rodger, *The Command of the Ocean: A Naval History of Britain 1649–1815* (Penguin, 2006)
An excellent book; well researched and a gripping read

J. Sugden, *Nelson: A Dream of Glory* (Pimlico, 2012)
The first of Sugden's two excellent books

J. Sugden, *Nelson: The Sword of Albion* (The Bodley Head, 2014)
Probably too detailed for most students but well worth reading the chapters on the naval battles

Chapter 2

M. Adkin, *The Waterloo Companion: The Complete Guide to History's Most Famous Land Battle* (Aurum Press, 2001)
A nice, well-illustrated and informative book

B. Cornwell, *Waterloo: The History of Four Days, Three Armies and Three Battles* (William Collins, 2014)
Not a typical history book but a tremendous read by an author who knows more than most historians about Wellington's army and the warfare of the period

C. Esdaile, *The Peninsular War: A New History* (Allen Lane, 2002)
Probably the best single scholarly book on the war

P.J. Haythornthwaite, *The Armies of Wellington* (Brockhampton Press, 1996)
A detailed account of the make-up, training, recruitment and disposition of troops in the Peninsular and Waterloo campaigns

R. Knight, *Britain Against Napoleon: The Organization of Victory* (Allan Lane 2013)
Knight brilliantly examines the way the whole British population was involved in the war against France

E. Longford, *Wellington: The Years of the Sword* (Weidenfeld & Nicolson, 1969)
The first of Longford's two volumes on Wellington's life. Her biography is still the best

R. Muir, *Britain and the Defeat of Napoleon 1807–1815* (Yale University Press, 1996)
An excellent account of the strategic and political aspects of Britain's struggle with Napoleon

R. Muir, R. Burnham, H. Muir and R. McGuigan, *Inside Wellington's Peninsular Army 1808–1814* (Pen & Sword Books, 2006)
An excellent collection of essays. The first, 'Wellington and the Peninsular War: The Ingredients of Victory' by R. Muir, is particularly good

I.C. Robertson, *Wellington at War in the Peninsula, 1808–1814: An Overview and Guide* (Pen & Sword Books, 2000)
A good, readable, well-illustrated account

J. Weller, *Wellington in the Peninsula 1808–1814* (Frontline Books, 2012)
This book was first published in 1962 and I include it because it sparked my interest in Wellington and the Peninsular War and it has stood the test of time

Chapter 3

O. Figes, *Crimea: The Last Crusade* (Penguin, 2011)
A lucid account of the war

C. Hibbert, *The Destruction of Lord Raglan: A Tragedy of the Crimean War, 1854–55* (Pelican, 1963)
It may be dated but this remains an excellent read

D. Judd, *The Crimean War* (Book Club Associates, 1976)
A short, well-illustrated account of the war

T. Royle, *Crimea: The Great Crimean War 1854–1856* (Abacus, 2000)
A splendidly written and thorough account of the war

H. Small, *The Crimean War; Queen Victoria's War with the Russian Tsars* (Tempus, 2007)
An interesting, thought-provoking book

Chapter 4

D. Judd and K. Surridge, *The Boer War: A History* (I.B. Tauris, 2013)
A very good introduction to the war

B. Nasson, *The South African War 1899–1902* (Hodder Education, 1999)
A good narrative account

T. Pakenham, *The Boer War* (Abacus, 1991)
The Boer War on a grand scale. Well worth reading

E.M. Spiers, *The Late Victorian Army 1868–1902* (Manchester University Press, 1992)
An overview of the late Victorian army

E. van Heyningen, *The Concentration Camps of the Anglo-Boer War: A Social History* (Jacana Media, 2013)
A recent, in-depth coverage of this topic

Chapters 5 and 6

A. Gregory, *The Last Great War: British Society and the First World War* (Cambridge University Press, 2008)
An excellent book on the effect of the war on British society

P.G. Halpern, *A Naval History of World War I* (UCL Press, 1994)
A very good study of the war at sea

J.P. Harris, *Douglas Haig and the First World War* (Cambridge University Press, 2009)
A book critical of Haig

J. Horne, editor, *A Companion to World War I* (Wiley-Blackwell, 2012)
A very useful collection of short articles that reflect recent scholarship

J.H. Morrow Jr, *The Great War in the Air: Military Aviation from 1909 to 1921* (The University of Alabama Press, 2009)
This provides a detailed account of the air war

G. Sheffield, *A Short History of the First World War* (One World, 2014)
The finest short history of the war: superbly informed

G. Sheffield, *Forgotten Victory: The First World War – Myths and Realities* (Headline Review, 2012)
This focuses on Britain and the British Army and stresses the strengths of that army by 1918

G. Sheffield, *The Chief: Douglas Haig and the British Army* (Aurum, 2012)
A book defending Haig

A.G.V. Simmonds, *Britain and World War One* (Routledge, 2011)
A very useful history of the home front in the First World War

D. Stevenson, *1914–18: The History of the First World War* (Penguin, 2012)
Probably the best analytical history of the war

H. Strachan, *The Oxford Illustrated History of the First World War, New Edition* (Oxford University Press, 2014)
An interesting collection of well-illustrated essays on the war

S.C. Tucker, *The Great War 1914–18* (Routledge, 1997)
A good, fairly short narrative history

J.M. Winter, *The Great War and the British People* (Palgrave, 2003)
Excellent coverage of the domestic front

Index

The Publishers would like to thank the following for permission to reproduce copyright material:

Photo credits: p10 http://www.gutenberg.org/files/16914/16914-h/16914-h.htm; **p45** https://commons.wikimedia.org/wiki/File:Phillips-Arthur_Wellesley,_1st_Duke_of_Wellington.jpg; **p84** SSPL/Getty Images; **p92** https://commons.wikimedia.org/wiki/File:Florence_Nightingale_three_quarter_length.jpg; **p94** Wellcome Library, London; **p109** Popperfoto/Getty Images; **p112** Corbis; **p124** Library of Congress, 3c11781; **p125** Hulton Archive/Getty Images; **p143** Topham Picturepoint; **p160** S. Forster/Alamy; **p161** Library of Congress, LC-DIG-ggbain-24478; **p172** John Warwick Brooke/Getty Images; **p188** Library of Congress, LC-USZ62-133019; **p194** Universal History Archive/Getty Images; **p199** Library and Archives Canada, Acc. No. 1983-28-1396.

Acknowledgements: Aurum Press, *The Telegraph Book of the First World War* by G. Fuller, editor, 2014. Bodley Head, *Nelson: The Sword of Albion* by John Sugden, 2012. Book Club Associates, *The Crimean War* by Denis Judd, 1975. David & Charles, *Tales from the Front Line: Trafalgar* by Peter Warwick, 2011. Greenhill Books, *Wellington in the Peninsula* by Jac Weller, 1992. Harper Perennial, *Tommy: The British Soldier on the Western Front 1914–1918* by Richard Holmes, 2005. Oldhams Press, *War Memoirs* by David Lloyd George, 1938. Oxford University Press, *The Oxford Popular History of Britain* by Kenneth O. Morgan, editor, 1993; *The Oxford Illustrated History of the British Army* by David Chandler, editor, 1994. Pen & Sword Books, *Wellington at War in the Peninsula 1808–1814* by Ian C. Robertson, 2000; *Inside Wellington's Army 1808–1814* by R. Muir *et al.*, 2006; *Light Dragoons: The Making of a Regiment* by A. Mallinson, 2012. Penguin, *Britain Against Napoleon: The Organization of Victory 1793–1815* by R. Knight, 2014; *Crimea* by Orlando Figes, 2011; *The Destruction of Lord Raglan* by Christopher Hibbert, 1963. Sphere Books, *Wellington as Military Commander* by Michael Glover, 1973. *The Times*, 1854 and 1855. Weidenfeld & Nicolson, *Empire of the Deep* by Ben Wilson, 2013. World Books, *The Years of the Sword* by E. Longford, 1971.

Every effort has been made to trace all copyright holders, but if any have been inadvertently overlooked the Publishers will be pleased to make the necessary arrangements at the first opportunity.